GATEKEEPERS
OF
BLACK CULTURE

GATEKEEPERS OF BLACK CULTURE

BLACK-OWNED BOOK PUBLISHING IN THE UNITED STATES, 1817–1981

DONALD FRANKLIN JOYCE

Contributions to Afro-American and African Studies,
Number 70

Greenwood Press
Westport, Connecticut • London, England

Z
471
.J69
1983

Library of Congress Cataloging in Publication Data

Joyce, Donald F.
  Gatekeepers of black culture.

  (Contributions in Afro-American and African studies,
ISSN 0069-9624; no. 70)
    Bibliography: p.
    Includes index.
    1. Publishers and publishing—United States.
2. Book industries and trade—United States.   3. Afro-
American business enterprises—United States.   I. Title.
II. Series.
Z471.J69   1983   070.5'08996073   82-9227
ISBN 0-313-23332-2   (lib. bdg.)   AACR2

Library of Congress Catalog Card Number: 82-9227
ISBN: 0-313-23332-2
ISSN: 0069-9624   8475194

First published in 1983

Greenwood Press
A division of Congressional Information Service, Inc.
88 Post Road West
Westport, Connecticut 06881

Printed in the United States of America

10 9 8 7 6 5 4 3 2 1

To my mother, Pearl Jackson Joyce, who sacrificed many of the luxuries of life and endured many of its hardships to provide me with the opportunity to acquire a fine education; my sister Marjorie Joyce Mims, who was the family pacesetter and a guiding light; my brother, Raleigh Walter Joyce, Jr., who instilled in me at an early age an appreciation of art, music, and literature; and to Fisk University

Contents

Graphs

Tables

Acknowledgments

Many persons, too numerous to mention here, assisted me at various stages of this study's development. To all of them I am grateful, especially the many Black publishing executives who took time from their busy schedules to grant me two-hour interviews. I would, however, like to cite personally some of the individuals who played key roles in helping me to bring this study to completion.

Dr. Abraham Bookstein, Associate Professor in the Graduate Library School of the University of Chicago, shared with me his remarkable vision and expertise in research methodology. Dr. Howard W. Winger, formerly Dean and presently Professor Emeritus in the Graduate Library School of the University of Chicago, allowed me to benefit from his authoritative knowledge of book publishing. From Dr. John Hope Franklin, formerly John Matthew Manly Distinguished Professor in the Department of History of the University of Chicago and presently Senior Fellow at the National Humanities Center, I received guidance into several little-known areas of Black cultural history. Dr. Eliza Atkins Gleason, formerly Assistant Chief Librarian of Regional Library Centers at the Chicago Public Library, prodded and encouraged me at every step of the way. Mary Ann Stephens and Dorothy Lyles, my former colleagues in the Vivian G. Harsh Collection of Afro-American History and Literature at the Carter G. Woodson Regional Library of the Chicago Public Library, gave invaluable assistance in checking innumerable facts and dates in Black history. Dr. Dorothy B. Porter-Wesley, through her extensive knowledge of Black bibliography, illuminated for me many areas on the subject which I had not considered.

The staffs of many libraries graciously assisted me in researching unique and pertinent sources in their collections. Notable among them were: Special Collections Department, Mugar Memorial Library, Boston University, Boston: Special Collections Department, Boston Public Library, Boston; the Schomburg Center for Research in Black Culture, New York Public Library, New York City; the Vivian G. Harsh Collection of Afro-American History and Literature, Carter G. Woodson Regional Library, Chicago Public Library, Chicago; the Newberry Library, Chicago; Joseph Regenstein Library, University of Chicago; Peabody Collection, Collis P. Huntington Library, Hampton Institute, Hampton, Virginia; the Moorland-Spingarn Research Center, Howard University, Washington, D.C.; the University Archives and the Slaughter Collection, Atlanta University, Atlanta, Georgia; Tuskegee Historical Collection, Tuskagee Institute, Tuskegee, Alabama; the Negro Collection, Fisk University, Nashville, Tennessee; Library, Sunday School Publishing Board of the National Baptist Convention, U.S.A., Nashville, Tennessee.

And, finally, I would like to thank Lillie J. Shelton, Executive Secretary to the Director of Libraries, Tennessee State University, for typing and, when necessary, retyping the manuscript.

GATEKEEPERS
OF
BLACK CULTURE

Introduction

Although Black book publishers have been active in the United States since 1817, when the African Methodist Episcopal Church established the A.M.E. Book Concern in Philadelphia, no systematic study has ever been made of Black-owned book publishing in the United States. Only a few published sources have appeared on the subject. Notable among them was a series of seminal articles authored by Bradford Chambers of the Council of Interracial Books for Children, which was published in *Publishers Weekly* in early 1971.[1] The present work is a ground-breaking study into this almost neglected, but extremely fascinating as well as important, area of American book publishing.

Most Black book publishers are small book publishers. They experience many of the same problems as other small book publishers. Black book-publishing executives and Black librarians, however, suggest in the scant literature available that Black book publishers also face unique problems related to acquiring capital, to gaining experience and expertise in book publishing, and to getting their books reviewed by the major white reviewing media. Alfred E. Prettyman, president of the New York City-based Emerson Hall Publishers, cited some reasons seemingly underlying the difficulties encountered by Black publishers seeking capital from financial institutions. "At best the business is a difficult one in which to stay afloat. For investors the payoff can only be over the long haul. Our problem is that in too many quarters, whether for good intentions or ill, they would keep us out.[2] The problem of acquiring capital may also be related to the lack of publishing expertise among Black book publishers, since many publishers identified in this study came into existence after 1960. Doris E. Saunders, formerly director of the Book Division of Johnson Publishing Company and presently book publishing consultant to the firm, alluded to this problem in an interview. Ms. Saunders cited problems related to production and emphasized that there was too little practical knowledge of book publishing among Blacks.[3]

But one of the most discouraging of problems experienced by Black book publishers is the neglect of their books by the major white reviewing media. Ann Allen Shockley, Associate University Librarian at Fisk University, urged her fellow librarians to agitate for a positive resolution of this problem. "Now is the time for the library profession to pressure the book reviewing media to index Black publications and to review books by and about Blacks. These should include those published by Black publishers.[4]

This study has four objectives: (1) to cite the activities of pioneering Black book publishers of the nineteenth century in the light of emerging Black institutions; (2) to survey the growth of Black book publishing from 1900 through 1959; (3) to investigate in particular detail its subsequent development between 1960 and 1974; and (4) to discuss the state of Black book publishing in 1981 through observations and comments of representative book-publishing executives. To realize these objectives, data have been gathered to discuss the following four hypotheses.

1. The growth of Black book publishing after 1960 accelerated in the number of publishers and the diversity of their publishing activities, reflecting the growing social and cultural roles of Black Americans in American society.

2. One of the factors which has inhibited the growth and development of Black publishing has been the inability of executives with Black book-publishing enterprises to secure adequate capital for growth and development, which is a need shared by all business enterprises.

3. The lack of experience and expertise in the administrative and technical aspects of book publishing has been another factor limiting the growth and development of Black book publishing.

4. In addition, the neglect of books published by Black book publishers by the major white reviewing media, reflective of the small impact made by Black book publishing industry, has discouraged the growth and development of Black book publishing.

Primarily two methods of investigation were employed to gather data. The literature and documents on and related to Black book publishing were examined and the executives of Black book-publishing enterprises who were active between 1960 and 1974 were interviewed. When circumstances arose that prevented interviews, as was the case when data were gathered on the state of Black book publishing in 1981, or when there were conflicting schedules between the interviewer and interviewee, executives were interviewed via telephone or sent mail questionnaires.

Publishers were identified by examining: imprints in selected major bibliographic works on Black Americana; book advertisements in numerous Black journals and periodicals published between 1900 and 1975; periodical literature on Black book publishing; directories, histories, yearbooks and encyclopedias on Black institutions and organizations; Black business directories; and biographical encyclopedias.[5]

Statistical and factual data gathered in this study are reported in three appendixes. Portraying selected characteristics of Black-owned book publishing from 1817 through 1974, appendix A includes graphs and a table based on information gleaned from personal interviews with publishing executives as well as an examination of published and unpublished documents and the related literature on Black-owned book publishing. Based on data obtained from personal interviews with Black book-publishing executives, appendix B tabulates on charts and tables statistics relative to specific problems that these executives experienced between 1961 and 1974. Profiles of the sixty-six publishers and two printers that engaged in book publishing between 1817 and 1981, based on the aforementioned data gathering methods and mail questionnaires, are included in appendix C.

Included in this study are all Black publishing enterprises, publishing books of Black interest, that could be identified as engaging in book publishing between 1817 and 1981. To be included, a publisher had to publish or finance the publication of at least one book and use the imprint of the enterprise on the title page. Excluded from this study are: Black publishers who engaged primarily in the publication of sheet music, pamphlets, or pictures; Black fraternal organizations or secret societies which engaged in book publishing; publishing divisions owned or financed by white-owned book publishing enterprises but headed by Blacks and publishing primarily books by and about Blacks; and Black publishers who released books between 1817 and 1981 about whom too little information could be found in published or unpublished sources.

Some terms and phrases used in this study might be subject to various interpretations. "Active book-publishing years" are the number of years between the first and last titles released by a publisher. "Book" is defined as a monograph of forty-nine or more pages or a volume of poetry or a children's book of any number of pages. "Book-publishing objective" is the intellectual objective which a publisher intends to achieve with the publication of a book. Any publisher who released three or more titles in any of the periods 1817–1899; 1900–1959; 1960–1974; 1975–1981 is a "major publisher." A "minor publisher" is a book-publishing enterprise that published fewer than three titles in the aforementioned four periods. A "title" is an edition of a book that has been published.

NOTES

1. These articles were: Bradford Chambers, "Book Publishing: A Racist Club?" *Publishers Weekly*, February 1, 1971, pp. 40–47; and Bradford Chambers, "Why Minority Publishing? New Voices Are Heard," *Publishers Weekly*, March 15, 1971, pp. 35–50.
2. Dudley Randall, "Negro Publishers for Black Readers," *Publishers Weekly*, October 22, 1973, p. 50.
3. Ibid., pp. 49–50.
4. Ann Allen Shockley, "Black Book Reviewing: A Case for Library Action," *College and Research Libraries*, 35 (January 1974): 20. Generally, publishers of periodical indexes sent lists of periodicals to be considered for inclusion in their indexes to librarians and other information specialists with the request that they indicate which periodicals they think, because of use, should be included. These lists are returned to the publishers who make the final decision.
5. Two publishers were identified through serendipity.

1

Beginnings: The Foundation of Major Black Institutions in the United States, 1775–1900

INTRODUCTION

The promise of freedom and equality which the Constitution of the United States insured all of its citizens can hardly be said to have been realized in the last decades of the eighteenth century when the vast majority of the new nation's Black Americans were living in bondage.[1] Excluded from the American mainstream, leaders of the "free" Black communities, joined and sometimes led by sympathetic leaders from the liberal white community, began in the late eighteenth and early nineteenth centuries to develop institutions within the Black community to meet the specific needs and aspirations of Blacks. A study of the growth of these Black institutions— fraternal organizations, financial, institutions, religious denominations, civil rights groups, cultural organizations, and educational institutions—provides a background for understanding the status of the Black community as a whole at the dawn of the twentieth century. The development of Black-owned book publishing, the subject of this study, was intimately tied to the history of other Black institutions, social, economic, and cultural, and to the forces both internal and external which affected their growth.

FRATERNAL ORGANIZATIONS

Denied membership in white fraternal organizations, Black Americans began establishing their own fraternal organizations just before the Revolutionary War. The first of these was the Freemasons. On March 6, 1775, Prince Hall and fourteen other Afro-

Americans were initiated into Freemasonry by a Lodge of English Freemasons attached to General Gage's regiment in Boston.[2] In that same year Prince Hall petitioned the Provincial Grand Master of Modern Masons of Massachusetts for a charter to allow his lodge to enjoy the fullest Masonic rights and powers shared by other Masonic bodies in the United States. The petition was denied, "on account of color." Not discouraged, the Black Masons decided to apply to foreign Masons for a charter. In 1787, a charter was granted from the Grand Lodge of England ("Moderns") to form African Lodge No. 459.[3] Before the Civil War a number of lodges of Black Freemasons, including seven grand lodges, were organized in many free Black communities.[4] Other fraternal organizations were also active in the free Black community during these years; in 1843 the Grand Order of the Odd Fellows established a chapter in New York City.[5]

In the fifty years following the Civil War, Black fraternal organizations, providing their members not only with outlets for entertainment and recreation but also with life and burial insurance through their beneficial programs, increased rapidly in number. By the end of 1870, the Grand United Order of Odd Fellows of America, for example, had established 770 lodges throughout the United States. And many newer fraternal organizations, like the Grand United Order of Saint Luke, founded in Baltimore in 1867, were coming into existence. These fraternal organizations, collecting dues from large memberships which also enrolled in their beneficial programs, controlled large sums of money within the Black community. It is estimated that between 1870 and 1920 Blacks paid $168 million into Black fraternal organizations.[6] Because of their strong financial position, these fraternal organizations played a strategic role in the establishment of the first Black-owned banks.

FINANCIAL INSTITUTIONS

In the last decades of the eighteenth century, beneficial and benevolent societies, the earliest financial institutions in the Black community, began to appear. Unable to secure loans or insurance from white banks and insurance companies, Black Americans, recognizing their precarious financial position, organized benevolent societies for mutual assistance. Generally, these societies were affiliated with church or fraternal organizations. Members were usually required to pay dues and received such benefits as life and health insurance and, in some cases, loans. The capital was generally deposited in a local bank. Many of the benevolent societies provided support for the destitute and newly escaped slaves.

The Free African Society of Philadelphia, organized by Richard Allen and Absalom Jones in 1778, was one of the first benevolent societies organized by Black Americans. Established to cater to the social, religious, and economic needs of free Blacks, it was a socioreligious and economic society from which eventually sprang the African Methodist Episcopal Church.

Similar societies were organized during this period in Afro-American communities in New York, Boston, Newport, Charleston, and Baltimore. Reportedly, by 1838 there were one hundred beneficial and benevolent societies in Philadelphia, for example, with an aggregate membership of 7,448. And in that year these societies collected $18,851 in dues and expended $14,172 in benefits.[7]

As the nineteenth century progressed, and particularly in the years following the Civil War, churches and fraternal organizations multiplied rapidly, and many of them organized beneficial and benevolent units as part of their programs. The number of Blacks enrolled in such units soared. Abram Harris saw this rapid post–Civil War expansion as a result of emancipation. "Since the freed Negro could no longer look to his master for support during illness or burial at death, these agencies were developed on a self-help basis to provide economic security.[8] Consequently, by 1900 the beneficial and benevolent units of Black churches and fraternal organizations controlled a considerable amount of capital in the Black community.

The story of the establishment, development, and demise of the Freedmen's Savings and Trust Company, the United States' first bank for Black Americans, is one of the tragic episodes in the banking and financial history of Afro-Americans. During the Civil War, military banks were established in the South by Union generals as depositories for the savings of Black soldiers and free laborers. After the war, in an effort to consolidate the deposits in these banks and to provide Blacks with special banking privileges, Congress in 1865 passed legislation creating the bank along with the Freedmen's

Bureau. The bank had thirty-four branches, thirty-two of them in the South. Between 1865 and 1869, the Bank's central office was in New York City; from 1869 to 1874, it was in Washington, D.C. The Bank was controlled and managed by white "friends" of the Afro-American, employing some Afro-Americans as tellers. In 1866 its total deposits were $305,167; by 1872 total deposits had risen to $31,260,499.97.[9]

The Freedmen's Savings and Trust Company ended in scandalous failure. Mismanagement, reckless investments, and fraudulent practices by several of its trustees and major officers forced the bank to close on June 28, 1874, with a deficit of $217,886.50.[10] Frederick Douglass, appointed president of the bank in a last-ditch effort to regain the confidence of its Black depositors, was unable to save the bank. Although the failure of the Freedmen's bank was a crushing blow to Black Americans who had entrusted their savings to it, a short fourteen years after its demise, as if to testify to the resilience of the human spirit, Blacks began opening their own banks.

In 1888 the first banks established and managed by Black Americans in the United States were opened. They were the Savings Bank of the Grand Reformers in Richmond, Virginia, and the Capital Savings Bank in Washington, D.C. By 1899 four other Black-owned banks had been established: the Mutual Bank and Trust Company, Chattanooga, Tennessee (1889); Alabama Penny Savings and Loan Company, Birmingham, Alabama (1890); Nickel Savings, Richmond, Virginia (1869); and Mutual Aid Banking Company, New Berne, North Carolina (1897). After 1900 the number of Black-owned banks continued to grow rapidly until by 1905 there were at least twenty-eight Black-owned banks in the United States.[11]

The rapid growth of Black-owned banks during this period was due largely to the expansion of the beneficial and benevolent units of churches and fraternal organizations, according to one observer. "As these societies increased in size and number there was a corresponding increase in their capital, their investments, and in the subsidiary businesses developed by them. The increasing financial resources led to the organization of banks as depositories."[12] Thus, as the twentieth century opened, the Black community was rapidly developing its own banking institutions. These institutions would in the twentieth century supply capital for the establishment and development of many Black-owned businesses including book publishing.

RELIGIOUS DENOMINATIONS

The rise of Black religious denominations in the nineteenth century was the result of the racist attitudes and discriminating practices of white church leaders toward Black Americans who worshipped in their churches. In 1794, for instance, Black worshippers in Philadelphia's Saint George Methodist Church, after being insulted by the church's clergy and laymen, withdrew and formed their own church under the leadership of Richard Allen: the Bethel African Methodist Church.[13] Other branches of this church were established in Baltimore, Wilmington, and other cities in New Jersey and Pennsylvania. In 1816 these churches organized into a formal religious denomination known as the African Methodist Episcopal Church with headquarters at Mother Bethel Church in Philadelphia.

In 1796 Blacks in New York City, experiencing similar treatment at the hands of white church leaders and their congregations, founded their own church under the leadership of John Varick: the Zion Church. This church was incorporated in the state of New York in 1801 as the African Methodist Episcopal Church of New York. At its General Conference in 1848, this denomination changed its name to the African Methodist Episcopal Zion Church.[14]

Both of these denominations established their publishing houses before the Civil War for the purpose of publishing religious materials such as disciplines and hymnals for their members. The African Methodist Episcopal Church formed the A.M.E. Book Concern in 1817 in Philadelphia.[15] The African Methodist Episcopal Zion Church established the African Methodist Zion Publishing House in New York City in 1840.[16] After the Civil War, the African Methodist Episcopal Church founded the A.M.E. Sunday School Union and Publishing House to publish primarily Sunday School literature, in 1882 in Bloomington, Illinois. In 1886, however, this publishing house was moved to Nashville, Tennessee.[17]

Another Black American Methodist denomination was established just after the Civil War when white southern Methodists
realized that they were losing their Afro-American communicants
to the two established Black Methodist denominations. Consequently, in 1870 Black communicants in the Methodist Episcopal
Church South were allowed to form their own denomination: the
Colored Methodist Episcopal Church. With headquarters in Jackson, Tennessee, this new Afro-American Methodist denomination
elected William J. Miles as its first bishop and established its own
publishing house to publish religious literature for its members.[18]

During the Revolutionary War, Black Baptists began organizing
their own independent churches. The First African Baptist Church
was founded in Savannah, Georgia, in 1778 by Rev. Abraham
Marshall, a white minister, and Jesse Peter, a Black.[19] Other independent Black American Baptist churches were organized throughout the United States in the decades which followed. As the nineteenth century progressed, many of the independent Black Baptist
churches formed conferences such as the Wood River Conference
in Illinois, which was established in 1840. It was not, however, until 1895 in Atlanta that all of the local and state Black Baptist conferences and independent Black Baptist churches organized into a
national denomination: the National Baptist Convention of America. In the following year, the denomination established its publishing house in Nashville.

By 1900 there were four national Black American religious denominations in the United States. Membership in these denominations was expanding rapidly. At the turn of the century the Black
American church was the most powerful organization among
Blacks in the country and wielded considerable influence both inside and outside the Black community.

COMMERCIAL PUBLISHING ENTERPRISES

In the late 1820s, as Black Americans were growing more prominent in the abolitionist movement, Black leaders began to feel the
need to articulate the Afro-American's cause themselves in print as
well as in the public forum. To fulfill this need the first Black
American newspaper, *Freedom's Journal*, was established in New

York City in 1827 by John Russwurn, the second Black to graduate from an American college, and Samuel Cornish. The following excerpt from an editorial in the first issue of *Freedom's Journal* cites reasons why the newspaper and its many successors came into existence.

> We wish to plead our own cause. Too long have others spoken for us. Too long has the public been deceived by misrepresentations in things which concern us dearly, though in the estimation of some mere trifles; for though there are many in society who exercise towards us benevolent feelings; still (with sorrow we confess it) there are others who make it their business to enlarge upon the least trifle, which tends to discredit any person of color; and pronounce anathemas and denounce our whole body for the misconduct of this guilty one.[20]

Freedom's Journal was widely circulated. This newspaper had, reportedly, over thirty agents in the United States, Canada, and England.[21] It influenced public opinion in the free Black community as well as the liberal white community by publishing news items of activities in the free Black communities throughout the United States and editorial commentaries by Black leaders on the plight of the Black American.

Although *Freedom's Journal* ceased publication in 1829, two years after it was founded, it set the tone for future Black American journalistic efforts in the United States.[22] In its wake, other Black newspapers sprang into existence before the Civil War to champion the cause of the Afro-American. Among some of them were: the *Colored American*, New York City (1837–1842); the *North Star*, Rochester, New York (1847–1855); and the *Mirror of the Times*, San Francisco, California (1855–1862).[23]

Between 1865 and 1900, a plethora of Black newspapers was founded. Some of these newspapers were directed toward regional audiences such as the *Elevator*, San Francisco, California (1865–1889); and the *Weekly Louisianian*, New Orleans, Louisiana (1870–1882).[24] Other newspapers, however, enjoyed a national audience and were very influential on the national level, such as the *New York Age*, New York City (1887–1937) and the *Washington Bee*, Washington, D.C. (1882–1922).[25]

These Black newspapers not only provided the Black community with a means of reporting its news and articulating its response to the larger society, but they also contributed to the growth of Black business. In these newspapers, Black American businessmen advertised their services and products to the grass roots of the Black community.

In 1838, eleven years after *Freedom's Journal* made its appearance, the first Black-owned commercial periodical made its debut in New York City: the *Mirror of Liberty*, a quarterly magazine. Published by David Ruggles, the *Mirror of Liberty* contained articles by a core of able Afro-American writers who advocated the moral, social, political, and intellectual elevation of Black Americans. Although it lasted for only three numbers, it was a pioneering effort among Black Americans in commercial periodical publishing. Before the end of the Civil War, other commercial Black-owned periodicals appeared, such as *Douglass' Monthly*, Rochester, New York (1858–1863); and the *Anglo-African Magazine*, New York City (1858–1865). From 1865 through 1900 other Black-owned commercial periodicals appeared. Some were short-lived while others had relatively long publishing histories. Some examples of them were *Howard's American Magazine*, Harrisburg, Pennsylvania and New York City (1889–1901); and the *Southland*, Winston-Salem, North Carolina. (1890–1891).[26]

These commercial Black-owned periodicals provided opportunities for the publication of the essays, poems, and articles by Black Americans. In the nineteenth-century tradition, they serialized novels and longer works. Many of them were widely read in the Black community and some of them enjoyed a following in the liberal white community.

During the nineteenth century, several Black Americans, seeking to express themselves in print, had books privately printed. Two Blacks, however, did develop commercial book-publishing firms during this period when many of the major white American book-publishing houses were, also, being established.

The firm of John W. Leonard and Company of New York City was the most prolific Black-owned book-publishing firm in the nineteenth century. Unlike most Black publishers in any medium during the period, Leonard published only books on Freemasonry. An active book publisher for only two years, 1855 and 1856, Leonard published at least eleven volumes of the *Universal Masonic Library*. In addition to this work, Leonard also published twelve other works on Masonry during these two years. In 1856 Leonard sold his firm to Jonathan R. Neall, a white publisher.[27]

Thomas Hamilton, Sr., publisher of the *Anglo-African Magazine*, (q.v.) until his death in 1861, was also a book publisher.[28] Hamilton, and his brother and son, who managed his business after his death, seemed to have developed a book-publishing program centered on various aspects of Black-Americana and Africana. Before his death in 1861, the senior Hamilton published Robert Campbell's *A Pilgrimage to My Motherland: An Account of a Journey Among the Egbas and Yorubas of Central Africa, 1859-60*. This work was the firsthand narrative of Campbell's experiences traveling in Africa as Martin Robison Delaney's assistant on the Niger River Exploration Expedition in 1859 and 1860.

After the senior Hamilton's death, his brother, Robert Hamilton, and his son, William Hamilton, published another book indicative of the firm's publishing objectives, a collective biography of prominent Black Americans entitled *The Black Man, His Antecedents, His Genius, and His Achievements*, by William Wells Brown (1863). Ten years earlier William Wells Brown had become the first Afro-American to publish a novel. It was *Clotel; or The President's Daughter, a Narrative of Slave Life in the United States*, which was not published in the United States, but in England by a London publisher, Partridge and Oakey, in 1853.

As commercial publishers, Black Americans entered successfully the arena of newspaper and periodical publishing in the nineteenth century, providing their fellow Blacks with avenues of self-expression which would have otherwise been denied to them, and, perhaps more importantly, providing channels of written communication between Black leaders and other Blacks as well as the white community. As the twentieth century dawned, Black American journalism, as evidenced by commercial newspapers and periodicals, had become an entrenched institution in the Black community. But Black-owned commercial book publishing was still a novelty to the Afro-American community in 1900.

CIVIL RIGHTS ORGANIZATIONS

The development of the Black press was catalytic to the rise of another Black institution: the civil rights organization. In several numbers of *Freedom's Journal* in 1827 and 1828 there were accounts of plans for cooperative actions among Blacks, and in one number, there was even a suggestion of a plan for national action.[29]

Although such a plan was not enacted immediately, it became a reality in 1830 when a national convention of free Blacks was called to devise plans to aid the expatriation to Canada of Black citizens of Cincinnati who were being required by law to post an exorbitantly high bond to remain in the city, because the city's leaders had grown weary of altercations between skilled Black artisans and white immigrants over jobs.[30] Under the leadership of the Reverend Richard Allen, senior bishop of the African Methodist Episcopal Church, the first of a series of national conventions met in Philadelphia in 1830 from September 20 through September 24 at Mother Bethel African Methodist Episcopal Church. The convention had twenty-six delegates from seven states and fourteen honorary members from seven states.[31] The delegates voted to support those Black citizens of Cincinnati desiring to emigrate to Canada, but took a firm stand against emigration to Liberia, which was being advocated for Black Americans by the American Colonization Society at the time. Delegates at the convention also made plans for their next annual meeting.

These national assemblies were called by prominent Black leaders. From 1830 to 1835, six of these national assemblies were called. However, because of disunity among Black leaders, no national assemblies were called from 1836 through 1842. In 1843 there was sufficient cooperation among Blacks to hold a national assembly in Buffalo, New York. Thereafter and before the end of the Civil War, national Black assemblies were held in Troy, New York (1847); Cleveland, Ohio (1848); Rochester, New York (1852); Philadelphia, Pennsylvania (1855); and Syracuse, New York (1864). According to Howard Holman Bell, these national Negro conventions "performed acceptably in so many areas that it could well be said to be the first National Association for the Advancement of Colored People."[32]

Afro-Americans held state as well as national conventions during this period. In these conventions Black Americans discussed and acted upon problems facing them in education, equality before the law, anti-slavery, and emigration. To a lesser extent they considered problems of temperance and women's rights.

Each of the national conventions and many of the state conventions published the minutes of their proceedings including a roster of the delegates attending: transcriptions of each session; committee reports; and the all-important convention address. In the national conventions this address was generally entitled "To the Free People of Colour of the United States, a State of the Black Community Message." These minutes were widely distributed among the Black community and the liberal white community in the North by delegates attending the assemblies. They were antecedent to the annual reports and other publications which would be published in later years by the National Association for the Advancement of Colored People, the National Urban League, and other civil rights and social welfare organizations which were formed in the interest of Black Americans in the twentieth century.

The delegates to the national and state conventions shifted their strategies with each decade from 1830 through 1864 in their attempt to deal with the Black American's problems, according to Bell.

> The decade of the "fifties" was one in which the Negro sought in various ways to work out his own destiny. During the "thirties" he had tried moral suasion techniques, and found them wanting. In the "forties" he had sought equality of citizenship by working through political channels, but in cooperation with established parties dominated by whites. By 1850 that effort had also grown to be unproductive. In fact, the decade preceding the Civil War opened with the passage of the Fugitive Slave Law which made it apparent to Negro leaders that the United States was far from ready to protect the rights of its colored citizens. Increasingly thereafter, organized activities of the Negro tended to become more radical, more self-contained, more independent. Under these circumstances many turned to plans for emigration, and the development of a Negro empire.[33]

In the last national convention before the end of the Civil War, held in 1864, Bell observes that, again, the delegates were using moral suasion.

If any one reason for calling a convention in the fall of 1864 is
to be named, it is that the fate of the Negro and the fate of the
nation hung in delicate balance. . . . In one of the most challenging passages of the entire thirty-five years, the convention
once more reminded the nation of the discrepancy between
the claims of the democracy and the actions of that democracy; they reminded the nation that Negro troops, although at
first refused the privilege of defending their country, had,
when belatedly given the opportunity, acquitted themselves
well. And once again they reminded America that the debasement of one was the debasement of all.[34]

Although the passage of the Thirteenth, Fourteenth, and Fif-
teenth amendments secured for all Black Americans the rights for
which the antebellum national and state conventions agitated, and
although the years following the Civil War witnessed an unprece-
dented growth of educational opportunities for Blacks, during the
Reconstruction and post-Reconstruction years Blacks recognized
the need for continued agitation in their behalf through state and
national civil rights organizations to insure that their newly won
rights were not abrogated. The Tennessee State Convention of
Negroes held in Nashville in 1865 was typical of the many state
conventions convened after the Civil War to petition and agitate
for the protection of the Black American's rights at the state level.
Similar state conventions were held during these years in Louisiana, Kansas, Rhode Island, Texas, and Georgia.

On the national level, after the Civil War, perhaps the most ambitious effort by Blacks to form an ongoing national civil rights organization was the founding of the Afro-American National League
in Chicago in 1890. To its ranks were drawn some of the most able
Black Americans of the day, such as Alexander Walters, who later
became a bishop of the African Methodist Episcopal Zion Church,
T. Thomas Fortune, editor of the *New York Age*, and J. C. Price, a
prominent North Carolina educator. The objectives of the league
were outlined in Article II of its constitution.

The objects of the League are to protest against taxation; to
secure a more equitable distribution of school funds in those
sections where separate schools exist; to insist upon a fair and

impartial trial by a judge and jury of peers in all causes of law
wherein we may be a party; to resist by all legal and reason-
able means mob and lynch law whereof we are made the action; and to insist upon the arrest and punishment of all such
offenders against our legal rights.[35]

Organized into local branches, the Afro-American National League
for the next ten years was the main vehicle for Black American ex-
pression in the area of civil rights.

Thus, in the seventy years from 1830 to 1900, Blacks had demonstrated their ability to establish and develop effective civil rights
organizations to agitate for their rights and the general uplift of all
Black Americans. With this tradition behind them it is little wonder
that Blacks continued to work vigorously to establish new civil
rights organizations in the twentieth century, which would continue to win and insure for them further participation in the opportunities which America offered.

CULTURAL ORGANIZATIONS

During the early 1830s free Blacks in northern cities began forming their own cultural organizations. Dr. Dorothy B. Porter-
Wesley explains why Afro-Americans began establishing these
organizations.

Some of the expressed reasons for the organization of these
institutions were the stimulation of reading and the spreading
of useful knowledge by providing libraries and reading
rooms, the encouragement of expressed literary efforts by
providing audiences as critics and channels of publication for
their literary productions and the training of future orators
and leaders by means of debate.[36]

Racial discrimination, according to Dr. Porter, was also one of the
contributing factors in the establishment of these organizations.

Apart from this, there were certain existing conditions inherent in the race relations of the times which led to the establishment of these societies. The Reverend Theodore S. Wright, a

prominent Negro of the day, was thrown out of a white literary meeting in Alumni Hall in New York. The presence of Negroes in white literary organizations was not wanted. . . . New institutions were formed in these places as a result of this discrimination.[37]

These cultural organizations were established in Philadelphia, New York, Boston, Pittsburgh, Buffalo, New Bedford Providence, Newark, and Washington, D.C. in the 1830s. In the 1840s they appeared in Rochester, Schenectady, Cincinnati, Columbus, and Detroit.[38] The membership of these organizations was restricted by sex. The Theban Literary Society in Pittsburgh, which was cofounded by Martin Robison Delany, for example, limited its membership to men;[39] the Minerva Literary Society and the Edgeworth Literary Association in Philadelphia only admitted women.[40] However, the all-male Phoenix Society in New York City had some white members.[41]

Most of these cultural organizations established substantial subscription libraries. The Philadelphia Library Company for Colored Persons was an example. "In 1833, the 'Philadelphia Library Company for Colored Persons' was organized and in 1841 had a hundred members notwithstanding the entrance fee was one dollar and the monthly dues, twenty-five cents."[42]

As the nineteenth century continued, some of these organizations died out but similar ones sprang into being. Their significance lies in the fact that they represent early efforts by Blacks to use their leisure time effectively to impart useful knowledge and develop communicative skills.

In the last decade of the nineteenth century the first national cultural organization was founded by Black Americans. It was the American Negro Academy. The activities of this organization, including its extensive publishing program, will be discussed later in this study.

EDUCATIONAL INSTITUTIONS

At the end of the eighteenth century, the restrictions of segregation barred Black Americans from attending most of the established educational institutions in the United States. Recognizing the plight faced by free Blacks, sympathetic liberal white leaders associated with the antislavery movement began in the late 1770s to establish private schools for the education of Black children and adults. These schools were organized in northern cities with substantial free Black communities such as New York, Boston, Philadelphia, and Newport. Typical of these private schools was the New York African Free School that was established in 1787 in New York City by the Society for Promoting the Manumission of Slaves. The school's enrollment grew so rapidly that in 1815 a building was erected and the name was changed to the New York African Free Schools.[43] Among the outstanding alumni who attended the New York African Free Schools were Ira Aldridge, the great Black Shakespearean actor who became the toast of the European stage in the nineteenth century and Dr. James McCune Smith, who graduated from the Medical College of the University of Glasgow.

During the first six decades of the nineteenth century the number of schools established for the education of Blacks increased. Even in such southern cities as Charleston and New Orleans, private schools were organized for free Black children and adults. Although most of these schools were established to provide students with a general elementary and secondary education, other schools and institutions were established to provide students with special education to equip them for a vocation or profession. The Peterboro Manual Labor School, for example, which was founded by the wealthy antislavery advocate Gerrit Smith in 1834 in Madison County, New York, and the Emlen Institute in Mercer County, Ohio, which was established in 1843, provided industrial training for their students. Another educational institution, The Institute for Colored Youth (presently known as Cheyney State University), which was founded in Philadelphia in 1842, prepared its students for careers in teaching and preaching.[44]

In the last two decades before the Civil War, white and Black leaders in the antislavery movement recognized the need for higher education for Afro-Americans and worked together to establish colleges. In 1849 Avery College was founded in Allegheny City, Pennsylvania, with a bequest of $300,000 from the Reverend Charles Avery.[45] This college, which had a faculty of Black and white instructors, was sustained by funds from the white community as well as the Afro-American community.

Three religious denominations were involved in the establishment of two colleges for Afro-Americans in the 1850s. The Presby-
tery of New Castle, Pennsylvania, established Ashum Institute,
presently known as Lincoln University, in Hensonville, Chester
County, Pennsylvania in 1854. In 1856 the Cincinnati Conference
of the Methodist Episcopal Church established Wilberforce University in Xenia, Ohio. Wilberforce University, after it closed briefly
during the early years of the Civil War, was purchased by the African Methodist Episcopal Church and reopened in 1862.[46]

Following the Civil War, numerous educational institutions were
established throughout the South for the Black American with the
aid of the Freedmen's Bureau, state government agencies, Black and
white religious denominations, and white philanthropists. These
institutions included day, night, evening, and Sunday schools.
Notable among some of the colleges and universities were Fisk University (1865); Atlanta University (1868); Tuskegee Institute
(1881); Kentucky State College (1886). By 1900 there were thirty-
four institutions for Afro-Americans giving college-level training
and 2,000 Black Americans had graduated from institutions of
higher learning in the United States.[47] Some of these institutions of
higher learning, such as Atlanta University, Howard University,
and Hampton Institute, developed publishing programs and
became active book publishers before the turn of the century.

CONCLUSION

Thus, as the twentieth century opened, the foundations of several
major Black American institutions had been firmly implanted within the Black community in the United States. Some of these institutions, as it has been noted, were active book publishers. Others
would become book publishers. And still others would be indirectly
supportive of Afro-American-owned book publishing.

Before 1900 the four national Black religious denominations had
established five publishing units which were actively publishing
books. Two Black colleges and universities were engaging in book
publishing in the last decades of the nineteenth century.

As the century unfolded, new Black civil rights organizations
would add book publishing to their programs. They would be
joined in this activity by the publishing units of Black cultural organizations and other Black colleges and universities.

In the commercial sector, Black periodical and newspaper publishers, having been established to publish in their respective media, would also become book publishers in the twentieth century. Black commercial publishers that only published books would also become very active in this sector.

Black fraternal organizations would indirectly be supportive of Black-owned book publishing. As it was noted earlier, these organizations were instrumental in the establishment and development of the first Black-owned banks: banks which would, as the twentieth century evolved, provide loans to some Black publishers who engaged in book publishing.

NOTES

1. In 1790, 757,181 Blacks were living in the United States. Of these, 697,624 (92.1%) were in slavery and 59,557 (7.9%) were free. U.S. Bureau of the Census, *Negro Population, 1790–1915* (Washington, D.C.: Government Printing Office, 1918).

2. Harold Van Buren Voorhis, *Negro Masonry in the United States* (New York: Henry Emmerson, 1940), p. 10.

3. Wm. H. Grimshaw, *Official History of Freemasonry* (New York: Negro Universities Press, 1969), pp. 73, 77, 78.

4. Voorhis, *Negro Masonry*, p. 109.

5. M. S. Stuart, *An Economic Detour* (New York: A. Wendell Malliet & Co., 1940), p. 22.

6. Ibid., pp. 21, 22, 33.

7. Abram L. Harris, *The Negro as Capitalist: A Study of Banking and Business among American Negroes* (Philadelphia: American Academy of Political and Social Science, 1936), p. 20.

8. Ibid., p. 46.

9. Ibid., p. 29.

10. Ibid., p. 42.

11. Ibid., pp. 46–48.

12. Ibid., p. 47.

13. Daniel A. Payne, *History of the African Methodist Episcopal Church*, vol. 1 (Nashville: A.M.E. Sunday School Union and Publishing House, 1891), p. 5.

14. William J. Walls, *The African Methodist Episcopal Zion Church* (Charlotte, N.C.: A.M.E. Zion Publishing House, 1974), pp. 42, 50, 52.

15. Charles Spencer Smith, *A History of the African Methodist Episcopal Church*, vol. 2 (Philadelphia: Book Concern of the A.M.E. Church, 1922), p. 340.

16. Walls, *African Methodist Episcopal Zion Church*, p. 336.

17. Payne, *History of the African Epsicopal Church*, p. 493.

18. M. C. Pettigrew, *From Miles to Johnson* (Memphis, C.M.E. Church Publishing House, 1970), p. 12.

19. E. K. Love, *History of the First African Baptist Church* (Savannah, Ga.: The Morning New Print., 1888), p. 1.

20. "To Our Patrons," *Freedom's Journal*, 16 March 1827, p. 1.

21. Bella Gross, "Freedom's Journal" and the "Right of All," *Journal of Negro History* 17 (July 1932): 249.

22. *Freedom's Journal* suspended publication with its March 28, 1829, issue. The first issue of *Rights of All*, another Afro-American newspaper published in New York City, was released initially on May 29, 1829. Some researchers regard *Rights of All* as a continuation of *Freedom's Journal*, because John Russwurn edited both newspapers. Ibid., p. 259. In this study, however, the author considers them as two separate publications.

23. I. Garland Penn, *The Afro-American Press and Its Editors* (Springfield, Mass.: Willey & Co, 1891), pp. 35–47, 67–70, 76.

24. Ibid., pp. 96, 113.

25. New York Public Library, *Dictionary Catalog of the Schomburg Collection of Negro History and Literature*, 9 vols. (Boston: G. K. Hall, 1962), 6: 5561, 5547.

26. Penelope Laconia Bullock, "The Negro Periodical Press in the United States 1838–1909," (Ph.D. diss., University of Michigan, 1971), pp. 25–32, 73–77, 81–88, 369, 392.

27. Peggy Jo Zemens Richmond, "Afro-American Printers and Book Publishers, 1650–1865," (Master's thesis, University of Chicago, 1970), pp. 82, 83, 38.

28. Ibid., p. 94.

29. "A National Convention of Free Persons of Colour," *Freedom's Journal*, 19 December 1828, pp. 296–97.

30. Howard Holman Bell, *A Survey of the Negro Convention Movement, 1830–1861* (New York: Arno Press, 1969), p. 12.

31. American Society of Free Persons of Colour. *Constitution of the American Society of Free Persons of Colour; Also the Proceedings of the Convention, with Their Address to the Free Persons of Colour of the United States* (Philadelphia: J. W. Allen, 1831), pp. 1v, 2. (The name "American Society of Free People of Colour" was used in the proceedings of the first convention, but not continued.)

32. Howard Holman Bell, ed., *Minutes of the Proceedings of the National Negro Conventions, 1830–1864* (New York: Arno Press and the New York Times, 1969), p. 1.

33. Bell, *Survey of the Negro Convention Movement*, p. 162.

34. Howard Holman Bell, ed., "The Convention of 1864," in *Minutes of the . . . Conventions*, p. 2.

35. Afro-American National League, *The Birth of the Afro-American National League, Chicago, Illinois, January 15-17, 1890* (Chicago: Afro-American National League, 1890), p. 1.

36. Dorothy B. Porter, "Activities of Literary Societies, 1828-1846," *Journal of Negro Education* 5 (October 1936): 557.

37. Ibid.

38. *American and Foreign Anti-Slavery Reporter* (New York: The Society, 1846), p. 103.

39. Dorothy Sterling, *The Making of an Afro-American: Martin Robinson Delany, 1812-1885* (New York: Doubleday, 1971), p. 45.

40. Richard R. Wright, *The Negro in Pennsylvania: A Study in Economic History*, (New York: Arno Press and the *New York Times*, p. 43.

41. Porter, "Literary Societies," p. 565.

42. Wright, *The Negro in Pennsylvania*, p. 42.

43. Carter G. Woodson, *The Education of the Negro prior to 1861* (Washington, D.C.: Association for the Study of Negro Life and History, 1919), pp. 97, 98.

44. Ibid., pp. 292, 269, 270.

45. Ibid., p. 271.

46. Ibid., pp. 271-73.

47. John Hope Franklin, *From Slavery to Freedom: A History of Negro Americans*, 3d. ed. (New York: Knopf, 1967), p. 389.

2

Proud Protectors and Vindicators of the Race: Black Secular Institutional Book Publishers, 1900–1959

INTRODUCTION

In addition to the Black institutions discussed in chapter 1 which directly or indirectly influenced the early growth of Black-owned publishing, powerful, if adverse, forces outside of the Black community were also catalytic in its early development. During the last decade of the nineteenth century and the early decades of the twentieth century, a host of scholarly books based on the assumption of the inferior mental and social abilities of the Black American flowed from the pens of several influential white American scholars and were published by the scholarly book publishing sector of the American book publishing industry. In *Reconstruction: Political and Economic* (New York: Harper & Brothers, 1907) William Archibald Dunning, one of the leading historians of the day, described the Black American as an intellectually and socially inferior human being and lauded slavery as a benign institution with which Blacks were contented. Howard Odum, a prominent twentieth-century sociologist, concluded:

> The Negro has few ideals and perhaps no lasting adherence to an inspiration towards real worth. He has little conception of the meaning of virtue, truth, honor, manhood, integrity. He is shiftless, untidy and indolent; . . . Thus with mental stupidity and moral insensibility back of them the children are affected already, in deed and speech.[1]

That Columbia University Press published *Social and Mental Traits of the Negro: A Study of Race Traits, Tendencies and Pro-*

spects, where this passage appears, illustrated the trend of some scholarly presses of the period to publish books discrediting the Afro-American. Another example of a commercial firm releasing a scholarly book discrediting the Afro-American is Ulrich Bonnell Phillips's *American Negro Slavery: A Survey of the Supply, Employment and Control of Negro Labor as Determined by the Plantation Regime* (New York: D. Appleton, 1918). The underlying assumption of this work, according to historian Stanley Elkins, is Phillips's conception of the racial inferiority of the Afro-American. He writes; "The basic assumption of *American Negro Slavery* was that of innate and inherited racial inferiority. There is no malice toward the Negro in Phillips's work. Phillips was deeply fond of the Negroes as a people; it was just that he could not take them seriously as men and women; they were children."[2]

The demand for such scholarly works discrediting the Afro-American was enhanced by the intellectual, political, and social forces which prevailed during the early years of this period. Some of these forces were: the widespread acceptance by many of the nation's intellectual and political leaders in both the North and South of an interpretation of social Darwinism which viewed Blacks as mentally and socially inferior; the enactment of rigid "Jim Crow" laws against the Afro-American by legislators throughout the South, who used the assumptions advanced in these works to justify the need for such laws; and the wide-ranging influence in academic and intellectual circles of certain prominent Southern scholars who authored these works. Howard University historian Michael R. Winston assessed the scholarly efforts of these historians and social scientists.

> While the nation's leading historians were busy showing how "disastrous" it had been during Reconstruction for Negroes to be allowed minimal legal freedoms, a formidable body of purportedly "objective scholarship" was being produced in emerging disciplines of sociology and psychology (at that time strongly under the influence of Social Darwinism) to show that Negroes were innately incapable of rising above the status imposed by white terrorism.[3]

Within the Black community, a reaction to the many scholarly books discrediting the Black American developed in the last years of the nineteenth century and continued, gathering momentum, into the twentieth century. Led by a small group of emerging Black and white scholars, this reaction was characterized by a small, but persistent, demand for scholarly books which treated objectively the Black American.

As the twentieth century dawned and lengthened into decades, this demand grew. Its growth was influenced by several educational, social, and intellectual developments which occurred in the early decades of the period. For example, in 1897 W.E.B. Du Bois assumed a professorship at Atlanta University where he directed a series of annual conferences on various phases of Afro-American life that were among the earliest sociological researches conducted in the South and did much to set the stage for the objective and systematic study of the Blacks in the United States. Monroe N. Work in 1908 set up the Department of Records and Research at Tuskegee Institute, which began to collect systematically data on Blacks on a nationwide basis. At Fisk University in 1910, a department of sociology was established under the direction of George Edmund Haynes to train Black social workers. Between 1897 and 1915 four Black national organizations were founded with research and publishing departments devoted to the study of various phases of Afro-American life and culture: the American Negro Academy (1897); the National Association for the Advancement of Colored People (1910); the National Urban League (1911); and the Association for the Study of Negro Life and History (1915). By 1930, 102,755 Black Americans were listed in specific professional services, as compared to 62,245 in 1910, thus increasing the number of Blacks active in the nation's professional life.[4] And, equally significant, there was an erosion of social Darwinism by environmentalism in American intellectual thought that was changing white attitudes toward Black Americans. "The environmentalism of Boas, Dewey, and Thomas (even of William Graham Sumner), launched well over a decade before, was coming to be the accepted position on race."[5]

Some white-owned publishing firms and the book-publishing units of white institutions made attempts to satisfy the demand for scholarly books during the period that treated Blacks objectively. A few of the titles these publishers released were: *History of the Negro Race in America from 1619 to 1880*, by George Washington Williams (New York: G. P. Putnam's Sons, 1883); *The Souls of*

Black Folk, by W.E.B. Du Bois (Chicago: A. C. McClurg Co., 1903); *The Negro Family in the United States,* by E. Franklin Frazier (Chicago: University of Chicago Press, 1939); and *Caste and Class in a Southern Town,* by John Dollard (New Haven: Published for the Institute of Human Relations by Yale University Press, 1937). But to a greater extent the demand for such books was met by the book-publishing units of Black cultural, professional, civil rights, social welfare, and educational institutions.

THE BOOK-PUBLISHING ACTIVITIES
OF BLACK CULTURAL AND PROFESSIONAL
ORGANIZATIONS, 1900–1960

Several Black cultural and professional organizations had book-publishing programs that reflected their general aims. Although these publishing programs had a variety of objectives, an important one, particularly in the early part of the twentieth century, was to respond to the attacks made on the mental and social characteristics of the Black American by white supremacist scholarly writers.

One of the early Black national cultural organizations of the period was the American Negro Academy. The Reverend Alexander Crummell, the prolific nineteenth-century Afro-American scholar, orator, and clergyman, founded the American Negro Academy in Washington, D.C., where it was permanently based. The academy's membership included such influential Black scholars, intellectuals, and writers as W.E.B. Du Bois, Paul Laurence Dunbar, W. S. Scarborough, John W. Cromwell, Kelly Miller, and A. A. Schomburg. The academy had five aims: "(1) the promotion of literature, science and art; (2) the culture of a form [*sic*] of intellectual taste; (3) the fostering of higher education; (4) the publication of scholarly works; and (5) the defense of the Negro of vicious assaults."[6]

From its inception, the academy's members recognized the importance of a publishing program in realizing these aims. At the academy's first general organizational meeting at the Lincoln Memorial Congregational Church in Washington, D.C., on March 5, 1897, several of its members, while ratifying ARTICLE IV of its constitution, which dealt with the organization's publishing pro-

gram, discussed the need for such a program. The minutes of that
meeting make clear the reactive nature of their publishing efforts.
William H. Ferris remarked, "There are some people who doubt
whether the Negro has any ability for scholarly work, and it seems
to me, that this is what the Academy needs to do. . . ."[7] Reacting
to Ferris's remarks, W.E.B. Du Bois, apparently seeking to refine
more sharply the objectives of the academy's publishing program,
said, "Mr. Du Bois moves to amend article four as follows: 'To aid
by publication a knowledge of the truth and the vindication of the
race against vicious assaults.' "[8] The Reverend Crummell, who
chaired the meeting, further elaborated on Mr. Ferris's remarks and
Dr. Du Bois's proposed amendment just before it was passed.

> Since Emancipation, if there has been one, there have been fif-
> ty publications by distinguished writers in this country,
> scholars, philosophers, eminent men of letters, which were
> assaults on this race. Not one of them has been answered.[9]
> Remember, in 1874, Dr. Tucker made a most vicious assault
> upon the race.[10] It is with this race as with all races; you have
> got to have good protectors.[11]

From 1897 to 1924, the American Negro Academy published
twenty-one numbers of its occasional papers and one full-length
book. The occasional papers were scholarly in nature and read at
the academy's meetings held annually in Washington, D.C., in late
December. Most of the occasional papers were published as
pamphlets. Two of them, however, do qualify as books in this
study because they contain forty-nine or more pages (see final para-
graph of the Introduction). They were *Occasional Paper No. 11*,
released as one volume in 1905 (85 pages) and *Occasional Papers
No. 18–19*, published as a single volume in 1915 (78 pages).

   The single full-length book published under the academy's imprint was *The Negro in American History*, by John Cromwell, its
corresponding secretary, in 1914. In the preface to the book
Cromwell cited his reason for writing it.

>   . . . confirmed by my own conclusion based on an experi-
> ence in the classroom covering twenty years, [this] leads me

to attempt the publication of a book which shall give to teachers and secondary school pupils, especially, the salient points in the history of the American Negro, the story of their most eminent men and women and a bibliography that will guide those desirous of making further study and investigation.[12]

The work served as a text for teaching Black history to subsequent generations. A reprint edition of the book appeared in 1968.

The publications of the academy were underwritten by its general membership and the individual authors of each manuscript. Every member was assessed five dollars as the initial membership fee and one dollar, thereafter, annually. A percentage of each initial membership fee was used to support the publishing program. Authors of individual manuscripts assumed one-half of the cost of editing and printing the manuscript and the academy paid the remaining costs, a practice in similar white organizations.

The academy's executive committee, composed of members who lived in Washington, D.C., and other elected members, selected and assigned topics for all papers to be presented at the annual conferences and exercised final authority on those papers selected for publication. These papers were proofread and edited by John Cromwell.

Imposing a limit of 4,500 words on individual manuscripts, the academy copyrighted all its publications with the exception of *The Negro in American History*, which John Cromwell copyrighted. The executive committee administered the sale and distribution of the academy's publications, sending copies to each member, many major public libraries, and to newspapers and journals for review. The academy reprinted none of its publications nor issued any revised editions.

The publications of the academy explored competently several areas of Afro-Americana. Rarely, however, were these publications long enough to be exhaustive. Most of the authors of the academy's publications, with the notable exceptions of W.E.B. Du Bois and Kelly Miller, although well read and articulate, had not been trained in the latest scientific methods of conducting research in history or the social sciences. The American Negro Academy did, nonetheless, pave the way for other Afro-American cultural organizations which would come into existence and publish books by authors fully capable of scholarly rigor.

After 1924 the activities of the American Negro Academy came to a close. Ernest Kaiser observed the significance of its passing. "Thus, by 1924, Negro scholarly writing of protest and history and the cultural fields was being done under other auspices than those of the Academy. Having passed its banners into other hands, the American Negro Academy quietly came to an end.[13]

One of the cultural organizations to which the American Negro Academy "passed its banners" was the Association for the Study of Afro-American Life and History (originally known as the Association for the Study of Negro Life and History). The association was founded in Chicago at the Wabash YMCA on September 3, 1915, by the Harvard-trained Black historian Dr. Carter G. Woodson with the assistance of four other Afro-Americans: Dr. George Cleveland Hall; W. B. Hartgrove; James E. Stamps; and A. L. Jackson.[14]

The publishing program developed by the association was more extensive and varied than the academy's. This cultural organization published a quarterly scholarly journal, a monthly magazine, and a host of exhaustive studies in many areas of Black Americana and Africana. Monographs that Dr. Woodson thought would be published at a loss, he published under the imprint of the association; those that he imagined would bring a profit, he published under the imprint of the Associated Publishers (discussed in chapter 3).

Upon the occasion of the twenty-fifth anniversary of the association in 1940, Dr. Woodson reviewed the significance of the association and its publishing program.

> This undertaking was the first systematic effort of the Negro to treat the records of the race scientifically and to publish the findings to the world. Up to that time no organization with this scientific objective and a program to attain this end had been able to function efficiently along this line in the United States.[15]

The publishing program of the association included employing and training investigators to research various aspects of Afro-Americana and Africana and publishing the findings of these and other investigators in the association's publications.

On January 1, 1916, the *Journal of Negro History*, the association's scholarly quarterly, began publication. By 1940 twenty-five volumes of this journal had appeared, containing 360 articles authored by 254 investigators, slightly more than half of whom were Blacks.[16]

In 1926 the association established the first annual observance of Negro History Week to dramatize the achievements of Blacks and to promote better racial understanding. This project was so well received by the general public that the association launched the *Negro History Bulletin* in 1937.[17] Published nine times a year from October through June to correspond with the months that schools and colleges are in session, this publication, aimed at the average young adult and adult reader, contains articles which popularize the research conducted by the association.

Presenting the findings of investigations into little-known areas of Black Americana and Africana, which most earlier scholars had ignored or neglected, the book-publishing activities of the association have had a significant impact on American historical scholarship that can hardly be measured. The development of this program was greatly influenced by: the fluctuating financial support the association received over the years from philanthropic foundations and private individuals; the administrative acumen and self-sacrificing efforts of Dr. Woodson; and the willingness of competent scholars, both Black and white, to perform investigations, in some instances at personal sacrifices. When these influences were in harmony, the association's book-publishing program flourished; when they were in discord, it went into a decline. The changing status and relationships of these influences allow the program's history to be divided into two periods: 1918 to 1940; and 1941 to 1953.

In 1918 the association issued its first two books: *A Century of Migration*, by Carter G. Woodson; and *Slavery in Kentucky*, by Ivan Eugene McDougle. By 1940 it had published under its imprint twenty-eight monographs.[18] Many of these have become classic studies, such as: *Anti-Slavery Sentiment in American Literature*, by Lorenzo Dow Turner (1924); *The Negro in South Carolina during Reconstruction*, by Alrutheus Ambush Taylor (1924); *The*

Negro Wage Earner, by Lorenzo J. Greene and Carter G. Woodson (1930); and *Negro Casualties in the Civil War*, by Herbert Aptheker (1939).

From 1918 through 1930 the association successfully solicited funds from several foundations. Among them were the Phelps Stokes Fund, the Julius Rosenwald Fund, the Social Science Foundation of the Rockefeller Foundation, and the Laura Spelman Rockefeller Memorial.[19] After 1930, Dr. Woodson stated that Jesse Jones of the Phelps Stokes Fund used his influence to stop these contributions. "Jones conducted a campaign against the Association for the Study of Negro Life and History because its Director questioned the wisdom of Jones' African policy. By 1930 he succeeded in lopping off all support of the Association from boards and foundations.[20] Dr. Woodson further stated that support, after 1930, came primarily from Afro-Americans.

> Observing as early as 1930 that such was the situation with respect to financial support, the Director began to organize the Negroes of the country to obtain from them what support the interracialists had succeeded in diverting from this effort. . . . The success thus achieved is a credit to the Negro race and serves as eloquent evidence of the capacity of the Negro for self-help.[21]

Undoubtedly, the greatest influence on the association's book-publishing program during these years was the presence of Dr. Woodson. In the early years of the association's existence Dr. Woodson made up its deficits from his personal funds. His leadership ability and business sense guided it successfully through the depression years when many of the monographs were published.

From 1941 through 1953 the book-publishing activities of the association declined sharply. Dr. Woodson in his annual reports from 1941 to 1949 cited several reasons. Prominent among these were the lack of funds, the rapidly rising costs associated with publishing, and the paper shortages during World War II.

Dr. Woodson died in 1950. Three years later, as provided by Woodson's will, the association assumed control of Associated Publishers, a private book-publishing firm founded by Dr. Woodson and his associates in 1921. The Associated Publishers became, thereafter, the official book-publishing unit of the Association for the Study of Afro-American Life and History.

During the 1930s, while the association spearheaded investigations into various areas of Black Americana and Africana, another Black cultural organization, the Blyden Society, sprang into being, focusing its efforts on disseminating information about war-stricken Ethiopia and Africa. Founded in Harlem in 1935 by Willis Huggins, a New York City high school history teacher, the Blyden Society achieved its goals through its well-attended meetings, public forums, and publishing program. Professor John Henrik Clarke of Hunter College, a former member of the society, discussed the objectives of its publishing program: "The publishing objectives were to bring out manuscripts relating to Africa from a different perspective than those which already existed. Part of our intent was to publish old works too, like those of Leo Frobenius."[22] The society published one book, *Ethiopia and the Origin of Civilization*, by John G. Jackson (1939), and several pamphlets. These publications were sold through advanced subscriptions originating from its membership, which numbered about 150, and mail advertisement sent to leaders in Black communities throughout the United States, Europe, the West Indies, and Africa. In the summer of 1939, Willis Huggins met a mysterious death. Found in the Hudson River near the George Washington Bridge, it is a matter of conjecture whether he committed suicide or encountered foul play.[23] One year later the Blyden Society folded.

The Associates in Negro Folk Education realized a more ambitious publishing program in the 1930s than the Blyden Society. Based in Washington, D.C., the Associates in Negro Folk Education was established in 1935 by Dr. Alain LeRoy Locke, a Howard University philosophy professor.[24] Under the direction of Dr. Locke, the associates, composed of a group of Black scholars and intellectuals, published nine titles in its Bronze Booklet Series between 1935 and 1937 and in 1940, one quarto volume on the history of Afro-American art.

Dr. Locke secured funds for launching the Associates in Negro Folk Education's publishing program from the Adult Education Association. These funds covered the cost of publishing the books and provided a small honorarium for the authors.

Dr. Robert Martin, Professor of Political Science at Howard University, described Dr. Locke's objective in establishing the publishing program of the associates.

Dr. Locke's basic objective was to provide authentic information on major aspects of American Negro life written by recognized, highly qualified authors for a wide spectrum of readers, especially Black Americans, at a low cost, so that the books could be afforded by the masses. The books sold for twenty-five cents, paperbound, and fifty cents, hardbound.[25]

Serving as a general editor, Dr. Locke decided the subject areas for the books, selected the authors and worked closely with them, assisted by Dr. Martin, in developing their manuscripts. Examples of some of the books published by the Associates are: *Adult Education among Negroes*, by Ira D. Reid (Bronze Booklet n. 1) (1935); *A World View of Race*, by Ralph J. Bunche (Bronze Booklet n. 4) (1936); *Negro Poetry and Drama*, by Sterling Brown (Bronze Booklet, n. 7) (1937); and *The Negro in Art*, by Alain LeRoy Locke (1940). After 1940 no titles were identified as publications of the Associates in Negro Folk Education.

As the decade of the 1940s unfolded, another Black cultural organization devoted to the publication of books and a journal for the dissemination of information about Afro-Americans was organized: the Communist-supported Negro Publication Society of America. William A. Nolan described the circumstances surrounding the founding of this publishing venture. "Not long after the Nazi invasion of Russia, the Communists set up the Negro Publication Society of America, which provided for the integration of Negro and white fellow-travelers and for the publication of their writings in the *Negro Quarterly*."[26]

Established in New York City in 1941, the society began publishing the *Negro Quarterly* in the spring of 1942. Edited by Angelo Herndon, an Afro-American for whom the Communist-sponsored International Labor Defense had won an appeal before the Supreme Court for his supposed violation of an 1886 Georgia law for leading a relief march in Atlanta in 1933, and Ralph Ellison, a budding young Afro-American writer, the *Negro Quarterly* set forth the aims of the society in its first issue. "The Negro Publication Society of America is a non-profit-making organization formed for the purpose of disseminating and promoting the publication of literary and scientific works giving information in and interpreting the history and contributions of Negro life." The society planned to organize its publications into six categories: history, literature, labor, government, science, music and art. "These six categories govern series in which books and other publications will be issued. Each series containing a number of selected volumes covering varied phases of the Negro experience."[27]

Unfortunately, these stated ambitious aims of the society were scarcely realized. Only two books seem to have been published. In Series No. 1, History, one title appeared: *The Kidnapped and the Ransomed*, by Kate Picard (1941), a reprint of a novel based on the life story of two Black Americans who were sold into slavery and finally set free, which was originally published in 1856. A second title was published in Series No. 2, Race and Culture: *Jim Crow's Last Stand*, by Langston Hughes (1943), a volume of poetry.

The Negro Publication Society of America apparently died with the last number of the *Negro Quarterly* in the spring of 1943. William A. Nolan sums up in the significance of the society and its journal in the following way: "Like many other Communist intellectual efforts, this magazine was short-lived; but while it lasted it enabled a few Negro writers to promote their careers.[28]

Another non profit, predominately Afro-American, cultural organization which enabled many Black American as well as white writers to publish their works was the Free Lance Poetry and Prose Workshop of Cleveland. Unlike the Negro Publication Society of America, the Free Lance Poetry and Prose Workshop was not affiliated with any political organization. Organized in 1950, by Casper L. Jordan and Russel Atkins, it was an interracial writers group, mostly Afro-Americans, which met regularly to read and discuss the manuscripts of its members.[29] In that same year the workshop launched the Free Lance Press with the publication of *Free Lance*, a semiannual journal of prose, poetry, and drama. Nine years later, Free Lance Press began publishing books authored by members of the workshop with the publication of *Perchance to Dream, Othello*, a book of poems by Conrad Kent Rivers (1959). The book publishing objectives of Free Lance Press, unique among the publishers thus far considered, are, as indicated by one of its editors, to publish books which articulate and portray various aspects of Afro-American culture for highly literate audiences and to publish works which celebrate through literature various aspects of the human experience unrelated to Afro-Americana or Africana. The book publishing activities of the Free Lance Press continued mainly after 1960. They will be discussed later in this study.

The National Dental Association was the only professional organization identified as an active book publisher during this period. With headquarters in Charlottesville, Virginia, the association was founded in 1913 to work for the equal rights of Black American dentists in all aspects of the dental profession. In 1941, the association began publishing the *Bulletin of the National Dental Association*, a quarterly. One book was released by the association: *The Growth and Development of the Negro in Dentistry*, by Clifton Orrin Dummett (1952), a history of the contributions of Afro-Americans to dentistry.

THE BOOK-PUBLISHING ACTIVITIES OF BLACK CIVIL RIGHTS, POLITICAL, AND SOCIAL WELFARE ORGANIZATIONS

Between 1910 and 1914, four national organizations devoted variously to the political, legal, cultural, and economic uplift of Black Americans were established in the United States. Each of them developed publishing programs with objectives supportive of their overall goals.

The National Association for the Advancement of Colored People (NAACP), organized in 1910, was one of these organizations. Under the directorship of W.E.B. Du Bois, this organization's Department of Research and Publicity developed a very ambitious publishing program that included the publication of a monthly periodical, pamphlets, and books. These publications contributed to this organization's goals by realizing the following publishing objectives: informing Blacks of various aspects of their past and present culture; apprising Blacks of their contemporary legal, political, and social status; providing information to persons and organizations interested in the welfare of Blacks; and publicizing the philosophy and programs of the NAACP.

The broadest realization of the publishing objectives of the NAACP is *Crisis Magazine*. Published since 1910 and intended for a mass audience, *Crisis Magazine* is the official organ of the NAACP. Articles by many knowledgeable leaders in the Black American's struggle for equality have appeared within its pages reporting on the legal, political, and social status of the Black American as well as fiction, poetry, and book reviews on Black American life by aspiring and leading Black and white writers. By 1919 *Crisis Magazine* reached its highest monthly circulation, 104,000, making it the most widely read Black publication in the first two decades of the twentieth century.[30] Throughout its long history the NAACP has been a prolific publisher of pamphlets, such as *The Fantastic Case of the Trenton Six* (1951) and *Stop That Bully* (1950), which, like *Crisis Magazine*, were illustrative of its publishing objectives. Book publishing, however, was not a major publishing effort of the NAACP. It did, nonetheless, release some important books like *Thirty Years of Lynching* (1919), *Prince Hall and His Followers*, by George Williamson Crawford (1914), *The Awakening*, by Mary White Ovington (1923), and *A Child's Story of Dunbar*, by Julia L. Henderson (1913). The NAACP advertised its publications in the *Crisis Magazine*. They were generally ordered by the readership and distributed through the mail.

Concerned primarily with the social, economic, and cultural betterment of Blacks in urban areas, the National Urban League (NUL), organized in 1911, developed one of the most extensive publishing programs of any Black civil rights, political, or social welfare organization between 1900 and 1960.[31] The objectives of this organization's publishing program were to publish books, periodicals, and pamphlets to improve the social, economic, and cultural conditions of Blacks in urban areas by informing them of significant developments in their present culture, documenting contemporary social and economic problems facing them, providing individuals and organizations interested in the Black American with authoritative information about his social life, and publishing the philosophy and programs of the NUL.

The first book published by NUL, *Ebony and Topaz*, edited by Charles S. Johnson (1927), reflected its efforts to diffuse knowledge about significant developments in Black culture. This anthology of works by leading and aspiring Black writers, artists, and intellectuals was one of the major books published by Blacks during the Harlem Renaissance.

To a greater extent, however, the NUL published studies conducted by its research department documenting problems facing the urban Black. Directed primarily at sympathetic white individuals and organizations interested in the welfare of urban Blacks, these studies have had a profound effect on urban race relations as well as the development or urban sociology. *Unemployment Status of Negroes: A Compilation of Facts and Figures Respecting Unemployment among Negroes in the United States and Its Cost: 1932-1933* (Color Line Series) (1933), *Racial Conflict: A Homefront Danger* (1946), and *Race, Fear and Housing in a Typical American Community* (1946) are examples of these studies.

Books publicizing the philosophy and programs of the NUL appeared from time to time between 1911 and 1959. *And the Pursuit of Happiness: 40th Anniversary Yearbook* (1950) is indicative of such publications released by the NUL.

Like the NAACP, the NUL published periodicals and pamphlets which reflected the objectives of its publishing program. From 1921 to 1922, it published the *Urban League Bulletin*, which was superseded by *Opportunity: A Journal of Negro Life* from 1923 through 1949, a broader-based periodical carrying not only articles on the League's research but also fiction, essays, poetry, and book reviews. Of notable interest was the Color Line Series of pamphlets released by the League. Begun in 1933, this series, composed of mostly vocational pamphlets, like *Guiding Negro Youth toward Jobs*, by Ann Tanneyhill (1938), was widely distributed throughout the country.

Most of the League's publications were advertised in *Opportunity* and purchased through the mail by its readership. Many of them, however, were distributed through the League's affiliates in various cities throughout the country.

Established in Jamaica in 1914 by Marcus Garvey and moved to Harlem in 1916, the Universal Negro Improvement Association (UNIA), which advocated a more militant philosophy for the political, social, and economic improvement of Black Americans than did either the NAACP or the NUL, had a very active, though relatively short-lived, publishing program in the United States. Advancing in its publications, which included newspapers, books, and pamphlets, the philosophy of racial separatism as the only means of equality for the Afro-American, the UNIA developed a publishing program with a distribution system through its chapters so effective that its publications reached the masses of Blacks in the United States and many foreign countries.

The most widely distributed publication of the UNIA was the *Negro World*, a weekly newspaper and its official organ. It reportedly reached a circulation in the early 1920s of almost 200,000.[32]

The book and pamphlet publications of the UNIA, although not as widely circulated as the *Negro World*, illustrated the organization's effort to publicize its programs and philosophy in extended works. For example, *Philosophy and Opinions of Marcus Garvey*, Volume 1, compiled and edited by Garvey's second wife, Amy Jacques-Garvey, was released in 1923; a pamphlet *Selections from the Poetic Meditations of Marcus Garvey*, also edited by Amy Jacques-Garvey, was published in 1924.

In Memphis the energetic Reverend Sutton E. Griggs, pastor of the city's Tabernacle Institutional Baptist Church, organized the National Public Welfare League in 1914. Advocating a philosophy of social efficiency among Blacks and interracial cooperation as a means of improving Blacks economically and socially, this organization published literature which communicated its philosophy to Afro-Americans and concerned white Americans. All of the publications issued by the National Public Welfare League were authored by the Reverend Sutton E. Griggs. Illustrative of the several books published by this organization was *Guide to Racial Greatness; or, The Science of Collective Efficiency*, by Sutton E. Griggs (1923), a book which outlined his philosophy of social efficiency for Blacks. It was well received by the white Memphis press and the Colored Teachers Association of Texas adopted it as a text for the instruction of Black teachers in the state.[33]

The Black community of Memphis, however, was skeptical of Griggs and his philosophy, which had won the favor of many prominent white leaders of the city. In 1930 Grigg's career in Memphis came to an end when his Tabernacle Institutional Baptist Church fell into serious financial trouble. Griggs left Memphis and the National Public Welfare League folded. David Tucker summed up Griggs's exodus from Memphis: "His church was sold by the holders of the mortgage, and Griggs retreated in embarrassment to Denison, Texas, where he died on January 3, 1933, an intellectual in exile, a despondent man, almost unwept and unhonored."[34]

THE BOOK-PUBLISHING ACTIVITIES OF BLACK COLLEGES AND UNIVERSITIES, 1900–1960

Black colleges and universities that engaged in book publishing between 1900 and 1960 did so without the benefit of a university press replete with an editorial office and professional staff such as those that were being established during this period at several major American universities such as Columbia, Johns Hopkins, and the University of Chicago. Book publishing at most Black colleges and universities was not an ongoing campus activity. It was given low priority and was generally assigned, with other duties, to the institution's public relations officer, who worked closely with individual authors and the institution's printing department or a commercial printer to develop the manuscript into a published book.

Nonetheless, several significant scholarly books were published by Black colleges and universities during this period. The book publishing objectives of these colleges and universities were broader in scope than those of the publishing units of Black cultural, professional, and civil rights organizations. Like these organizations, Black colleges and universities included among their publications books to vindicate Blacks and to document various aspects of Black culture and history as well as to publicize their particular programs; but they also published books to serve as textbooks for courses unique to their curricula, to document various aspects of local history, and to explore specific subjects unrelated to Black Americana but of appeal to adult audiences. As we shall see, these presses were also outlets for significant faculty research at most of the colleges and universities as were similar presses at major white colleges and universities.

The Hampton Institute Press, which began publishing in 1871, had one of the most varied book publishing programs of any of the

Black colleges and universities. Ruth M. Tolson in her bibliography, "Hampton Institute Press Publications," discusses two of the publishing objectives of this press.

> The press was used by the school's founder, General Armstrong, in publicizing the school and its philosophy. As can be seen from the list, the Press published mostly regional books, pamphlets and works of writers who lived in the community. Its publications dealt chiefly with the local scene and the greater part of its authors were from this area.[35]

One of this press's early books, *Twenty-Two Years of the Hampton Normal and Agricultural Institute at Hampton, Virginia: Records of Negro and Indian Graduates and Ex-Students* (1893), did, indeed, publicize this institution's educational program by documenting the achievements of its students. Another early title, *Visitors' Handbook of Old Point Comfort, Va. and Vicinity*, by Charles Betts (1883), does describe the local region. However, there are books in Tolson's bibliography which reflect publishing objectives not discussed by her. *On Habits and Manners: Written Originally for the Students at Hampton N. and A. Institute*, by Mary Frances Armstrong (1888), and *The Hampton Arithmetic*, by Flora F. Low (1909), for instance, were books obviously published for the instruction of students in courses taught at Hampton. *Virginia's Contribution to Negro Leadership*, edited by William M. Cooper (1936), illustrates the press's attempt to publish books which document an aspect of Afro-American history.

No titles with the "Hampton Institute Press" imprint were identified as being published after 1939. Publishing at Hampton Institute on a large scale seems to have ceased after that year. For example, the *Southern Workman*, a monthly journal published by the press for sixty-eight years, ended its run in that year. In the late 1930s Hampton, as viewed by one writer, went through a period of financial entrenchment.[36] Book publishing was, undoubtedly, a casualty of this financial crisis.

Manned by students under the supervision of an instructor, the Printing Department of Atlanta University began printing books published under the "Atlanta University Press" imprint in 1896.

The Atlanta University Press, though to a lesser extent than the Hampton Institute Press, published books to publicize the educational program of the university with the aim of winning northern philanthropy and new students to the university. Three titles were published for this purpose: *The General Catalogue of Atlanta University*, compiled by Myron Adams (1918), a semicentennial publication describing the achievements and the general development of the university and its students; *The General Catalogue of Atlanta University, 1867–1929*, revised edition (1929); and *A History of Atlanta University*, by Myron Adams (1930).

However, the Atlanta University Press, to a greater degree, focused on publishing exhaustive sociological studies documenting the social and cultural conditions of Afro-Americans in the South and books to serve as textbooks in various courses taught at the university. In 1896 the Atlanta University Press began publishing the Atlanta University Publications. These pioneering studies, regarded by many as the earliest researches in sociology conducted in the South, were the results of annual conferences held on the Black American at Atlanta University from 1896 to 1918. Between 1897 and 1910, they were directed by W.E.B. Du Bois, then teaching at the university. The Atlanta University Publications, composed of twenty-two monographs, included such studies as *Social and Physical Conditions of Negroes in Cities*, No. 2 (1897), *Some Efforts of American Negroes for Their Own Betterment*, No. 3 (1898), *The College-Bred Negro*, No. 5 (1900), and *The Negro Common School*, No. 6 (1901). The Atlanta University French Series, which the press issued in 1936, was a group of textbooks for use in French courses at the university. Edited by Mercer Cook and Guichard Parris they included *Les Singes De Dieu Et Les Hommes Du Diable*, by Alexandre Privat d'Anglemont (Atlanta University French Series, No. 1, 1936) and *Ourika*, by Madame de Duras (Atlanta University French Series, No. 2, 1936).

No books with the "Atlanta University Press" imprint were identified after 1936. A search through the University Archives did not give any clues for the cessation of book publishing activities at that time.

Tuskegee Institute, like its mentor Hampton, advocated industrial education as a panacea for the Black American and published books to publicize the success of its program. In 1908, Tuskegee's Hampton-trained founder and principal, Booker T. Washington, upon the recommendation of sociologist Robert E. Park, who was working at Tuskegee at the time, brought University of Chicago-trained Monroe N. Work to Tuskegee to establish the Department of Records and Research. Work compiled a record of Tuskegee's students and graduates, which resulted in the first book published by the Tuskegee Institute Press in 1911: *Industrial Work of Tuskegee Graduates and Former Students during the Year 1910.*[37]

Over the years other publishing objectives were realized by the press. Among the many titles published by the press with the obvious objective of documenting the accomplishments of the Black American was John Kenny's *The Negro in Medicine* (1912), a detailed history of the Afro-American's role in American medicine. Jesse Parkhurst Guzman's *Lynching by States, 1882–1958* (1958) is an example of a book published by the press to document the plight of Afro-Americans in the United States. The press also published books unrelated to Black Americana or Africana but of interest and appeal to an adult audience, such as *Graphic Arts Survey*, by William E. Boone (1955).

No titles were identified as publications of the Tuskegee Institute Press after 1958. After that year the press became inactive.

In 1910 another Black book-publishing enterprise, the Negro Year Book Publishing Company, sprung into being on the campus of Tuskegee Institute. This firm began publishing *The Negro Year Book* in 1912. Funds for the publication of the first edition of *The Negro Year Book* were obtained from the Committee of Twelve for the Advancement of the Interest of the Negro Race. Underwritten by Andrew Carnegie, the Committee of Twelve was founded in 1904. It was composed of prominent Black Americans who were concerned with improving civil rights for Blacks in the South. By 1910 the funds of the committee had dwindled to one thousand dollars. Booker T. Washington, who was chairman at the time, pursuaded the committee to use the remaining funds to publish a book documenting the progress of the Black American since Emancipation, thus winning funding for the first edition of *The Negro Year Book.*[38]

The Negro Year Book Publishing Company was a partnership

composed of Robert E. Park, president, Emmett J. Scott, vice-
president, and Monroe N. Work, secretary. In 1929, when the firm
fell into financial trouble, the publication of *The Negro Year Book*
was taken over by Tuskegee Institute. The deficit in *The Negro
Year Book's* account occurred when 25,000 copies of the 1918–1919
edition were put on the market at the beginning of the financial
depression of 1929.[39]

The outgrowth of Monroe N. Work's activities as head of the
Department of Records and Research at Tuskegee Institute, *The
Negro Year Book* was the most comprehensive source of facts and
statistics on the Black American to appear in the first four decades
of the twentieth century. Scrupulously edited, this serial monograph included a variety of subjects such as "Negro progress; the
Race Problem; the Negro World Distribution; Governments;
Chronology in America; Slavery; Abolition; the Church; Education; Music; Fine Arts.[40] The purpose of *The Negro Year Book* was
stated by Monroe Work:

> When I came to Tuskegee, educators and others seeking to
> advance the interest of the Negro were confronted with such
> questions as: What had the Negro accomplished? What can
> he do? Does it pay to educate him? Morally is he deteriorat-
> ing? Has his emancipation been justified? The publication by
> Hoffman in 1896 of *Race Traits and Tendencies of the Negro*
> presented a more or less hopeless view. To the indictment by
> this publication there was at hand no effective answer. From
> 1908 on I was compiling a day by day record of what was tak-
> ing place with reference to the Negro. Thus it became possible
> to answer in a factual manner questions relating to all matters
> concerning him.[41]

Apart from vindicating the Afro-American, *The Negro Year Book*
became a source of inspiration and uplift for every Black American
who read it.

From 1912 to 1952, *The Negro Year Book* was published in
eleven editions. Monroe N. Work edited nine of them; Jessie Parkhurst Guzman, his successor, edited the tenth and eleventh editions.

Many of the nation's leading newspapers published sections of *The Negro Year Book* annually. The research departments of the National Urban League and the National Association for the Advancement of Colored People relied heavily on it for many of their research projects. Today, *The Negro Year Book* is a classic reference tool on the Afro-American in libraries around the world.

Two books published in 1901 and authored by Jeremiah E. Rankin, president of Howard University from 1890 to 1903, were identified as the earliest books published by the university: *Seeking God Early and Other Sermons;* and *Esther Burr's Journal.* In 1914 another title was released under the "Howard University Press" imprint: *Commercial College Studies of Negroes in Business.* Yet, the board of trustees of the university did not formally authorize the establishment of the Howard University Press until its meeting on February 17, 1919.[42] However, no press was organized as a result of this official authorization. Nonetheless, although no administrative unit was charged with book publishing at the university, Howard University continued to be an active book publisher during the period under consideration.

In 1922 the university's history department began publishing the Howard University Studies in History. This series, which consisted primarily of pamphlets, did include books like Walter Dyson's *Founding of the School of Medicine of Howard University* (1929). In the late 1920s the Howard University Studies in Urban Sociology began to appear with such titles as *The Housing of Negroes in Washington, D.C.*, by William H. Jones (1929) and *Recreation and Amusement Among Negroes in Washington, D.C.* (1927).But, perhaps, the most widely heralded book publication of the university during these years was the *Journal of Negro Education Yearbook.* Begun in 1932 by Charles H. Thompson, a professor in the university's department of education and later dean of its college of liberal arts, the *Yearbook* was first published as the second number of the *Journal of Negro Education* in April 1932. Dr. Thompson states its purpose in this first volume: "This yearbook issue is conceived and launched in accord with the expressed editorial policy of the *Journal* to make a rather comprehensive study of some particular aspect of Negro education each year."[43]

Many other titles were published during this period under the "Howard University Press" imprint by members of the university's faculty. Among some of them were: *Howard University, the Capstone of Negro Education,* by Walter Dyson (1941); *The Negro in the Americas,* edited by Charles Wesley (1940); *Trust and Non-Self-Governing Territories,* edited by Merze Tate (1948); *The Negro Thirty Years Afterwards,* edited by Rayford Logan (1955); and *A Catalogue of the African Collection in the Moorland Foundation, Howard University Library,* compiled by Dorothy Barrett Porter-Wesley.[44]

Fisk University, like Howard, had no organized administrative unit within the university with the responsibility of publishing books. Notwithstanding, the "Fisk University Press" imprint did appear on several scholarly books published by the university. All of them, however, were printed by a local commercial printing firm in Nashville.

One of the earliest titles identified with the "Fisk University Press". imprint was a prime example of the university's effort to publish books documenting an aspect of Afro-American culture: John W. Work's *The Negro and His Song* (1915), a history and criticism of Afro-American songs. Curiously, this title was not copyrighted by Work or the university but by Fayette McKenzie, president of Fisk University at the time of its publication.

During the 1930s and 1940s the university's social science department, under the direction of Charles Spurgeon Johnson, conducted several original researches into various areas of Black American sociology which the university published. For example, *The Free Negro Family,* by E. Franklin Frazier, at the time a member of the faculty, was published in 1932; Herman Long and Charles Spurgeon Johnson collaborated on *People versus Property,* which was released in 1947. These studies were indicative of the university's commitment to publishing books that scientifically documented aspects of the Black American's social, legal, and economic conditions.

One of the books published by the university which was of great scholarly interest, but unrelated to Black Americana of Africana, was Fanny Bandelier's translation of *History of Ancient Mexico,* by Fray Bernadino de Sahagun (1932). Bandelier was a member of the faculty when the book was released.

Build the Future: Addresses Marking the Inauguration of Charles Spurgeon Johnson (1949) was the last book identified with the "Fisk

University Press" imprint. After that year book publishing seems to have been discontinued by the university.

Although not as prolific as Fisk, Xavier University of Louisiana in New Orleans was also a book publisher. However, C. Tilger, acting university librarian, when queried about the presence of a press at Xavier, made the following statement: "Xavier University does not have a university press and never did have a Xavier university owned press. Books have been published by Xavier, but printed for Xavier by a private printing press.[45]

The three books identified with the "Xavier University Press" imprint reflected the university's interests in publishing books on local Black American history, Black Catholicism, and vocational guidance. They were *The Negro in Louisiana: Aspects of His History and His Literature*, by Charles B. Rousseve (1937), *Occupational Opportunities Monographs*, by John Patrick Corcoran (1938), and *Arrows of Gold: An Anthology of Catholic Verse from America's First College for Colored Youth*, edited by Peter Clark (1941). No books published by the university were identified with imprints after 1941.

Afro-American institutional book publishers, although small in number between 1900 and 1960, made, as has been shown in this chapter, a significant contribution to American book publishing. To a greater extent, however, the books released by these publishers, while enriching the cultural and intellectual life of Afro-Americans, improved the intellectual life of the country as a whole. Several titles published by these publishers were classics and established trends in their respective disciplines.

NOTES

1. Howard Odum, *Social and Mental Traits of the Negro: A Study of Race Traits, Tendencies and Prospects*, Studies in History and Public Law 37 (New York: Columbia University Press, 1910), pp. 39–41.

2. Stanley M. Elkins, *Slavery: A Problem in American Institutional and Intellectual Life*. (Chicago: University of Chicago Press, 1959), p. 10.

3. Historian George M. Fredrickson summarized the impact of Darwinism on racialism in the United States during the period: "By 1900 Darwinism provided the basis for a necessary reformulation of the set of

racist concepts originally developed in the middle of the nineteenth century as a rationale for slavery" *The Black Image in the White Mind* [New York: Harper & Row, 1971], p. 25.

4. In the 1910 census, 64,245 Afro-Americans were listed as being employed in the following professional services: clergymen, college presidents and college teachers, dentists, lawyers and judges, musicians and music teachers, physicians and surgeons, school teachers, and trained nurses. U.S., Department of Commerce, Bureau of the Census, *Negroes in the United States, 1920-1932.* (Washington, D.C., Government Printing Office, 1936), p. 498.

5. Elkins, *Slavery: A Problem,* p. 16.

6. Mignon Miller, "The American Negro Academy: An Intellectual Movement During the Era of Negro Disenfranchisement, 1897-1924" (Master's thesis, Howard University, 1966), p. 17.

7. American Negro Academy, *Minutes of the Meetings, 1897-1922, Washington, D.C.* (Boston: Microfilm by Dr. Adelaide Cromwell Gulliver, 1975), reel 1.

8. Ibid.

9. Contrary to this statement by Rev. Crummell, some Afro-American leaders did answer the assaults made on Afro-Americans by white supremacist writers during this period, such as Frederick Douglass, George Washington Williams, and, as noted below, Rev. Crummell, himself.

10. This reference is to Dr. Joseph L. Tucker who read a paper at the "Church Congress" (Protestant Episcopal Church) in Richmond, Va., on October 1882 entitled "On Relations of the Church to the Colored Race," which Crummell considered a vicious attack on Afro-Americans. Crummell answered the attack in the following work: "A Defense of the Negro Race in America from the Assaults and Charges of Rev. J. L. Tucker, D.D., of Jackson, Mississippi" (in Alexander Crummell, *Africa and America* [Springfield, Mass: Wiley & Co., 1891], pp. 85-125).

11. American Negro Academy, *Minutes of Meetings,* reel 2.

12. John Cromwell, *The Negro in American History* (Washington, D.C.: American Negro Academy, 1914), p. xii.

13. Ernest Kaiser, "Preface," *The American Negro Academy Occasional Papers,* 1-22 (New York: Arno Press, 1969), p. ii.

14. Carter G. Woodson, "An Accounting for Twenty-five Years," *Journal of Negro History* 25 (July 1940): 422.

15. Ibid., p. 432.

16. Luther P. Jackson, "The First Twenty-Two Volumes of the *Journal of Negro History* Digested," *Journal of Negro History* 25 (July 1940): 432, 422.

17. Woodson, "An Accounting," pp. 428, 429.

18. Ibid., p. 424.

19. Ibid., p. 425.

20. Carter G. Woodson, "Thomas Jesse Jones," *Journal of Negro History* 35 (January 1950): 108.

21. Woodson, "An Accounting," p. 425-26.

22. Professor John Henrik Clarke, interview held at Hunter College, New York, N.Y., November 24, 1975, reel 1.

23. Ibid.

24. Dr. Robert Martin, Professor of Political Science, Howard University, to the author, May 31, 1976, p. 2.

25. Ibid., p. 1.

26. William A. Nolan, *Communism versus the Negro* (Chicago: Regnery, 1951), p. 157.

27. "Aims of the Negro Publication Society," *Negro Quarterly* 1 (Summer 1942): vi.

28. Nolan, *Communism versus the Negro*, p. 157.

29. Casper L. Jordan, interview held at Atlanta University, Atlanta, Ga., 10 January 1976, reel 1.

30. Charles Flint Kellog, *N.A.A.C.P.: A History of the National Association for the Advancement of Colored People* (Baltimore: Johns Hopkins University Press, 1967), vol. 1, *1909-1920*, p. 153.

31. The National Urban League's original name was the National League on Urban Conditions among Negroes. Its present name was adopted in 1920.

32. Theodore G. Vincent, *Black Power and the Garvey Movement* (Berkeley, Calif: Ramparts Press, 1971), p. 127.

33. David M. Tucker, *Black Pastors and Leaders: Memphis, 1919-1972* (Memphis: Memphis State University Press, 1975), p. 84; *Memphis Commercial Appeal*, 30 March 1924, p. 18.

34. Tucker, *Black Pastors*, p. 86.

35. Ruth M. Tolson, comp., "Hampton Institute Press Publications," mimeographed, 1959, Hampton Institute Archives, Publications," Hampton, Va., p. 1.

36. William Hannibal Robinson, "The History of Hampton Institute" (Ph.D. diss., New York University, 1953), pp. 174-220.

37. Linda Elizabeth Ott Hines, "A Black Sociologist in a Time of Trouble: Monroe Nathan Work," (Master's thesis, Auburn University, 1972), p. 14.

38. Booker T. Washington—Committee of Twelve Correspondence, Tuskegee Institute Historical Collection, Tuskegee, Ala.

39. "*Negro Year Book* Historical Statement," Monroe Nathan Work Papers, Tuskegee Institute Historical Collection, Tuskegee, Ala.

40. Monroe N. Work, ed., *The Negro Yearbook*, 1st ed. (Tuskegee, Ala.: Negro Yearbook Publishing Co., 1912), p. 1.

41. Monroe N. Work, "An Autobiographical Sketch, February 7, 1940," Monroe Nathan Work Papers, Tuskegee Institute Historical Collection, Tuskegee, Ala.

42. Rayford W. Logan, *Howard University: The First Hundred Years, 1867-1967* (New York: New York University Press, 1969), p. 281.

43. *Journal of Negro Education*, Yearbook no. 1 (Washington, D.C.: Howard University Press, 1932), p. 99.

44. The publishing activities of the Howard University Press, after it was organized as an administrative unit within the university with a professional staff trained and experienced in book publishing in 1972, will be discussed later in this study.

45. C. Tilger, to the author, January 15, 1976.

3

Valiant Purveyors of Black Americana: Black Commercial Book Publishers, 1900–1959

INTRODUCTION

At the same time as a host of scholarly books discrediting the Black American was being published by the scholarly sector of the American book-publishing industry, an equally large number of books portraying the Afro-American in demeaning stereotypes, authored by some of the country's leading writers, was published by the industry's commercial sector for popular distribution. Joel Chandler Harris's popular *Uncle Remus Tales* (rev. ed., New York: Appleton, 1908) and Charles Carroll's *The Negro as Beast* (St. Louis: American Book and Bible House, 1900) were examples. Similarly, *The Clansman*, by Thomas Dixon, Jr. (New York: Doubleday, 1905) was so well received that it was made into one of the early classic films in American motion picture history in 1915: *Birth of a Nation*. When opposition developed against releasing the film, because of its racist theme, Dixon was successful in securing a positive appraisal of it from President Woodrow Wilson, who viewed it at a private showing at the White House. President Wilson is quoted as saying: "It is like writing history with lightning. And my only regret is that it is all so terribly true." With this blessing the film was released immediately and became a box office success. Books like *The Clansman* were widely read and were very influential in shaping the image of the Black American in the nation's popular culture.

A reaction, articulated by the Black intellectual community and some quarters in the white liberal community, to these books developed in the early decades of the twentieth century. This reaction was characterized by a small but ever-increasing demand, paralleling that in the scholarly sector, for books which portrayed the Black American as a human being endowed with the dignity, integrity, and intelligence shared by all humanity.

As the twentieth century progressed, several developments occurred which increased the growth of this demand for popular books objectively portraying the Black American. Illiteracy rates among Black Americans decreased from 45.5 percent in 1900 to 7.5 percent in 1958.[2] Blacks between 1910 and 1960 migrated from rural to urban communities in substantial numbers, thus exposing themselves to better library facilities, bookstores, and greater educational opportunities.[3] There was, as the twentieth century lengthened into decades, a growing interest in Black American culture and history by Blacks and white Americans as evidenced in such movements as the Harlem Renaissance, the Negro History Week Celebrations, and the development and acceptance of jazz and Gospel music. The civil rights movement gained undiminished momentum and wider support from Blacks and white Americans in the first decades of the century. And, finally, there was increased visible participation of prominent Black people in many areas of American life which stimulated segments of the reading public to seek information about the Black Americans.

A small number of white commercial book-publishing firms attempted to satisfy the demand during the period for books which treated the Black Americans objectively. In general, however, white firms published relatively few books by and about Blacks. Black poet-critic Sterling Brown, writing in 1941, commented on this situation.

> One of our leading critics used to characterize the New Negro Movement as the time when "every publisher wanted a Negro book." This was a peeved exaggeration. A few new and liberal publishers were genuinely interested in Negro expression; a few attempted to create and/or cash in on a fad; but when all was said and done comparatively few books on the Negro were published.[4]

The work, as Brown suggests, of Black book publishers should not go unnoticed. "One aspect of the Negro [author] and his publisher that must be noticed is the work of Negro publishers. . . . Aiming to publish books within the purchasing power of a poor people and to develop an audience, these Negro enterprises are highly commendable."[5]

Black commercial book-publishing firms that published books between 1900 and 1960 can be classified into four categories: (1) commercial book publishing firms; (2) newspaper firms that occasionally published books; and (3) periodical publishing firms that occasionally published books; and (4) commercial printing firms that engaged in book publishing as job printers to Black authors who published privately, but with the firm's name as the imprint.

Although publishing books to earn a profit and for a more diverse audience than the publishing units of Black organizations and institutions, these commercial publishing firms and the Black authors who paid Black printing firms to print their books often had motives similar in substance to those of the institutional publishers. Their books were published for general Black audiences with the ultimate goals of informing them of their past and present culture and articulating their response to the larger society and for general white audiences with the purpose of vindicating the Black American of the vicious attacks made on his moral, mental, and social abilities by popular white supremacist writers.

BLACK COMMERCIAL
BOOK-PUBLISHING FIRMS

The Orion Publishing Company, established in Nashville in 1901 by the Reverend Sutton E. Griggs, exemplified a one-man publishing firm that came into existence to publish the works of its founder. Because of Griggs's shifting race relations philosophy, the firm had divergent publishing objectives.

In the firm's early years Griggs authored and published militant novels directed toward the average adult Black American articuating the Afro-American's response to the injustices he experienced at the hands of a white racist society. *The Overshadowed*, a protest novel portraying the injustices encountered by Blacks living in the South, which was released in 1901, is an example of one of the early books published by the firm. The zenith of Griggs's militancy seems

to have come in 1905 when, with the blessings of the National Baptist Convention, he published *The Hindered Hand, or the Reign of
Repression*. Included in this protest novel, depicting the cruel
aspects of miscegenation, is a chapter that answered the vicious attack on Black Americans by the Reverend Thomas Dixon, Jr. in
The Leopard's Spots: A Romance of the White Man's Burden (New
York: Doubleday, 1902). Although *Hindered Hand* was released in
three printings in 1905, this novel, like others published by the
Orion Publishing Company, was a financial failure. Griggs
lamented the fact. "The promised support of the National Baptist
Convention never came. Thus, *The Hindered Hand* was a financial
failure."[6]

After 1907 Griggs's race relations philosophy shifted radically.
David M. Tucker noted, "Thus the militant Griggs became an ac-
commodating Black, a move which many of his friends failed to
understand."[7]

Griggs now authored and published books aimed at the white
Southerner as well as the Black American. Although these books
attempted to mildly vindicate the Black American, to a greater extent they advanced the philosophy of accommodation in the mold of
Booker T. Washington. *Wisdom's Call*, released in 1911, illustrated
Griggs's new race relations position. In this collection of essays he
outlines his accommodationist views on the race problem. According to Griggs, Northern and Southern whites as well as Blacks
received the book well.

> As confident as I was of the strength of the case which I made
> out for the Negro race, I confess that the character of the im-
> pression made by the book has taken me by surprise. The
> Northerner, the Southerner and the Negro find a common
> meeting ground in the book. Though the first thirty-five
> pages of *Wisdom's Call* are devoted to a discussion of the Fif-
> teenth Amendment, and much hated in the South, Southern
> white men are its outspoken champion. I count that a
> victory.[8]

In 1913 Griggs moved to Memphis where he became pastor of
Tabernacle Institutional Baptist Church and continued his book

publishing under the auspices of his National Public Welfare League, which was discussed earlier.

In the same year that Griggs went to Memphis, Robert W. Coleman organized a publishing company in Baltimore bearing his name and began publishing a series of annual directories about prominent Afro-Americans and businesses in that city entitled *The First Colored, Professional, Clerical, Skilled, and Business Directory of Baltimore City*. Coleman stated the publishing objectives which he hoped to achieve with the publication of the directory in the preface of the fourth edition. "I have tried to establish a method of a 'real effective' medium of advertisement, and at the same time to collect a directory of the colored professional, clerical, skilled and business people. I aim to uplift men to give them credit for what they do."[9] In 1918 Coleman expanded his directory to include Washington, D.C., and Annapolis: thus the sixth and subsequent editions were known as the *First Colored Professional, Clerical, Skilled and Business Directory of Baltimore City, with Washington, D.C., and Annapolis, Maryland Annex*. Published until 1927, the directory went through fifteen editions.

Having the longest publishing history, forty-three years, of any Black commercial book-publishing firm, which published only the books of its founder during the period, J. A. Rogers Publications of New York City had very definite publishing objectives. Writing in 1946, J. A. Rogers, after twenty-nine years of operating his own firm, recounted his reasons for studying Black history and making the results of his research available in books which he authored and published.

> However, I noticed that books alleging inherent Negro inferiority continued to appear. Dixon's *Clansman* had now been made into a flaming attack on Negroes in a motion picture *The Birth of a Nation*. All of these, I felt, should be answered not with sentiment, as I noticed certain white friends of the Negro and Negroes themselves were doing in the Chicago Press, but with facts.[10]

Not just content with publishing books to vindicate the Black American, Rogers also believed that his books should be a source of uplift for Blacks, especially the youth. "In conclusion, let me say that my intention was not to write highly critical and psychoanalytical or even literary essays, but rather principally success stories, chiefly for Negro youth. And not only young people, but adults need encouragement to be had from the lives of the great."[11]

All of the titles published by the firm from its beginning in 1917 through 1959 illustrated Rogers's attempt to realize these publishing objectives. For example, *From Man to Superman*, which by 1924 had been issued in five editions since its original publication in 1917, refuted, using extensive documentation, the doctrine of white racial superiority. *Nature Knows No Color Line*, published in 1952 with a second edition in 1960, is a well-researched treatise on Black ancestry in the white race from early Greece to modern-day America. And *World's Great Men of Color*, released in several editions since it was first published in 1940, documents the achievements of famous and little-known Blacks in the history of Western civilization.

Rogers reached the masses of Afro-Americans through his syndicated column "Know Your History" in the *Pittsburgh Courier* and other Afro-American newspapers. Largely because of the popularity of this column, Rogers was able to distribute many of his books by mail from his home in New York City.

Associated Publishers of Washington, D.C., stands as the most prolific Afro-American commercial book-publishing enterprise of this period. A private corporation founded and headed by Carter G. Woodson, this firm's publishing objectives represented the collective thinking of members of this corporation. From its inception, the firm's incorporators clearly stated these objectives.

> This firm will publish books of all kinds, but will direct its attention primarily to works bearing on Negroes so as to supply all kinds of information concerning the Negro race and those who have been interested in its uplift. . . . During the recent years the Negro race has been seeking to learn more about itself and especially since the social upheaval of the World War [I]. The Negro's reading has been largely increased and the number of persons interested in the Negro have so multiplied that any creditable publication giving important facts about the race now finds a ready market throughout the

United States and even abroad. To supply this demand these gentlemen have launched the enterprise, THE ASSOCIATED PUBLISHERS.[12]

From 1921 through 1960, the Associated Publishers published numerous titles, many in several editions, indicative of these objectives. The firm's first book, released in 1921, Carter G. Woodson's *History of the Negro Church*, was the first composite history of the development of all Black religious denominations ever published. *Negro Musicians and Their Music* by Maud Cuney-Hare, published in 1936, is a landmark study in Black musicology. For the young reader this firm also released a host of books such as: Jane D. Shackelford's *The Child's History of the Negro* (1939); *Negro Art, Music and Rhymes for Young Folk*, by Helen Whiting (1938); and Gertrude P. McBrown's *The Picture-Poetry Book* (1935).

In 1952, resulting from directions in Carter G. Woodson's will, the Associated Publishers (of which he had been the major stockholder), was transferred to the control of the Association for the Study of Afro-American Life and History. Its activities after 1959 will be discussed in a later chapter.

A careful search through records in Memphis revealed very little information about the Pictorial History Publishing Company of that city. This firm was apparently short-lived and probably owned by Dr. Thomas O. Fuller, the author of its only publication: *Pictorial History of the American Negro* (1933). A former member of the South Carolina Senate, a distinguished minister, and an educator, Fuller states in the book's preface the reasons for its publication. "Negro History is necessary for the proper education and inspiration of the youth of the race. Examples of thrift, of patriotic loyalty to the country and success along various lines, have a stronger appeal when they rise out of the group [of] which individual readers are members."[13] *Pictorial History of the Negro* was used for many years as a text in secondary school courses in Afro-American history.

Similarly, little information could be found on the Bi-Monthly Negro Book Club of Columbus, Ohio, apparently a book club publishing and distributing books to an Afro-American audience. Only one title was identified as the firm's publication. O'Wendell Shaw's *Greater Need Below* (1936), a novel about life on the campus of a

southern Black college.[14] Based on the literary genere and subject
matter of this book, it might be concluded that the Bi-Monthly
Negro Book Club intended to publish books portraying various
aspects of the Black experience for an adult Black audience.

Because of the lack of sufficient documentation in the literature
on A. Wendell Malliet and Company and the unavailability to this
researcher of persons who were associated with the firm, its exact
founding date could not be determined. The firm, however, is listed
in the *Cumulative Book Index 1938–1942* and in subsequent editions of this work through 1956.[15] It is also listed annually in "A
Directory of United States Publishing Firms Issuing Books," in *Publishers Weekly* from 1939 through 1946.[16] And Black critic Sterling
Brown, writing in 1943, cites the firm and the Associated Publishers as examples of two contemporary Afro-American book publishers.[17]

Jamaican-born Afro-American Arnold Mehew Wendell Malliet,
founder of the firm, came to the United States in 1917. In 1927 he
wrote a series of articles for the *Pittsburgh Courier* on his impressions of the political and social plight of Afro-Americans.[18]

Although no statement by Malliet regarding the objectives of his
publishing firm could be found, it seems, judging from the nine
titles identified as publications of his firm, that he intended to
publish books informing Blacks of their past and present culture,
articulating their response to the larger society and portraying
various aspects of the Black experience. *The Negro Handbook*,
edited by Florence Murray (1942), for example, is a comprehensive
reference work containing facts and statistics about Black American life covering twenty-nine specific categories. M. S. Stuart's
Economic Detour (1940), a history of insurance in the lives of Black
Americans, is a classic work in Afro-American insurance history.
And *A Traipsin' Heart*, by Mildred Martin Hall, is a collection of
poems depicting the Black American experience.

NEWSPAPER FIRMS THAT
OCCASIONALLY PUBLISHED BOOKS

One of the earliest newspaper firms to engage in book publishing
was the Afro-American Publishing Company in Baltimore. Eight
years after this firm was established to publish the weekly *Afro-*

American, it released its first book: *The White Man's Failure in Government*, by Harvey Elijah Johnson (1900), a treatise on race relations in the United States. Like this title, other books published by this firm indicated that it was committed to publishing works to document some aspect of Black history or Black Americana such as: *The Ethiopian's Place in History*, by John William Norris (1916); *This Our War Too*, by the *Baltimore Afro-American* Staff (1945); and *Baltimore, America's Fifth Largest Negro Market*, by the *Baltimore Afro-American* Staff (1946).

A less active book publisher was the Fortune and Peterson Publishing Company of New York City, which published the weekly *New York Age* from 1887 to 1905. This firm released only one book, *Dreams of Life*, by T. Thomas Fortune (1905), one of its owners and the editor of the *New York Age* at the time. This title is a volume of poems extolling the virtues of nature in Fortune's native Florida.

Like the Fortune and Peterson Publishing Company, the Iowa State Bystander Publishing Company was a partnership established in 1894 by John Lay Thompson and J. M. Shephard to publish the weekly *Iowa State Bystander*. Occasionally, this midwestern firm published books documenting Black history. Two of these titles were: John Lay Thompson's *History and Views of Colored Officers Training Camp for 1917 at Fort Des Moines* (1917), a title detailing a little-known aspect of Black American military history; and *The History of the Order of the Eastern Star among Colored People*, by Sue M. Wilson (1925), a history of a secret society among Afro-American women.

The Dabney Publishing Company of Cincinnati, identified as the only one-man newspaper firm that published books, produced books written by its owner. Founded by the fiery Wendell P. Dabney in 1907, this firm published the *Union*, a weekly newspaper with regional readership, from that year until Dabney's death in 1952. The *Union* was a crusading newspaper through which Dabney propounded the social and political needs of Cincinnati's Black community. The three books published by this firm are indicative of its efforts to produce titles documenting Black history and describing the Afro-American response to the larger society.

The first book released by this firm, Dabney's *Colored Citizens of Cincinnati* (1926), was well received by the local white press.

The *Times-Star* praised Dabney's knowledge of his subject. "Dabney's knows his subject and he reveals his knowledge. Every resident of Cincinnati, every citizen of the United States, should be informed of this matter, for it concerns the whole nation."[19] And the *Enquirer* carried the following comment: "As Cincinnati's foremost Negro citizen, he speaks with authority on the conditions which have affected other citizens of his race throughout its history in the city."[20] The book went through three editions.

In 1927 the Dabney Publishing Company published *The Life of Maggie L. Walker*, a biography of the first Afro-American woman banker. And in the same year *Chisum's Pilgrimage and Others*, a collection of articles Dabney had published in the *Union* about the political, social, and economic life of the Cincinnati Afro-American community, appeared. The firm published no other titles.

Four years after Dabney started his firm, Plummer B. Young, Sr., established the Guide Publishing Company in Norfolk and began publishing the weekly *Journal and Guide*. Occasionally, the Guide Publishing Company produced books documenting local Black history. Two of these books were Luther Porter Jackson's *A History of the Virginia State Teachers* (1937) and his *Virginia's Negro Soldiers and Seamen in the Revolutionary War* (1944). Jackson was a leading Black historian, a columnist on the *Journal and Guide*, and a faculty member at Virginia State College in Petersburg.

Founded in 1912 to publish the regional *St. Louis Argus*, a weekly, the St. Louis Argus Publishing Company was also an active book publisher and issued a few books portraying Black American life. In 1919 this firm published *The Immediate Jewel of His Soul*, by Herman Dreer, a militant novel depicting the new wave of militancy that exploded among Black Americans in Chicago and various other northern cities in the wake of World War I. It brought out a volume of poems by Thomas Atkins, *The Eagle*, in 1936.

PERIODICAL FIRMS THAT
OCCASIONALLY PUBLISHED BOOKS

The earliest twentieth-century Black periodical publisher to publish books was the Colored Cooperative Publishing Company in Boston. Organized in 1900 as a publishing cooperative, this firm began publishing in that year the *Colored American Magazine*, a monthly periodical devoted to Blacks with the aim, as stated in an early issue, of uplifting and vindicating the Black American. "To the encouragement of those who are faint, or would slavishly bend under the weight of a mistaken popular prejudice; and to the inspiration and aid of all our noble men and women who are fearlessly and successfully vindicating themselves and our people the *Colored American Magazine* is published."[21]

In September 1900 this firm released a book consistent with the publishing objectives of its magazine: *Contending Forces*, by Pauline Hopkins, a novel about the struggles of a middle-class Black American family adjusting to life in postbellum Boston. In the novel's preface the author sets forth her views on the value of fiction for Afro-Americans.

> Fiction is of great value to any people as a preserver of manners and customs—religious, political and social. It is a record of growth and development from generation to generation. No one will do this for us; we must ourselves develop the men and women who will faithfully protray the innermost thoughts and feelings of the Negro with all the fire and romance which lie dormant in our history, and, as yet, unrecognized by writers of the Anglo-Saxon race.[22]

Contending Forces was the only book actually published by the Colored Cooperative Publishing Company, although three other titles were announced in the *Colored American Magazine: In Free America; or, Tales from the Southland*, by Ellen T. Wetherell; *The Story of the American Negro as Slave, Citizen, and Soldier*, by Theophilus G. Stewart; and *Progress or Reversion, Which?*, by Joseph E. Hayne.[23] No evidence could be found to support that these titles were ever published.

In 1904, after experiencing financial difficulties, the Colored Cooperative Publishing Company was dissolved. The *Colored American Magazine* was purchased by Fred Moore, an agent for Booker T. Washington and later editor and publisher of the *New*

York Age, and was moved to New York City where it was published until November 1909.[24]

James Ephraim McGirt, a rising young Afro-American poet, organized a public corporation, the McGirt Publishing Company, in Philadelphia and began publishing *McGirt's Magazine,* an illustrated monthly devoted to art, science, and literature, in 1903. In its first issue McGirt stated its publishing objectives. "I publish this magazine in order that we may have a paper that will be read by the white race as well as the colored so that they may know the great men of our race and what they are doing."[25]

One book was published by this firm. In 1907 it released James Ephraim McGirt's *The Triumphs of Ephraim,* a volume of short stories, which did not reflect the aforementioned publishing objectives of the periodical. The book was a specimen of protest literature. Black American critic John W. Parker critically assessed the book. "This group of stories, everywhere indicative of the limited locale, stems from the problem of the Negro's juxtaposition with the white majority in America—color prejudice, exploitation, the operation of restrictive covenants and the frustration-aggression phenomenon."[26] The McGirt Publishing Company published *McGirt's Magazine* until December, 1907, when the firm seems to have gone out of existence.[27]

W.E.B. Du Bois and Augustus Granville Dill organized a publishing company bearing their names in 1919 to publish a pioneering magazine for Black American children: the *Brownies' Book.* Based in New York City, the Du Bois and Dill Publishing Company published the magazine from January, 1920, through December, 1921.[28] The publishing objectives of the *Brownies' Book* were outlined in its first issue. "It will seek to teach universal love and brotherhood for all little folk—black and brown and yellow and white."[29] This firm published one book: *Unsung Heroes,* by Elizabeth Haynes (1921), a collective biography of outstanding Blacks.

The Du Bois and Dill Publishing Company folded with the last issue of the *Brownies' Book.* In his autobiography Du Bois recounts the reasons for the magazine's demise. "In those days, 1920 and 1921, I made an effort toward which I look back with infinite satisfaction: an attempt in the *Brownies' Book* to furnish a little magazine for Negro children, in which my efforts were ably seconded by Augustus Dill and Jesse Fauset; it was really a beautiful publication, but it did not pay its way."[30]

With the purpose of publishing short fiction by Black writers depicting facets of the Black experience, two Black women writers, Alice C. Browning and Fern Gayden, established the Negro Story Publishing Company in Chicago in 1944 to publish *Negro Story*, a bimonthly magazine.[31] Published from May-June, 1944, through December-January, 1945–1946, *Negro Story* carried short stories by such notable and budding writers as Richard Wright, Nick Aaron Ford, Ralph Ellison, and Chester Himes.

In 1945 this publisher released its sole book publication: *Lionel Hampton's Swing Book*, by Alice Browning. Although this book was nonfiction and did not reflect the publishing aims of the magazine, it does illustrate a move by the firm to publish books celebrating one aspect of Black culture. No other titles were published by this publisher, which went out of existence with the last issue of *Negro Story*.[32]

Another Chicago-based Black periodical publishing firm that engaged in book publishing was the Negro Digest Publishing Company. Founded by John H. Johnson in 1942, the firm published the *Negro Digest*, a monthly periodical carrying previously published condensed articles by and about Afro-Americans. Aimed at Black and white adult audiences, the editors stated the periodical's aims in its first issue: "*Negro Digest* is published in response to a demand for a magazine to summarize and condense the leading articles and comments on the Negro now current in the press of the nation in ever-increasing volume."[33]

The Negro Digest Publishing Company released its first book in 1945: *The Best of Negro Humor*, edited by John H. Johnson and Ben Burns, the white associate editor of *Negro Digest*.[34] In an advertisement for the book, the publisher claimed it to be a "first." "*The Best of Negro Humor*, a pocket-size, slick-covered 106-page book, represents the first collection of Negro jokes, ancedotes, cartoons and other wit placed between the covers of a book."[35] In the same year this firm launched *Ebony*, a monthly pictorial magazine modeled on the format of *Life*.[36] The name of the firm was changed to Johnson Publishing Company in 1949. *Negro Digest* was discon-

tinued in 1951 in favor of the pocket-size weekly, *Jet*, although it
was resumed in 1961.[37] It was not, however, until 1962 that this
highly successful firm engaged in book publishing again. Its career
as a book publisher from that date will be discussed later in this
book.

COMMERICAL PRINTING FIRMS
PUBLISHING BOOKS AS
JOB PRINTERS

Many Black authors, unable to get their books published by
white or Black publishing firms, published their works privately.
These authors generally contracted Black commercial printing
firms as job printers and distributed their books themselves. In
many instances these firms used their name on the title page as the
imprint. The most active of these firms were located in such large
Black American cultural centers as Washington, D.C., Nashville,
and Chicago.

The Murray Brothers Printing Company, located in Washington, D.C., is illustrative of such a printing firm. Founded in 1908,
the firm continues to be an active business enterprise.[38]

Freeman Henry Morris Murray's *Emancipation and the Freed in
American Sculpture* (1916) is an example of a book job-printed by
the firm for an author who, incidently, was a partner in the firm.[39]
A critique of the works of several Black and white sculptors who
used Black Americans as the subjects of their creations, this book is
one of the earliest extensive studies to seriously consider the artistic
achievements of Black sculptors. Its publication was the subject of
lengthy letters between Murray and George Washington Forbes,
who had reviewed the book in the *A.M.E. Church Review* favor-
ably. Murray thanked Forbes for the review, but commented rather
disparagingly on the economics surrounding the book's publication.

> Perhaps I need not tell you that I do not hope to get even
> expenses out of my book. Only 500 copies were printed. If I
> sold every one at full net price, I'd get back actual cost—not
> to mention my own work of typesetting, etc. But if what I

have done is worthwhile—as your review indicates—I am satisfied. I am encouraged to push on.[40]

Emancipation and the Freed in American Sculpture was reprinted in 1972 by Books for Libraries.

Several other titles, privately published by authors, were identified with this firm's name used as the imprint. These titles were generally in four genres: poetry; Black history; social commentaries and treatises; and art criticism.

Like Murray Brothers Printing Company, the Press of R. L. Pendelton, located in Washington, D.C., served as a job printer to several Black authors, who published privately. In 1919, for instance, this firm job-printed Laura Eliza Wilkes's *Missing Pages in American History, Revealing the Services of Negroes in the Early Wars in the United States of America, 1641–1815,* a unique work in Black military history. Several other Afro-American authors contracted this firm as a job printer and published privately works in Black history, Black cookery, and Afro-American poetry.

It would be difficult to identify all Black commercial firms which engaged in book publishing as job printers for authors who published privately. Upon examining citations, however, in *Black American Writers 1773–1949; a Bibliography and Union List,* compiled by Geraldine O. Matthews and the Afro-American Materials Project Staff (Boston: G. K. Hall, 1975), the job-printing work of several commercial printing firms was identified in the imprints of several books. Some of the firms that appeared frequently were: Hemphill Press, Nashville, Tennessee; West Hamilton Press, Washington, D.C.; and Black Cat Press, Chicago, Illinois.

The Black commercial sector of the American book industry, as has been shown in this chapter, was very small during the period of 1900 to 1960. Of the eighteen firms identified, the Associated Publishers and J. A. Rogers Publications were the most successful. These two publishers had the longest active book-publishing histories of the eighteen publishers; they successfully published titles in many editions; and, in the case of Associated Publishers, released titles in a wide variety of literary genres.

In forming a picture of the overall output of Black-owned commercial publishing during this period, however, the role of Black

commerical printing firms must not be overlooked. As has been
noted, they did provide an outlet for many Afro-American authors
who had no other means for getting their books into print.

NOTES

1. Milton MacKaye, "Birth of a Nation," *Scribner's Magazine*,
November 1937, p. 46.
2. U.S., Bureau of the Census, *Negro Population, 1790–1915* (Washington, D.C.: Government Printing Office, 1948), p. 236; idem, *Statistical
Abstract of the United States, 1974* (Washington, D.C.: Government Printing Office, 1975), p. 115.
3. In 1910 only 27.4 percent of the total Afro-American population
lived in urban communities. This figure rose in 1920 to 34 percent and in
1930 to 44.7 percent. By 1960, 13,808,000 Afro-Americans were living in
urban communities and 5,064,000 in rural communities. These figures
were reported in: Bureau of the Census, *Negro Population, 1790–1915*
(Washington, D.C.: Government Printing Office, 1918), p. 88; U.S.,
Bureau of the Census, *Negroes in the United States, 1920–1932*
(Washington, D.C.: Government Printing Office, 1936), p. 48; U.S.,
Department of Commerce, *Statistical Abstract of the United States, 1974*
(Washington, D.C.: Government Printing Office, 1974), p. 30.
4. Sterling Brown, "The Negro Author and His Publisher," *Negro
Quarterly* 1 (Spring 1942): 16.
5. Ibid., pp. 19–20.
6. Sutton E. Griggs, *The Story of My Struggles* (Memphis: National
Public Welfare League, 1914), p. 12.
7. David M. Tucker, *Black Pastors and Leaders* (Memphis: Memphis
State University Press, 1975), p. 78.
8. Griggs, *The Story of My Struggles*, p. 14.
9. Robert W. Coleman, ed., *The First Colored, Professional, Clerical,
Skilled, and Business Directory of Baltimore City* (Baltimore: Coleman
Publishing Co., 1917), p. 1.
10. J. A. Rogers, *World's Great Men of Color*, 2 vols. (New York: J. A.
Rogers, 1946), 1:6.
11. Ibid., p. 4.
12. "Notes," *Journal of Negro History* 6 (July 1921): 380.
13. T. O. Fuller, *The Pictorial History of the American Negro.*
(Memphis: Pictorial History, 1933), p. ii.
14. O'Wendell Shaw is the pseudonym for Oliver W. Shaw. Howard

University, *The Dictionary Catalog of the Arthur B. Spingarn Collection of Negro Authors*, 2 vols. (Boston: G. K. Hall, 1970), 1:422.

15."Directory of Publishers, 1938–1942," *Cumulative Book Index, 1938–1942*, 4th ed. (New York: H. W. Wilson, 1945), p. 2713; "Directory of Publishers, 1943–1948," *Cumulative Book Index, 1943–1948*, 5th ed. (New York: H. W. Wilson, 1950), p. 2554; "Directory of Publishers, 1949–1952," *Cumulative Book Index, 1949–1952*, 6th ed. (New York: H. W. Wilson, 1952), p. 2112.

16. "Directory of United States Publishers Issuing New Books," *Publishers Weekly*, pp. 137–143 (third week in January number annually from 1939 to 1946 inclusive), various paging.

17. Brown, "The Negro Author and His Publisher," p. 16.

18. A. M. Wendell Malliet, "A. M. Malliet from Jamaica Gives Experiences That Turned Him against Americanization," *Pittsburgh Courier*, 9 July 1927, pp. 7, 8.

19. *Cincinnati Times-Star*, 3 April 1926, p. 18.

20. *Cincinnati Enquirer*, 10 April 1926, p. 30.

21. R. S. Elliot, "The Story of Our Magazine," *Colored American Magazine*, May 1901, p. 43.

22. Pauline Hopkins, *Contending Forces* (Boston: Colored Cooperative Publishing Co., 1900), pp. 13–14.

23. "Books in Press," *Colored American Magazine*, June 1901, p. 23.

24. For further information on the fate of the *Colored American Magazine* between 1904 and 1909 see August Meier, "Booker T. Washington and the Negro Press: With Special Reference to the *Colored American Magazine*," *Journal of Negro History* 38 (January 1953): 67–90.

25. James E. McGirt, "Announcement," *McGirt's Magazine*, September 1903, p. 1.

26. John W. Parker, "James Ephraim McGirt: Poet of 'Hope Deferred'," *North Carolina Historical Review*, 16 (July 1954): 322.

27. Ibid., p. 334.

28. Elinor Desverney Sinnette, "*The Brownies' Book:* A Pioneer Publication for Children," in *Black Titan, W.E.B. Du Bois, An Anthology*, ed. Editors of *Freedomways* (Boston: Beacon Press, 1970), pp. 166, 168.

29. W.E.B. Du Bois, "Opinion—The True Brownies," *Crisis Magazine*, October 6, 1919, p. 286.

30. W.E.B. Du Bois, *Dusk of Dawn* (New York: Harcourt, Brace & Co., 1940), p. 256.

31. Alice C. Browning and Fern Gayden, "A Letter to Our Readers," *Negro Story*, May-June, 1944, p. 1.

32. Alice C. Browning, interview held in the Vivian G. Harsh Collection

of Afro-American History and Literature at the Carter G. Woodson Regional Library Center, Chicago, Illinois, November 16, 1976.

33. "Introducing," Negro Digest, November 1942, p. 2.

34. Although the firm was Chicago-based, this title bears the imprint of its New York City office.

35. John H. Johnson and Ben Burns, eds., *The Best of Negro Humor* (New York: Negro Digest Publishing Co., 1945), p. 2.

36. Roland E. Wolseley, *The Black Press, U.S.A.* (Ames, Iowa: Iowa State University Press, 1971), p. 62.

37. "Copyright Notice," Negro Digest, June 1949, pp. 2, 63.

38. Norma M. Jorgensen, Secretary, Murray Brothers Printing Co., Washington, D.C., to the author, November 27, 1975.

39. Freeman Henry Morris Murray was one of the founders of Murray Brothers Printing Company.

40. Freeman Henry Morris Murray to George Washington Forbes, June 10, 1919, George Washington Forbes Papers, Boston Public Library, Boston, Mass.

4

"Go Tell It on the Mountain": The Book-Publishing Activities of Black Religious Publishers, 1900–1959

INTRODUCTION

No group of Black publishers has produced more books of interest to Black Americans and other persons of African descent than Black religious publishers. Their books, circulated primarily through the home and foreign missions of Black religious denominations, have reached millions of people of African descent in the United States and throughout the world. Illustrative of the large volume of religious literature published and distributed by one of these publishers is the statement by D.C. Washington, the late executive director of the Sunday School Publishing Board of the National Baptist Convention, U.S.A., Inc. :. "As we pause to evaluate the fiscal year just closed, it is gratifying to note that we have distributed over two and two-thirds millions of pieces of literature to approximately twenty-six thousand churches throughout the United States and overseas."[1]

Black religious publishers, publishing books between 1900 and 1959, fall into two categories: publishers of books only on religious subjects; and publishers of books on religious and secular subjects.

From the last decade of the nineteenth century to 1960 many of the general external forces cited earlier in this study as influencing the demand for books treating the Black American objectively in other sectors of Black book publishing also operated in this sector. In addition, other developments occurred within the Black religious community which greatly influenced the publishing programs of Black religious publishers. In 1891 the American Baptist Publication Society, the nation's largest Baptist publishing house, dropped, for undisclosed reasons, Black Baptist clergymen and writers from its list of contributors, which resulted in Black Baptists organizing their own publishing house.[2] As the twentieth century evolved there was a dramatic growth of urban churches within Black religious denominations, with congregations experiencing greater exposure to better educational opportunities and libraries than the congregations of the rural churches that had previously dominated these denominations. Benjamin E. Mays and Joseph W. Nicholson noted this development.

> The shift of the Negro population has led to a rapid increase in the number of urban churches and increase in membership, especially in northern centers. According to the *Federal Census of Religious Bodies*, there were in 1916 a total of 127 Negro Baptist churches in Chicago, Detroit, Cincinnati, Philadelphia and Baltimore. In 1926, the *Federal Census of Religious Bodies* reported 319 Negro Baptist churches in these five cities, an increase of 151 percent. The reported membership of the 127 churches in 1916 was 59,863; the membership in 1926 was reported to be 178,637, an approximate increase of 200 percent.[3]

And lastly, the clergy and laymen in specific denominations became increasingly involved in the civil rights movement, which resulted in many books published by Black religious publishers presenting the views and opinions of Black religious leaders and laymen on American race relations.

PUBLISHERS OF RELIGIOUS SUBJECTS ONLY

Established in New York City in 1841 by the African Methodist Episcopal Zion Church, the A.M.E. Zion Publishing House was moved to Charlotte, North Carolina, in 1894 where the denomination built in 1911 "the first publishing house in the country built by Negroes."[4] The program of this publisher, as reflected by the books published, was to instruct and assist the denomination's laymen and clergy, adult and juvenile, in their understanding and performance of the church's rituals and doctrines; to record the history of the denomination; and to provide religious literature for adults seeking spiritual uplift.

Revised quadrennially from 1868 through 1959, *The Doctrine and Discipline of the African Methodist Episcopal Zion Church* is undoubtedly the most important work released by this house. Robert Morris's *The Children's Catechism*, released in 1892, achieved the same instructive goal for the denomination's younger members. In 1947 this publisher issued the denomination's official hymnal, *The A.M.E. Zion Hymnal*.

Numerous titles recording the denomination's history were published between 1841 and 1960. In 1895 Bishop James Walker Hood's classic *One Hundred Years of the African Methodist Episcopal Zion Church; or The Centennial of African Methodist* appeared. William H. Davenport's *The Anthology of Zion Methodism* was released in 1936.

During these years relatively fewer titles, by comparison, were published by the A.M.E. Zion Publishing House which reflected its effort to publish books for the general spiritual uplift of the denomination's membership. An example of such a title was *Birthday, Horoscopes, Dictionary on Thoughts, Biblical Standpoints, True Facts and Daily Helps*, by Lawrence S. King (1925).

Another Methodist publisher that published books only on religious subjects was the C.M.E. Publishing House. Organized in Jackson, Tennessee, in 1870 by the Colored Methodist Episcopal Church, this house published books to assist the church's clergy and membership in the understanding and performance of its doctrines and rituals and to record its history.

One of the earliest histories of the denomination published by this house was C. H. Phillips's *The History of the Colored Methodist Episcopal Church* (1898). Later editions of this work appeared in 1900 and 1925. Another important history of the denomination issued by this house was *History of the Woman's Missionary Society in the Colored Methodist Episcopal Church*, by Sara Jane McAfee (1934).

Numerous handbooks and songbooks were issued by this publisher for use in the church. *Songs of Love and Mercy*, compiled by Bishop L. H. Holsey and F. M. Hamilton was released in 1900.

*Handbook of Church Government of the Colored Methodist Epis-
copal Church* appeared in 1908. Earlier, in 1888, the first edition of
Discipline of the Colored Methodist Episcopal Church was published.

A less prolific publisher that seems to have published only denominational literature was the Church of God in Christ Publishing
House. Located in Memphis, where the denomination was reorganized as a national assembly in 1907, no exact date for the establishment of this house could be determined.[5] In that year Elder D. J.
Young, however, was elected editor of the *Whole Truth*, the denomination's newspaper. Hence, for purposes of this study, we will
consider the year of Elder Young's election to the editorial post as
the beginning of this house.

Only one book was reportedly issued by this publisher before
1960: *The Yearbook of the Church of God in Christ* (1923), a collection of annual statistics and facts about the denomination.

The Sunday School Publishing Board of the National Baptist
Convention, U.S.A., was organized in Nashville in 1916 as a result
of the split in the National Baptist Convention in 1915 over the
ownership of the National Baptist Publishing Board.[6] On August
15, 1898, two years after it had been established in Nashville, the
National Baptist Publishing Board received a charter from the state
of Tennessee as a nonprofit closed corporation. In 1915 when a dis-
pute arose over its ownership between members of the board and
the leaders of the National Baptist Convention at the annual meeting in Chicago, a court battle ensued. The supreme court of the
state of Tennessee decided in favor of the members of the National
Baptist Publishing Board, which left the convention with a substantial number of sympathetic members.[7] Without a publishing
house, leaders who remained in the convention set out to establish
a new one: the Sunday School Publishing Board of the National
Baptist Convention, U.S.A., Inc.

From 1916 to 1920 several prominent leaders of the National
Baptist Convention, U.S.A., Dr. E. C. Morris, Reverend S. P.
Harris, and Reverend William Haynes, played strategic roles in
shepherding the new publishing venture. In 1920 Dr. A. M.
Townsend was elected executive director of the Sunday School
Publishing Board.

Serving until his death in 1959, Dr. Townsend developed a book publishing program for the convention with a central thrust toward producing not only Sunday school literature but also books to instruct clergy and adults in Baptist doctrine and to record the history of the Afro-American Baptist denomination.

How to Study and Teach the Bible: Teacher Training Book, National Baptist Convention, by Samuel N. Vass (1922); *Principles and Methods of Religious Education*, by Samuel N. Vass (1932); and *Commentary on the International Uniform Lessons for 1940*, by J. T. Brown and M. A. Talley (1941) are examples of titles released by the Sunday School Publishing Board to instruct and assist the denomination's laymen in the administrative and teaching aspects of its Sunday schools. The board's objective of publishing titles during this period that recorded the history of the denomination was realized by such books as: *The Colored Baptist's Family Tree*, by William H. Moses (1925); and *Negro Baptist History, U.S.A., 1750–1930*, by Lewis Jordan (1930). Edited by Mrs. A. M. Townsend. *A New Book for All Services* (1924) and Lewis Jordan's *The Baptist Standard Directory and Busy Pastor's Guide* (1929) were examples of handbooks published for the clergy in their performance of church services.

PUBLISHERS OF RELIGIOUS AND SECULAR SUBJECTS

Founded in 1817 by the African Methodist Episcopal Church, the A.M.E. Book Concern, the first publishing firm founded by Black Americans in the United States, had by 1900 an unusually diversified book-publishing program. This publisher released books on religious as well as secular subjects.

Most of the books identified as publications of the A.M.E. Book Concern, however, were religious works. *A Manual of the A.M. E. Church*, by Bishop Benjamin T. Tanner (1901) and *The African Methodist Episcopal Hymn and Tune Book* (1904) are illustrative of the many denominational handbooks and hymnals published for the assistance of clergy and laymen in practicing the church's doctrines and rituals. *Centennial Encyclopedia of the African Methodist Episcopal Church*, edited by Bishop Richard Robert Wright

(1916) and *Bishop Richard Allen and His Spirit,* by Daniel Minort Baxter (1917) represent the Book Concern's attempt to publish works to record the denomination's history.

The A.M.E. Book Concern also published works for the use of clergy and laymen outside of the denomination. *Digest of Christian Theology for the Use of Beginners in the Study of Theological Service,* by James Crawford Embry (1890), is a textbook in general theology. *The Yearbook of Negro Churches,* edited by Bishop Reverdy C. Ransom and James H. Robinson (1939–1940), records statistics and facts about all Afro-American religious denominations.

A wide variety of books on secular subjects was published by this publisher. These titles generally documented some aspect of Black Americana or portrayed, in fiction, Black life. Bishop Richard Robert Wright's monumental *The Negro in Pennsylvania: A Study in Economic History* (1912) is a classic study of the economic history of Black Americans in Pennsylvania. *The Question before Congress: A Consideration of the Debates and Final Action by Congress upon Various Phases of the Race Question,* by George Washington Mitchell (1918) is an example of the many works released by the Book Concern that documented the Black Americans political plight. Mary Etta Spencer's novel, *The Resentment* (1921), and Irvin Underhill's *Daddy's Love and Other Poems* (1930) are titles of fiction and poetry, respectively, that portray and articulate aspects of Afro-American life.

In 1952 the A.M.E. Book Concern's operations were discontinued by the General Conference of the African Methodist Episcopal Church. This action, reportedly, resulted from a deterioration in its financial management.[8]

Another religious publishing enterprise founded by the African Methodist Episcopal denomination was the A.M.E. Sunday School Union and Publishing House. After several attempts by Charles Spencer Smith, a minister in the denomination, to persuade the General Conference of the African Methodist Episcopal Church to establish a publishing unit to publish Sunday school literature, the A.M.E. Sunday School Union and Publishing House was finally established in 1884. Originally located in Bloomington, Illinois, it was moved to Nashville, Tennessee, in 1886. This publishing house developed early a strong publishing program and was soon publishing books of a broader scope than Sunday school literature. The Sunday school literature was composed primarily of periodicals, pamphlets, and lesson manuals of less than forty-nine pages. Some books were published, however, for Sunday school teacher instruction. *Sunday School Problems*, by William Henry Shackelford (1950), was an example.

This house released several books treating various historical aspects of the African Methodist Episcopal Church. In 1891 it published Bishop Daniel A. Payne's *History of the A.M.E. Church*, volume 1, the most authoritative history of the denomination. A later history, John T. Jenifer's *Centennial Retrospect History of the A.M.E. Church*, appeared in 1916. And Bishop Reverdy C. Ransom's *Preface to the History of the A.M.E. Church* was produced in 1950.

Numerous treatises on general religious subjects were published by the A.M.E. Sunday School Union and Publishing House, reflecting this publisher's attempt to publish nondenominational religious literature for clergy and laymen outside as well as within the denomination. Timothy D. Scott's *Sunday, The Christian Sabbath* (1928) is indicative of one of these titles.

From its founding years to 1960, this house was a relatively prolific publisher of secular titles. Most of these titles documented some areas of Afro-American history or described some aspects of the civil rights movement. *The Negro at Mount Bayou*, by Aurellis P. Hood (1910), for example, was a history and description of the unique, all-Afro-American town in Mississippi. And Bishop Reverdy C. Ransom's *The Spirit of Freedom and Justice: Orations and Speeches* (1926) is a compilation of orations in defense of better race relations.

Undoubtedly one of the most successful publishing ventures launched by Black Americans in the last years of the nineteenth century was the National Baptist Publishing Board. The board was established in Nashville, Tennessee, in 1896 by Dr. Richard H. Boyd under the auspices of the National Baptist Convention, but chartered in 1898 as a private corporation, as noted earlier. This publishing house was established by Black American Baptists in reaction to the decision by the American Baptist Publication

Society to discontinue publishing the writings of Black American Baptist clergy and laymen. By 1913 it had become one of the largest business enterprises owned and operated by Afro-Americans in the United States with a physical plant valued at $350,000;[9] and had developed a varied publishing program.

Like the other religious publishers, the primary publishing objective of the National Baptist Publishing Board was to publish literature for denominational use. *Golden Gems: A Song Book for the Church, the Pew, and Sunday School* (1901); *Preacher's Text and Topic Book with One Hundred Ordination Questions*, by H. M. Williams (1909); and *Baptist Pastor's Guide and Parliamentary Procedure*, by Richard H. Boyd (1900) are examples of a songbook and handbooks published for the denomination's clergy and laymen. Three books published by the board reflected its attempt to detail the denomination's history: *An Outline of Baptist History*, by N. H. Pius (1911); *History of Louisiana Negro Baptists, 1804–1914*, by William Hicks (1915); and *The Beacon Lights of Tennessee Baptists*, by Allen D. Hurt (1900).

Between 1896 and 1959 this religious publisher released several titles on a wide variety of secular subjects. In 1903 it published John H. Holman's medical textbook, *Methods of Histology and Bacteriology*. One of the many books produced by this house on Black American civil rights was *The Separate or "Jim Crow" Car Laws*, by Archard H. Boyd (1909). Many literary works portraying various aspects of Black American life were published by this house. Two examples are *Sentimental and Comical Poems*, by James H. Thomas (1913) and J. M. Grant's novel *Out of Darkness* (1909).

In the middle 1950s, another religious publisher sprang into being: Muhammad's Temple No. 2, Publications Department. The publishing arm of the Nation of Islam, this publisher, located in Chicago, issued its first book in 1956: *The Supreme Wisdom to the So-Called Negroes' Problem*, volume 1, by Elijah Muhammad.

The central objective of the publishing program of this religious publisher, as evidenced by the titles it released, seems to have been, unlike other religious publishers, to publish books to discuss the plight of the Black American as perceived by the leadership of this highly ideologically oriented denomination and to offer its doctrine of racial separatism as a solution. In 1957 this publisher released a revised edition of Elijah Muhammad's *The Supreme Wisdom to the So-Called Negroes' Problem.*

The book publishing activities of Black religious publishers, as we have seen, were wide and varied from 1900 to 1959. These book publishers constituted, unquestionably, the strongest category within the Black sector of the American book-publishing industry during this period. Most of them had longer publishing histories than book publishers in other categories. All of them, unlike publishers from other categories, enjoyed the support of a captive audience, strong financial support from their religious denominations, and a built-in distribution system.

NOTES

1. "A Message from Our Executive Director," in *Winning the World for Christ: Sunday School Publishing Board, National Baptist Convention, U.S.A., Inc., Seventy-seventh Annual Report, Fiscal Year, July 1, 1973 – June 30, 1974.* (Nashville: Sunday School Publishing Board, 1974), p. 6.

2. R. H. Boyd, *The Story of the National Baptist Publishing Board: The Why, How, When, Where and by Whom It was Established* (Nashville: National Baptist Publishing Board, 1924), pp. 142–46.

3. Benjamin E. Mays and Joseph W. Nicholson, *The Negro Church* (New York: Institute of Social and Religious Research, 1933), p. 96.

4. William J. Walls, *The African Methodist Episcopal Zion Church: Reality of the Black Church* (Charlotte, N.C.: A.M.E. Zion Publishing House, 1974), p. 343.

5. J. O. Patterson, Germain R. Ross, and Julia Mason Atkins, *History and Formative Years of the Church of God in Christ with Excerpts from the Life and Works of Its Founder—Bishop C. H. Mason* (Memphis: Church of God in Christ Publishing House, 1969), pp. iii, 63.

6. S. E. Grinstead, Sr., "Publishing Board Came Out of Unity to Strength," *Tennessean,* Nashville, Tennessee, January 11, 1976, p. 9.

7. Boyd, *The Story of the National Baptist Publishing Board,* pp. 34, 48.

8. Rev. Andrew White, executive secretary, A.M.E. Sunday School Union and Publishing House, interview held at the A.M.E. Sunday School Union and Publishing House, Nashville, Tennessee, January 13, 1976.

9. Boyd, *The Story of the National Baptist Publishing Board,* p. 137.

5
Reactors to a Revolution: Black Book Publishers, 1960–1974

INTRODUCTION

Never before in the history of the United States had the Black American and his allies pursued so aggressively, and on such a broad scale, the goals of securing for all Black Americans full political, social, and economic equality than in the period embracing the years between 1960 and 1974. The same motivations among Black Americans and sympathetic white Americans that had been at work in the founding of *Freedom's Journal*, of the NAACP, of the NUL, and of other civil rights organizations and institutions were in full play. Indeed, it was a period that has been characterized by many writers and scholars as "The Black Revolution."[1]

This movement combined with other forces to augment the demand for books that treated Black Americans objectively. The rising literacy rate among Blacks reached its highest peak in the first seven decades of the twentieth century in 1969 when only 3.6 percent of Black Americans were reported illiterate. By 1970 a record 18,367,000 Black Americans (or 81 percent of all Blacks) were living in urban areas and enjoying exposure to a wide variety of educational opportunities that encouraged reading.[2] During this period there was a spiraling increase in the number of Blacks enrolled in institutions of higher learning, with 287,000 reported in 1968 and 357,000 in 1970.[3] Blacks employed in professional pursuits in these years soared to 611,924 in 1969 compared with 64,245 in 1910.[4] Among Blacks in the 1960s and 1970s there was a growing self-awareness of their present and past culture that resulted in an increased demand for books about Black history and culture. And, finally, the greater investment in education and libraries by the federal government as evidenced by the National Defense Act (1958), the Library Services Act (1956), the Library Services and Construction Act (1963), and the Elementary and Secondary School Act (1965) provided millions of dollars for the purchase of books and supplemental materials, including books about Blacks.

Existing Black and White book publishers attempted to satisfy the increased demand for books about Black Americans. Added to the publishing efforts of these established book publishers were those of many new Black book publishers that sprang into being during the period.

BLACK CULTURAL ORGANIZATIONS

Associated Publishers, which had become the publishing arm of the Association for the Study of Afro-American Life and History, continued to publish books for adults and children documenting Afro-American history and culture.[5] In 1969 this publisher issued a revised edition of Carter G. Woodson's *The Mis-Education of the Negro*, edited with an introduction by Charles H. Wesley. That same year Charles Wesley's *Neglected History: Essays in Negro American History by a College President* was published. A revised and expanded *Word Pictures of Great Negroes* by Elsie Palmer Derricotte, et al., a classic work for children in Afro-American history, was released in 1964.

Another cultural organization that had been active in the earlier period and continued to publish books after 1961 was the Free Lance Writers' Workshop in Cleveland. Through its Free Lance Press, this organization expanded its book-publishing activities in this period to become a major publisher (see definitions in the Introduction). Publishing the poetry of members of the workshop, whose membership was overwhelmingly Black, Free Lance Press released a relative plethora of titles when compared to the single title it issued in an earlier period. Among some of the volumes of poetry, delineating the Black experience, released by this publisher were: *Phenomena*, by Russell Atkins (1961); *Dusk at Selma*, by Conrad Kent Rivers (1965); and *The Mantu Poets of Cleveland*, edited by Russell Atkins (1968). During this period, this publisher issued a volume of poetry by one of the workshop's white members: *Permit Me Voyage*, by Adelaide Simon (1964). In the 1970s, two volumes of poetry appeared: Russell Atkins's *The Nail* (1970) and his *Malefictium* (1971).

In Toledo, another Ohio-based cultural organization became a book publisher in the 1960s, the Black Hope Foundation. Founded by Don Benn Owens, Jr., in 1955 to "keep the Black ghetto clean morally and physically,"[6] this organization established its Commonsense Books Division in 1969 and began publishing books on Black Americana and other subjects of general adult interest. This publisher issued Don Benn Owens, Jr.'s *Dark Valor: The Man History Forgot* (1969), a historical novel about Columbus's Black first mate on the Niña during his first voyage to the New World. *The Most Controversial American and Why the Negro Lacks Unity*, a treatise on Black solidarity, by Don Benn Owens, Jr., was produced in 1970. In 1974, another book by Don Benn Owens, Jr., appeared on a subject unrelated to Black Americana entitled *You Can Become a Selling Writer Within 30 Short Days.*

Founded in 1961 by Dr. Margaret Burroughs and funded by voluntary contributions from local citizens and private foundations, Chicago's DuSable Museum of African American History seeks to preserve and disseminate the contributions of Africans and Afro-Americans to American and world culture. In 1965 the museum inaugurated its book-publishing program. Eugene Feldman, its director of public relations, stated: "Our publishing objectives are to publish materials on Black contributions to history and life."[7]

Illustrative of these objectives was the first title released by the museum, *Figures in Negro History*, edited by Eugene Feldman (1965), a collective biography. In 1968 Margaret Burrough's moving collection of poems, *What Shall I Tell My Children Who Are Black?*, was published. One of the most illuminating books to appear with this publisher's imprint was Eugene Feldman's *Black Power in Old Alabama: The Life and Stirring Times of James T. Rapier* (1968).

Another publisher within this category, the Alkebu-lan Books Association of the Alkebu-lan Foundation, a nonprofit organization, had similar objectives but focused primarily on the African

perspective. Dr. Yosef ben-Jochannan, who founded the organization in 1970 in New York City, made the following statement about
its book-publishing program: "Our objectives are mainly to propa-
gandize information on African and African-American matters
from an African perspective."[8]

A few of the titles, usually scholarly in tone, produced by this
publisher that reflected these objectives were: *African Origins of
the Major Western Religions*, by Yosef ben-Jochannan (1970); *The
Black Man's North and East Africa*, by Yosef ben-Jochannan and
George E. Simmonds (1972); and *The Black Man's Religion*, by
Yosef ben-Jochannan (1974).

The East is one of the most unusual new cultural organizations
developed by Blacks in the United States. Located in Brooklyn's
Bedford-Stuyvesant area, The East was organized in 1970. In one of
its publications appeared the following statement about its goals
and activities.

> (However, inside its doors burns the fiery embers of 400 years
> of strife, now kindled by the winds of new hope—The East, a
> model toward the foundation of a Black Nation.) . . . The
> East is a cultural and educational center built around "Uhuru
> Sasa," an independent Black school; *"Black News,"* an inde-
> pendent newspaper; and the "African-American Student As-
> sociation," a political organization of Black secondary school
> students.[9]

In 1972 The East became an active book publisher, publishing
books to change the attitudes Afro-Americans traditionally held
about themselves. Kasisi Jitu Weusi, director of The East, cited the
objectives intended to be realized in its publishing efforts. "Our
publishing objectives are to publish material that reflect the
thoughts, ideas, philosophies and ideologies of Black Revolution-
aries in this country."[10] During that first year three books appeared
with this publisher's imprint: *Three Speeches by Minister Louis
Farrakham*, a volume of orations by the fiery and articulate Black
Muslim leader; Kasisi Jitu Weusi's revolutionary manual for teaching in a Black secondary school, *A Message from a Black Teacher*;
and Herman B. Ferguson's perceptive analysis on the use of drugs

in the Black community, *Dope: An Agent of Chemical Warfare.*
Among other titles released by The East have been *The Young Black
Poets of Brooklyn,* edited by Yusef Kman (1973) and *African
Names—Why? Which? What? Where?* (1973).

A BLACK UNIVERSITY PRESS:
HOWARD UNIVERSITY PRESS

For the first time in the history of American book publishing an
Afro-American university established a university press as an
ongoing campus activity with a separate administrative unit, staff,
and budget, when Howard University launched the Howard University Press on April 8, 1974.[11] Dr. James E. Cheeks, the university's president, described the events which led to the formation of
the press.

> This launching of the Howard University Press signals the
> beginning of the realization of a goal we set for ourselves
> several years ago. In 1969 we began a self-analysis and evalu-
> ation to determine the adequacy of resources and programs in
> meeting the challenges of the next decades. This analysis and
> evaluation provoked us to develop a new direction for
> Howard University. It is a direction destined to commit the
> total resources of Howard University to engage the entire
> spectrum of social problems emerging as crises in national
> and international life. The entire development of Howard
> University Press, in this our 106th academic year, is part of a
> plan to give Howard parity with other major American uni-
> versities of the first rank. Howard University Press was for-
> mally authorized by the Board of Trustees in June of 1972. At
> that time, a fourteen-member commission was created, com-
> prising representatives from the faculty, student body, the
> administrative staff, and persons outside the Howard com-
> munity who are distinguished in public life. The purpose of
> this commission is to formulate policies and to systematically
> evaluate the execution of those policies by the staff of the
> Press.[12]

Headed by Executive Director Charles Harris, previously a
senior editor at Random House, the staff is composed of eleven

other seasoned professionals who have worked in book publishing at several established publishing houses in the United States. Book production for the press is handled by Leonard Shatzkin's Planned Production, and the press has a warehousing agreement with the National Labor Association Processing Company.

Harris commented on the publishing objectives of the press and outlined areas in which books would be published.

> The importance of the Press is that we haven't had a chance to speak for ourselves—to tell something about ourselves. We will be a Black press, yes. But we will also publish books by non-blacks. We hope to improve the intellectual condition of the country. . . . Howard will publish in certain areas—academic, general trade, reference and books for people interested in formal education. It will publish poetry, short stories and novels. There are some of each on our first list.[13]

Howard University Press's inaugural list in 1974 consisted of thirteen titles representative of these publishing objectives, formats, and areas of interest. Two novels were on the list: Lindsay Barrett's newly designed edition of *Songs of Mumu* and *Saw the House in Half*, by Oliver Jackman. Works of literature were: *A Poetic Equation: Conversations between Nikki Giovanni and Margaret Walker*; Arthur P. Davis's *From the Dark Tower: Afro-American Writers, 1900 to 1960*; *Bid the Vassal Soar: Interpretive Essays on the Life of Phillis Wheatley and George Moses Horton*, by Merle A. Richmond; *HooDoo Hollerin' BeBop Ghosts*, a volume of poetry by Larry Neal; *The Short Fiction of Charles W. Chesnutt*, edited with an introduction by Sylvia Lyons Render; and *Aiiieeee! An Anthology of Asian-American Writers*, edited by Rank Chin, Jeffrey Chan, Lawson Inada, and Shawn Wong. In history there were three titles: *Reluctant Reformers: The Impact of Racism on American Social Reform Movements*, by Robert Allen, with the collaboration of Pamela Allen; William Leo Hansberry's *Pillars of Ethiopian History*; and *How Europe Underdeveloped Africa*, by Walter Rodney. Education was represented by William E. Brazziel's *Quality Education for All Americans* and *Black Engineers in the United States: A Directory*, edited by James K.K. Ho, was the single reference work.

BLACK CIVIL RIGHTS
ORGANIZATIONS

During this period the National Urban League (NUL) narrowed its book-publishing activities to works documenting the Black American's social, political, and economic condition. It did not, as it had in 1927 when *Ebony* and *Topaz* were released, publish works celebrating Afro-American artistic and literary achievement. Instead, the NUL focused on the publication of numerous important studies such as: *When the Marching Stopped: An Analysis of Black Issues in the 1970s* (1970); *The Power of the Ballot; A Handbook for Black Political Participation* (1973); and *When the Lender Looks First: A Case Study of Mortgage Disinvestment in Bronx County* (1970).

Although the National Association for the Advancement of Colored People continued publishing *Crisis Magazine*, this organization was a less active book publisher than the NUL. The NAACP primarily published pamphlets such as *Brotherhood in Action* (1962) and *Let's March to the Voters Registration Desk* (1963). Its book publications were limited to its annual reports. *The Birth of Freedom: N.A.A.C.P. Annual Report for 1964* (1964) was an example.

BLACK COMMERCIAL
BOOK-PUBLISHING FIRMS

Educational Publishers

Afro Am Publishing Company. One of the most active educational book publishers of this period was Afro Am Publishing Company in Chicago. The firm and its publishing activities, according to President David P. Ross, were shaped largely by the expressed demands of teachers and librarians for books on Afro-Americana and Africana.

Our initial plan was not one of establishing a publishing company. Our initial plan was to put out an information booklet for the Emancipation Centennial Exposition that would be a memento and that would be of interest to the general public, not to the educational market, initially. But once we got the book, *Great Negroes, Past and Present* by Russell Adams (1965), out, the teachers and librarians who got a hold of it wanted to use it in the schools, especially here in Chicago. . . . It has been adopted by several state boards of education.[14]

To satisfy this demand Afro Am Publishing Company issued *Great Negroes, Past and Present* in three editions between 1963 and 1969 and expanded its list to include *The Meeting*, a play about Afro-American history for children, by Peggy Osborn (1968); and *Colors Around Me*, by Vivian Church (1972), a primary textbook designed to create positive self-images in children of different skin colors.

Lotus Press. In 1972 Lotus Press in Detroit was organized to publish a volume of poetry by Naomi Long Madgett: *Pink Ladies in the Afternoon*. Two years later this poetess, who is also a professor of English literature at Eastern Michigan University, acquired the firm with the aim of publishing quality Afro-American poetry for use in high school and college literature classes. Poet/Professor Madgett's goal was realized when the firm published *Their Deep Rivers* (1974), a portfolio of the poetry of twenty contemporary Black-American poets.

Edward W. Blyden Press. New York City's Edward W. Blyden Press was another educational publishing firm established by Afro-American educators to publish books on the Black experience for use in the classroom. Founded in 1967, this firm has published paperback and hardcover texts in Black history for use in elementary and secondary schools by teachers and students. One of its most widely used publications has been Beryle Banfield's *Africa in the Curriculum: A Resource Bulletin and Guide for Teachers* (1968).

Buckingham Learning Corporation. Another New York City-based educational publisher was Buckingham Learning Corporation. This short-lived firm was formed by Dr. Oswald White in 1968, but reportedly had gone out of existence by 1975.[15] One book and an accompanying teacher's manual were identified as its publications. In 1968 this firm released *Dear Dr. King*, a supplementary text on the great civil rights leader, and an accompanying teacher's manual, *Encounters with Dr. King*, for use in elementary classrooms.

General Trade Book Publishers:
Black Americana/Africana Subjects Only

J. A. Rogers Publications. J. A. Rogers Publications continued to publish books documenting various aspects of Black history and responding to the writing of racist historians and writers after 1960. Illustrative of this firm's publications during this period were revised editions of earlier published works such as: *Africa's Gift to America* (rev. and enl. Civil War Centennial Edition, 1961); and *100 Amazing Facts about the Negro* (24th rev. ed., 1963). Joel Augustus Rogers died in 1966. His widow, Helga Rogers, continues to issue his books in reprint editions. These editions, however, bear the imprint "Helga M. Rogers."

Broadside Press. One of the most successful Black general trade book publishers was Detroit's Broadside Press. Founded in 1965, the press celebrated its tenth anniversary from September 26 to September 29, 1975. On this occasion poet-founder Dudley Randall commented on the objectives he tried to realize with the firm.

> I have not locked myself in any rigid ideology in managing Broadside Press, but I suppose certain inclinations or directions appear in my actual activities. As clearly as I can see by looking at myself, which is not very clear, because of closeness, I restrict the publications to poetry, which I think I understand and can judge not too badly. An exception is the new *Broadside Critics*, which, even though prose, will be concerned with poetry. I reserve the press for Black poetry (except in "For Malcolm"), as I think the vigor and beauty of our Black poets should be better known and should have an outlet.[16]

Among the many volumes of poetry produced by this publisher were: *Think Black*, by Haki R. Madhubuti (Don L. Lee, 1967); *Black Judgement*, by Nikki Giovanni (1968); *We a BaddDDD People*, by Sonia Sanchez (1970); and *The Last Ride of Wild Bill*, by Sterling Brown (1974).

Agascha Productions. Agascha Productions is another Detroit-based book publisher. In an interview, Agadem I. Diara, who founded the firm with his wife in 1970, stated, "I think the major reason why we decided to publish is to better propagate the Pan Africanist ideology."[17] To achieve this goal, this firm had released six titles by 1974. Reportedly, its best-seller was Agadem I. Diara's *Islam and Pan Africanism* (1978).

Black Star Publishers. Black Star Publishers of Detroit was founded in the same year as Agascha Productions, but seems to have gone out of existence in 1974. In that year the *Inner-City Voice*, a monthly journal that this publisher began publishing in 1970, ceased. One book was identified as its publication: *The Political Thought of James Forman*, by James Forman (1970), a work describing the political philosophy of the famed civil rights leader.[18]

Path Press. Established in 1968, Chicago's Path Press was another firm which demised before 1974. Its founders, Attorney Lemuel E. Bentley, the late novelist Frank London Brown, novelist Herman Cromwell Gilbert, and Bennett J. Johnson, outlined the aims of the firm.

> We shall concentrate on works by and about Negroes, first, because we ourselves are Negroes, participants in and recorders of the struggles of our people for dignity and equality. Second, because of our intimate knowledge of the epic nature of our existence—from the battles of winning our daily bread to the skirmishes for acceptance in high places—we know that these struggles seldom are presented with honesty and integrity by the major publishing houses, even in books by authors who are perceptive and brave enough to put truth on paper. We also know that when a book which realistically

depicts Negro life is published, often it is promoted in a lacka-
daisical manner, as though the publisher preferred under-
cutting profit to proselytizing justice. . . . It is our aim,
through Path Press, to usher in a renaissance in Negro
literature.[19]

Only two titles were published by this firm: Herman Cromwell Gilbert's *Uncertain Sound* (1969), a novel about race relations in a
southern Illinois community, and *The Myth Makers*, by Frank
London Brown (1969), a novel portraying life in Chicago's Black
ghetto in the 1940s and 1950s.

Third World Press. A more prolific publisher was Third World
Press. Poets Haki R. Madhubuti, Johari Amini, and Carolyn
Rogers started the firm in 1967. In the words of Kofi Moyo, Third
World Press's production coordinator, it seeks to be: "An alterna-
tive outlet that reflects, understands, and in most cases, agrees with
the ideological directions of its authors."[20] And in one of its catalogues, it's founders state: "Third World Press came into being to
provide in-depth reflections of ourselves by ourselves."[21] Numerous titles for adults and children have emanated from this highly
innovative publisher. In 1972, for example, Third World Press published *Garvey, Lumumba, Malcolm: Black Nationalist-Separatists*,
by Shawna Magalanbayan, a classic comparative study of the three
Black leaders. Howard University history professor Chancellor
Williams's *The Destruction of Black Civilization* (1974) is a mile-
stone publication by this firm. And for juvenile readers it has published such books as Gwendolyn Brooks's *The Tiger Who Wore
Gloves; or, Who Are You?*

Vita Ya Watu Publishers. In a more militant way, Imamu Amiri
Baraka's Vita Ya Watu (People's War) Publishers in Newark seeks
to change the attitudes of Black Americans and persons of African
descent through its book publications. This publisher's philosophy
was assessed by Baraka's literary biographer, Theodore Hudson.
"Jihad [formerly the name of Vita Ya Watu Publishers] produces
Black communications for the evolving Black Nation."[22] This
philosophy is evidenced in several titles released by this publisher.

In 1972, for instance, *Spirit Reach*, a volume of militant poetry by Imamu Amiri Baraka, appeared. *Africa and Imperialism*, an address by President Ahmed Sekou Toure of Guinea detailing the injustices of Africa, given on the occasion of the death of Amilcar Cabral, was published in 1972. Not restricted to adult titles, Vita Ya Watu also published books for children of a Black cultural-nationalist nature such as *Reflection in the Sun* (1972), a coloring book intended to acquaint young readers with African images and Swahili names and definitions.

Sapphire Publishing Company. Focusing on a different aspect of the Black experience, Black feminism, Sapphire Publishing Company was organized in San Francisco in 1973 by a group of Black professional women. In a policy statement Sapphire Publishing Company's founders stated its goals. "The Sapphire Publishing Company is committed to the publication of works which reflect those aspects of life and history having particular relevance for the Black women."[23] In the year it was established this publisher released its first book: Carolyn Jetter Green's *70 Soul Secrets of Sapphire*, a lively critique on the state of Black womanhood in America.

Tarharka Publishing Company. By contrast, Tarharka Publishing Company, founded by the late Africanist William Leo Hansberry's research assistant, Phaon Sundiata, in Annapolis, Maryland, in 1971, was organized "To research and popularize the socio-psychological history of persons of African descent with particular emphasis on the Black male."[24] One book has been published by this firm: Phaon Sundiata's *Black Manhood: The Building of Civilization by the Black Man of the Nile* (1971), a well-researched account of the Black man's role in the early development of Egyptian civilization.

Energy Blacksouth Press. Seeking to explore a different aspect of the Black experience, Energy Blacksouth Press with offices in Washington, D.C. (Upsouth Office) and De Ridder, Louisiana (Deepsouth Office) was formed in 1972 by poet Ahmos Zu-Bolton to publish Black literary works. To realize his goal, this imaginative young publisher embarked on the publication of a projected thirteen-volume mini-anthology of Black literature entitled *The Hoo-Doo Blackseries*. *Hoo-Doo 1*, the first volume, appeared in 1972 and its first printing was completely sold out. *Hoo-Doo 2 & 3* was published in 1973 carrying fiction, poetry, and literary criticism by such established and new Black writers and poets as Alice Walker, Sara Webster Fabio, Dudley Randall, Jerry Ward and Virginia Lester, Lucille Clifton, Joe Johnson, and nineteen other Black writers.

Black Academy Press. By comparison, Black Academy Press, located in Bloomfield, New Jersey, publishes books of a scholarly nature on Black subjects from the Black perspective. Shortly after the press was founded in 1970, Dr. S. Okechukwu Mezu, its president, discussed the firm's philosophy. "Not that foreigners are incapable of accurately interpreting African and Black cultural values, Black Academy, Inc., merely wants to give opportunities to scholars from areas involved to express their conception of their own society, their way of life and the gigantic forces that appear to be reshaping those societies today."[25] Many Black scholars and writers have taken advantage of this opportunity and published some illuminating titles with this publisher. The popular *Black Leaders of the Centuries*, edited by S. Okechukwu Mezu and Ram Desai, a collection of essays on prominent Black leaders and their political philosophies in Africa and the New World, was released by this firm in 1970. *Topics in Afro-American Studies*, edited by Henry J. Richards (1971) and *African Students in Alien Cultures*, by Amechi Anumoya (1974) were among the several other titles produced by this publisher.

Emerson Hall Publishers. Publishing books primarily in the behavioral and social sciences focusing on the Black American, New York City's pacesetting Emerson Hall Publishers was founded in 1970 by Alfred E. Prettyman. A former executive with Harper and Row, publishers, Prettyman became dissatisfied with the firm's lack of commitment to publishing quality books about Black Americans and left that publishing house to start his own firm. The dynamic Prettyman outlined in an interview his original plans for the firm.

The original intention was to do books in the behavioral and social sciences which are education related so that they are trade, professional and educational social science books. The intention was to begin with that so that you could build up a backlist and then to underlay that eventually with textbooks, one or two textbooks, and some selected children's books.[26]

Emerson Hall Publishers has released several titles in the behavioral and social sciences since its founding in 1970. Among some of those which have been well received are Dr. Kenneth Clark's *Possible Reality: A Design for High Academic Achievement for Inner-City Students* (1972); Inez Smith Reid's *Together Black Women* (1972), one of the first comprehensive studies to appear on Black womanhood; Robert B. Hill's popular *Strengths of Black Families* (1972); and Dr. Alvin Poussaint's classic, *Why Blacks Kill Blacks* (1973). Although no children's books had appeared by 1974, several works of literature had been issued by this publisher such as *No*, a novel, by Clarence Major (1973); *New Days, Poems of Exile and Return*, by June Jordan (1974); and *The House of Blue Lightning*, a volume of poetry by Wilfred Cartey (1973).

Nuclassics and Science Publishing Company. Little information could be found on the elusive Nuclassics and Science Publishing Company in Washington, D.C. Reportedly, this firm was organized in 1969 by Carl Shears to publish his books, which included poetry, fiction, and autobiography portraying and documenting Afro-American Life.[27] Typical of the titles released by this publisher were *Niggers and Po' White Trash: A Collection of Stories*, by Carl L. Shears (1969) and *The Black Letters: Love Letters from a Black Soldier in Viet Nam*, by Rita Southall and Carl Shears (1972).

General Trade Book Publishers:
Black Americana/Africana and Other Subjects

Drum and Spear Press. The defunct Drum and Spear Press, which was started in Washington, D.C., in 1968, folded in the early 1970s. It was unique among Black American publishers, because it was a thriving bookstore as well as a book publishing enterprise.

Drum and Spear Press, according to its erstwhile director, Carolyn Carter, came into existence to fulfill a specific need within the Black community. "It is obvious to us that Black people of every educational level and background are very eager to read material relevant to their survival, if only it is made available. Drum and Spear exists to put such material in print. We don't have all of the answers, but we are seriously looking for them."[28]

The first title released by Drum and Spear Press was an appropriate embodiment of its *raison d'etre:* a revised edition of historian C.L.R. James's classic, *A History of Pan African Revolt* (1969), a historical analysis of Black revolts from 1793 (Santo Domingo) to 1969 (Curacao).[29] Other titles published by this firm seem to have fulfilled the need for cultural survival within the Black community, such as: *The Book of African Names*, by Chief Ofuntoki (1970); *Speaking Swahili: Kusema Kiswahili*, by Bernard K. Meganda (1971); and *Children of Africa: A Coloring Book* (1971).

One book of poems, however, produced by this publisher was on a subject unrelated to Afro-Americana or Africana. It was a collection of poems in support of the Palestinian Liberation Movement entitled *Enemy of the Sun: Poems of Palestinian Resistance*, edited by Naseer Aruri and Edmund Shareed (1971).

The Third Press, Joseph Okpaku Publishing Company. One of the most versatile and ambitious Black firms publishing books on Black Americana/Africana and other subjects was The Third Press, Joseph Okpaku Publishing Company in New York City. However, when queried about the publishing objectives of his firm, Joseph Okpaku confined his response to Third Press's involvement in Black-oriented book publications.

> Well, essentially, prior to our efforts in the area, there was really no Black input into the book publishing industry. I am sorry, there was Broadside Press, of course, essentially publishing poetry and broadsides. In a country where there are twenty million Blacks. And to count the Black publishers around the world. Yet, we are all influenced by books. The power of publishing cannot be underestimated. So I figured

the first objective was to make a Black input into the area. All of that to encourage the publishing of sophisticated Black writing.[30]

Contrary to Mr. Akpaku's observation, there was, as this study reveals, Black input into the American book-publishing industry prior to 1970, when his firm was established, although not a highly visible one.

The Third Press's efforts to encourage Black writing were realized by a variety of publications. Communist-activist Angela Davis's *If They Come for Me in the Morning* (1971) was one of several sociopolitical commentaries released by this firm. *Two Plays*, by Douglas Turner Ward (1971), was representative of its publications in Black drama. Sonia Sanchez's *Love Poems* (1973) was one of the many volumes of Black poetry published. Clarence Major's *The Dark and Feeling* (1974) is an example of a title of Black literary criticism issued by this publisher. And in 1972, this firm produced Ruby Dee's compilation *Glowchild and Other Poems for the Young Reader: An Odarkai Book*, a line of books started for children in 1973 by the firm.

The Third Press released several titles on subjects unrelated to Afro-Americana/Africana. Two of them were widely received because of their high topical interest. In 1970, after the widely publicized and sensational Chicago trial of eight nationally known activists accused of inciting riots at the 1968 Democratic National Convention in Chicago, *Verdict: The Exclusive Picture Story of the Chicago 8*, by Joseph Opaku, appeared. This publisher scooped other more established New York publishers in 1974, a few months before the national presidential election, when it published *Gerald Ford and the Future of the Presidency*, by J. D. ter Horst, President Ford's former press secretary who had resigned this post in protest to Ford's pardon of former President Richard M. Nixon.

In children's literature The Third Press also distinguished itself with the publication of a number of unusual titles unrelated to Afro-Americana/Africana. Notable among them was *Did the Sun Shine Before You were Born: A Sex Education Primer*, by Sol and Judith Chone (1974; An Odarki Book).

Balamp Publishing Company. By contrast, Detroit's Balamp Publishing Company, according to president James M. Jay, confined its
efforts to publishing biography.[31] Four of the five titles released by
this firm were either biography or autobiography. They were
Negroes in Science: Natural Science Doctorates, 1876–1969, by
James M. Jay (1971); *Black American Scholars—A Study of Their
Beginnings, 1876–1969,* by Horace Mann Bond (1972); *My World
of Reality: The Autobiography of Hildrus A. Poindexter,* by
Hildrus Poindexter (1973), and *You Don't Look Like a Musician,*
by Bud Freeman (1974). One of the titles published by the firm,
however, illustrates its attempts to produce a work on higher education administration. It is *The Academic Department or Division
Chairman: A Complex Role,* edited by James Brann and Thomas E.
Emmet (1972), a collection of papers, lectures, and seminar presen-
tations by twenty-four scholars on the role, function, duties, and
problems of academic department and division chairmen.

A BLACK PERIODICAL PUBLISHING FIRM: JOHNSON PUBLISHING COMPANY

The Book Division of Johnson Publishing Company in Chicago,
formerly the Negro Digest Publishing Company (discussed in chapter 3) was organized in 1961. In an interview, Doris E. Saunders,
formerly head of the Book Division, recalled the series of developments and decisions that led to its formation.

> Yes, in the period of time from 1949, when I came to
> *Ebony,* and in 1961, when we started the Book Division, I
> received avalanches of letters from students, teachers, librar-
> ians and from individuals wanting information that was not
> available in books at the time, wanting reprints of articles in
> *Ebony.*
> We had done an article on the fifteen outstanding events in
> Negro history. We received so many requests for it that we
> finally had it reprinted and sent it to anyone who asked for it.
> So it ultimately seemed to us that the best thing to do was to
> put these things together in a book or a booklet. And the
> more we talked the more we realized that to publish a booklet

would be as expensive as to publish a book, if we did it the way we wanted to do it. And it really would not solve our problem. So we decided that there were areas. We wanted to do something in politics. We wanted to cover a variety of fields. We saw that we really had our initial list.[32]

In 1962 the Book Division of Johnson Publishing Company made its debut in the American book-publishing industry with the publication of *Burn, Killer, Burn*, an autobiographical novel by Paul Crump, an inmate on death row in Illinois's Statesville Penitentiary who, after its publication, had his sentence commuted to life imprisonment, and Lerone Bennett, Jr.'s *Before the Mayflower: A History of the Negro in America, 1619–1962*, a popularized history of Afro-Americans so widely received that it went through four editions by 1969. A plethora of titles exploring many areas of Afro-Americana flowed from the Book Division following the publication of these two books. Freda DeKnight's *The Ebony Cookbook: A Date with a Dish* (1962) brought the secrets and recipes of Afro-American cookery into the homes of many Americans. *The Negro Handbook*, edited by Doris Saunders (1966), and *The Ebony Handbook*, edited by Doris Saunders (1974), reminiscent of Monroe Work's *Negro Year Book* and Florence Murray's *Negro Handbook*, reported up-to-date statistics and facts on vital areas of Black life. Important and popular commentaries on various aspects of Afro-American life were also published, such as Edward T. Clayton's *The Negro Politician* (1964) and *Confrontation in Black and White*, by Lerone Bennett, Jr. (1965). *Sonny Liston: The Champ Nobody Wanted*, by A. S. ("Doc") Young (1963), *What Manner of Man: A Biography of Martin Luther King, Jr.*, by Lerone Bennett, Jr., and Alex Poinsett's *Black Power, Gary Style: The Making of Richard Gordon Hatcher* (1970) were examples of the many biographies to appear. In 1970 the Ebony Classic Series of reprints was produced, including such titles as *Autobiography of a Fugitive Negro*, by Samuel Ringgold Ward (Foreword by Vincent Harding) and *Men of Mark*, by William J. Simmons (Foreword by Lerone Bennett, Jr.). Pictorial works, recording current events in Black history, were released like *The Day They March*, edited by Doris E. Saunders (1963) and *The Black Revolution*, by the editors of *Ebony* (1970).

In the area of children's books several notable titles appeared, such as Dorothy Robinson's prize-winning *Legend of Africana* (1974) and Helen King's *Soul of Christmas* (1972).

BLACK RELIGIOUS BOOK PUBLISHERS

Seven of the eight Black religious book publishers active between 1900 and 1959 were still in operation from 1960 to 1971. Although by the 1960s the influence of Black religious denominations was declining in the Black community, these religious publishers continued to flourish. As noted earlier, the A.M.E. Book Concern suspended operations in 1952.

The A.M.E. Zion Publishing House, Muhammad's Temple No. 2, Publications Department and the National Baptist Publishing Board continued to publish books in line with their original publishing objectives. The four other religious publishers, however, altered or expanded their publishing programs in the years from 1960 to 1974.

Christian Methodist Episcopal Publishing House. In 1968 the Christian Methodist Epsicopal Publishing House moved its offices from Jackson, Tennessee, to Memphis. Although this publisher continued to publish only religious literature, it expanded its publishing program to include in this period the publication of interdenominational literature. In 1974 this house finalized plans to co-publish with the African Methodist Episcopal Church, the African Methodist Episcopal Zion Church, the National Conference of Black Christians and the Consolidation of Church Union the first in a series of books: *Liberation and Unity: A Lenten Booklet for 1976.* To be issued with the imprint of the C.M.E. Publishing House, it is estimated that the first press run will be 50,000 copies.[33] The publication of *Liberation and Unity: A Lenten Booklet for 1976* represents the first effort of these religious bodies to participate in a co-publishing venture.

The A.M.E. Sunday School Union and Publishing House. After 1961 the A.M.E. Sunday School Union and Publishing House became a less active book publisher. This publisher continued to release religious titles but ceased to publish secular titles as it had in the pre-1960 period when it published several noteworthy books on a variety of secular subjects.

The Church of God in Christ Publishing House. This religious publisher became a much more active book publisher after 1960 than it had been in the previous period. Although still confining its publications to denominational literature, its annual lists have been expanded to include denominational manuals, histories, and biographies. For example, in 1969 *The History and Formative Years of the Church of God in Christ with Excerpts from the Life and Works of Its Founder—Bishop C. H. Mason*, by Bishop J. O. Patterson, Germain R. Ross, and Julia Mason Atkins was published. *Here Am I, Send Me: A Biography of Bishop J. O. Patterson*, by Frances Burnett Kelly and Germain R. Ross, was released in 1970. And the *National Church Directory* appeared in 1974.

Sunday School Publishing Board of the National Baptist Convention, U.S.A., Inc. A new dimension was added to the publishing program of the Sunday School Publishing Board in 1967 when it organized the Townsend Press Division, a commercial trade book unit. This new division was established to publish secular titles on various aspects of Afro-Americana. The first book to appear with the "Townsend Press" imprint was Joseph H. Jackson's *Unholy Shadows and Freedom's Holy Light* (1967), an analysis of the civil rights movement. In 1970 Kenny Williams's *They Also Spoke*, a critical survey of Afro-American literature from 1780 to 1830, was released.

The publishing activities of thirty-seven book publishers that flourished between 1960 and 1974 have been presented in this chapter. Although a small segment within the American book publishing industry, these publishers reacted to the varied demands of the period by producing original titles on various aspects of Black-Americana and Africana. Many of these areas were either ignored or superficially treated in books released by white book publishers during this period.

NOTES

1. John Hope Franklin, *From Slavery to Freedom*, 3d ed. (New York: Knopf, 1967), pp. 623–51.

2. U.S., Bureau of the Census, *Statistical Abstract of the United States, 1974*, (Washington, D.C.: Government Printing Office, 1975), pp. 114, 160.

3. U.S., Bureau of the Census, *Statistical Abstract of the United States, 1975* (Washington, D.C.: Government Printing Office, 1976), p. 137.

4. U.S., Bureau of the Census, *Statistical Abstracts, 1974*, p. 360; U.S., Department of Commerce, Bureau of the Census, *Negro Population in the United States, 1790–1915*, (Washington, D.C.: Government Printing Office, 1936), p. 510.

5. At its 57th Annual Meeting, October 19–22, 1972, the membership of the Association for the Study of Negro Life and History voted to change its name to the Association for the Study of Afro-American Life and History. "Annual Meeting," *Journal of Negro History 57 (January 1973): 117.*

6. Carl Martin, Director, Commonsense Books Division, Black Hope Foundation, Inc., Toledo, Ohio, to the author, 23 September 1975.

7. Eugene Feldman, interview held at the DuSable Museum of African American History, Chicago, Illinois, 23 September 1975.

8. Dr. Yosef ben-Jochannan, a telephone interview, Alkebu-lan Foundation, New York, N.Y. 9, February 1977.

9. "The East: A Model of Nationhood," in *The East* (Brooklyn, N.Y.: The East, 1971), *p. 3.*

10. Kasisi Jitu Weusi, interview held at The East, Brooklyn, N.Y., 22 November 1975.

11. Howard University Press, "Howard U. President Launches First Black University Press in U.S.," mimeographed press release, (Washington, D.C.: Howard University, 1974), p. 1.

12. James E. Cheeks, "Remarks at the Launching of the Howard University Press," Washington, D.C.: Howard University Press, 1974.

13. Susan Waner, "Howard University Launches Its Own Press," *Publishers Weekly*, March 4, 1974, p. 49.

14. David P. Ross, interview held at Afro-Am Publishing Company, Chicago, Illinois, March 6, 1975.

15. Bradford Chambers, interview held at the offices of the Council on Interracial Books for Children, New York, N.Y., 25 November 1975.

16. Dudley Randall, *Broadside Memories: Poets I Have Known* (Detroit: Broadside Press, 1975), pp. 2, 27.

17. Agadem L. Diara, interview held at Agascha Productions, Detroit, Michigan, 7 November 1975.

18. Dudley Randall, "Negro Publishers for Black Readers," *Publishers Weekly*, October 22, 1972, p. 49.

19. Path Press, "Introducing Path Press—Something New in Publishing," mimeographed press release (Chicago: n.d.), p. 1.

20. Kofi Moyo, interview held at the Third World Press, Chicago, Illinois, 13 June 1974.

21. Third World Press, *75 Catalog* (Chicago: Third World Press, 1975), p. 16.

22. Theodore Hudson, *From LeRoi Jones to Amiri Baraka* (Durham, N.C.: Duke University Press, 1973), p. 36. In 1974 the name of Jihad Productions was changed to Vita Ya Watu (People's War).

23. Sapphire Publishing Company, *Introducing Sapphire Publishing Company: A Unique Venture* (San Francisco: Sapphire Publishing Co., 1974), p. 2.

24. Phaon Sundiata to the author, 23 December 1975.

25. Black Academy Press, *Supplement, Containing Index to Black Academy Review* (Buffalo, N.Y.: Black Academy Press, 1970), p. 111.

26. Alfred E. Prettyman, interview held at Emerson Hall Publishers, New York, N.Y., 26 November 1975.

27. The author is indebted to James P. Johnson, reference librarian, Moorland-Spingarn Research Center, Howard University, for providing information on this firm.

28. Bradford Chambers, "Why Minority Publishers? New Voices Are Heard," *Publishers Weekly*, March 15, 1971, p. 46.

29. The first edition of this book was entitled *A History of the Negro Revolt*, by C.L.R. James (London: Fact, 1938).

30. Joseph Okpaku, interview held at the Third Press, Joseph Okpaku Publishing Company, New York, N.Y., 25 November 1975.

31. James M. Jay, president, Balamp Publishing Company, Detroit, Michigan to the author, 7 February 1976.

32. Doris E. Saunders, interview held at Johnson Publishing Company, Chicago, Illinois, 4 March 1975.

33. Toney Terrance, interview held at C.M.E. Publishing House, Memphis, Tennessee, 13 February 1976.

6

Yesteryear versus Yesterday: A Comparison of Black Book Publishing in Two Periods: 1900–1959 and 1960–1974

INTRODUCTION

As has been shown, the demand for books that treated the Black American objectively was greatly affected by dynamic social, religious, political, economic, educational, and cultural developments occurring inside as well as outside the Black community. This demand, which changed in nature and complexity as the twentieth century progressed, influenced the number, composition, and activities of publishers in the Black book-publishing sector active in the two periods 1900–1959 and 1960–1974.

After 1960 did the growth of Black book publishing accelerate in the number of publishers? Did the composition of the categories of publishers change? And, finally, was there greater diversity in the activities publishers pursued?

THE NUMBER AND COMPOSITION OF PUBLISHERS

At the dawn of the twentieth century there were thirteen active publishing enterprises in the Black book-publishing sector of the American book-publishing industry. These publishing enterprises had come into existence during various decades from 1810–1819 through 1890–1899.

Between 1900 and 1959, thirty-one more book-publishing enterprises were established. Of these six decades, the most prolific was the 1910–1919 decade when fourteen new book-publishing enterprises came into existence.

The period of greatest acceleration in the growth of Black book publishers in the twentieth century occurred, however, after 1959. In the 1960–1969 decade, for instance, eleven new publishers were established. In the following half decade, 1970–1974, twelve more new publishers began releasing books. Thus, the years from 1960 through 1974 witnessed the most rapid proliferation of new Black book publishers in the century. During these years the largest number of Black book publishers, thirty-four, in the history of American book publishing was simultaneously engaged in book publishing.

Different categories of publishers predominated as the twentieth century unfolded. During the earlier period, book publishing was not a profit-making business venture among Black Americans. The economic and educational levels of the majority of Black Americans were not sufficiently high to support a commercial book-publishing market. Consequently, most of the commercial enterprises that engaged in book publishing did not thrive. They were short-lived and produced relatively few titles. Even newspaper and periodical firms that published books only did so sporadically. In these years institutional publishers dominated the sector. They were the most prolific in title output and had, in most instances, the greatest longevity when compared with other categories of publishers. Not consciously seeking to make a profit, although a few like the National Baptist Publishing Board did, they had the advantages of drawing on institutional capital to underwrite their book-publishing activities and a built-in distribution system available to them through the large memberships of their parent organizations.

After 1960, however, there were marked changes in the composition of publishers. No newspaper publishers, for example, released any titles. Only one university publisher, as compared to six in the earlier period, was active: the Howard University Press. And the Book Division of Johnson Publishing Company was the only surviving periodical publisher actively engaged in book publishing. During these years, the most dramatic change in the sector was its domination by commercial book-publishing firms. For the first time, commercial book publishers outnumbered institutional publishers and published more titles than any other category of publishers. The success of commercial book-publishing firms during this period was undoubtedly the result of the rising economic and educational status of Black Americans as well as other factors related to the Black Revolution and the growing number of white Americans who were seeking new and authentic information about Black Americans being published in titles released by these firms.

THE DIVERSITY OF PUBLISHING ACTIVITIES

Overall there seems to have been, with some notable exceptions, greater diversity in the publishing activities of most publishers between 1960 and 1974 than in the earlier period. This augmented diversity becomes apparent when a comparison is made between the title output, the number of literary genres, and the publishing objectives.

Title Output

A tabulation of selected titles published by active publishers from 1900 through 1974 revealed that in every category, except newspaper publishers, there was an increase in the title output after 1959.[1] The most spectacular growth in title output was among commercial book publishers. In the earlier period, these publishers had two consecutive peak five-year spans, 1935–1939 and 1940–1944, when they released twenty-one titles collectively during each five-year span. After 1959 the title output began to rise steadily until it soared to 154 titles in the 1970–1974 five-year span. A marked acceleration in title output was also evident after 1959 in the categories of periodical publishers, university presses, the publishing units of cultural and professional organizations, and religious publishers. To a lesser extent, after 1959, there was an increase in the title output of the publishing units of civil rights organizations. In general, title output for the entire sector mushroomed after 1959 from 51 titles in the 1960–1964 five-year span to an amazing 240 titles in the five-year span from 1970 to 1974.

Literary Genres

Another measure of the diversity displayed by categories of publishers is the comparative number of literary genres in which publishers in the same categories released titles during each period.[2] In both periods, various categories released adult and juvenile fiction and nonfiction titles in such literary genres as textbooks, poetry, scientific treatises, biographies and autobiographies, reference books, speeches, annual reports, cookbooks, songbooks, folktales, readers, subject monographs for children, novels, short fiction anthologies, and picture books.

Commerical book publishers developed the most diversified annual lists of titles of any category. From 1900 through 1959 these publishers issued adult and juvenile fiction and nonfiction titles in nine literary genres. In the later period publishers in this category expanded the offering to include titles in eleven literary genres.

Similarly, Howard University Press, the only university press operating in the later period, released titles in more genres than publishers in this category had in the earlier period. College and university presses that had been active between 1900 and 1959 produced titles for adults in only six genres; while Howard University Press in the later period published titles for adults in the following seven genres: poetry, subject treatises, biographies, reference books, speeches, novels, and short fiction anthologies.

Like Howard University Press, the Book Division of Johnson Publishing Company was the only surviving active book publisher in its category in the later period. It released titles in more literary genres than did periodical publishers active from 1900 to 1959. Between 1963 and 1974 this periodical publisher issued fiction and nonfiction titles for adults and children in twelve literary genres as compared to the four genres in which publishers in this category had published titles in the earlier period.

Cultural and professional organizations, also, released titles in more literary genres in the later period. Publishing only works in adult nonfiction, publishers in this category produced titles in only five literary genres in the earlier period. From 1960 through 1974, however, publishers in this category issued titles in adult as well as juvenile fiction and nonfiction in eleven genres.

Religious publishers produced titles in six genres in adult fiction and nonfiction during the earlier period. In the later period this category of publishers did not publish any titles in adult fiction but issued titles in seven literary genres in adult and juvenile nonfiction.

The publishing units of civil rights organizations issued titles in adult nonfiction and juvenile fiction and nonfiction in seven literary genres in the earlier period. During the later period this category of publishers published titles only in adult nonfiction in three literary genres. Although newspaper publishers between 1900 and 1959 released titles in adult fiction and nonfiction in five literary genres, they were not active in the later period.

In summary, publishers in five of the seven categories published titles in more literary genres in the later period than publishers in the same categories in the earlier period. More categories of publishers in the later period issued titles in the adult fiction literary genres of novels, short story anthologies, and novelettes and in the juvenile fiction and nonfiction literary genres of textbooks, folktales, readers, poetry, autobiography and biography, reference books, storybooks, and picture books.

Publishing Objectives

Black book publishers, like other publishers, released titles indicative of specific publishing objectives. These objectives were generally related to some aspect of Black-Americana or Africana, although a few publishers did publish titles in other subject areas. Some publishers issued titles that were indicative of only a few publishing objectives while others developed lists that included a variety of titles covering a wide range of interests, thus adding to the diversity of their publishing activities. The percentage of active publishers in each period that published annual lists of titles indicative of a broad spectrum of publishing objectives varied. Comparing the percentage of publishers publishing books having various publishing objectives in each period gives some insight into this dimension of the diversity of publishing activities among active Black book publishers in the earlier and later periods.

Forty-two (95 percent) of publishers active between 1900 and 1959 published nonfiction titles for adults, and in some cases for children, to document some aspect of Black-Americana or Africana. By contrast, all thirty-seven publishers (100 percent) active in the later period released nonfiction titles for adults and children illustrative of this publishing objective. In both periods this goal was a dominating feature of Black book publishing.

In the earlier period, fifteen (31 percent) of the publishers issued fiction titles or volumes of poetry for adults and children that portrayed some aspect of the Black experience. This percentage included at least one publisher from each category. During the later period, however, a greater number and percentage, eighteen (49 percent), of the active publishers released titles of fiction and volumes of poetry that were examples of this publishing objective. Some of these publishers, like Broadside Press, came into existence with the initial intent of publishing only poetry by Black poets who articulated the Black experience.

Of the publishers flourishing between 1900 and 1959, eleven (23 percent) published nonfiction titles for adults to defend the Afro-American against racist-inspired writings. In the early decades of this period these publishers issued more titles indicative of this objective than they did in the later years of the period, because writings assaulting the moral and mental sensibilities of the Afro-American appeared with greater frequency between 1900 and 1920. From 1960 through 1974, only three (8 percent) publishers released titles illustrative of this publishing objective. Undoubtedly, the decline was due to the diminished frequency of titles demeaning the Black-American by white racist writers: a dramatic indication of changing social attitudes.

Six (14 percent) of the publishers operating in the earlier period published books to assist students and teachers in learning and teaching specific nonreligious academic subjects. Three of these publishers were Afro-American colleges and universities: Hampton Institute Press, Atlanta University Press, and Xavier University Press. One publisher was the publishing unit of the National Public Welfare League, which issued *Guide to Racial Greatness: The Science of Collective Efficiency*, by Sutton E. Griggs (1923), a title that was adopted by the Colored Teachers Association of Texas as a text for future teachers. Another was a religious publisher, the National Baptist Publishing Board, which issued *Laboratory Methods of Histology and Bacteriology*, by John H. Holman (1903). And, lastly, Associated Publishers, published *The Negro in Our History*, by Carter G. Woodson (1922), a book that has been used as a textbook in many secondary schools and colleges. In contrast, nine (24 percent) of the active publishers in the later period released textbooks or titles supplementary to classroom teaching.

The majority of these publishers were commercial publishing firms. Three of these publishers, however, were the publishing units of Afro-American cultural organizations and institutions.

Only two (5 percent) of the active publishers in the earlier period published titles for the general adult reading audience on subjects unrelated to Afro-Americana. Both of these publishers were university publishers. Fisk University Press issued *History of Ancient Mexico*, by Fray Bernadino de Sahagun, translated by Fanny Bandelier (1932) and Tuskegee Institute Press released *Graphic Arts Survey*, by William E. Boone (1955). In the later period a larger number of publishers, six (16 percent), published titles unrelated to Afro-Americana or Africana. Notable among some of these titles were: *Permit Me Voyage*, by Adelaide Simon (Cleveland: Free Lance Press, 1964), a volume of poetry by a white poetess; *Aiiieeeee! An Anthology of Asian-American Writers*, edited by Frank Chin, Jeffrey Chan, Lawson Inada, and Shawn Wong (Washington, D. C.: Howard University Press, 1974); and *Verdict: The Trial of the Chicago 8*, by Joseph Okpaku (New York: Third Press, Joseph Okpaku Publishing Co., 1970).

Between 1900 and 1959 seven (15 percent) of the active publishers produced titles with the objective of publicizing the programs and philosophies of their parent organizations, institutions, or religious denominations. Examples of a few of these titles were: *Industrial Work of Tuskegee Graduates and Former Students during the Year 1910*, by Monroe N. Work (Tuskegee, Alabama: Tuskegee Institute Press, 1910); and *The Supreme Wisdom to the So-called Negroes' Problem*, volume 1, by Elijah Muhammad (Chicago: Muhammad's Temple No. 2, Publications Dept., 1956). During the later period, only three (7 percent) of the active publishers released titles reflective of this publishing objective. Two of these titles were: *Emancipation's Unfinished Business: 545th Annual Convention Souvenir Program Book* (New York: N.A.A.C.P., 1963); and *The Urban League Story, 1910–1960, Golden Fiftieth Anniversary Yearbook* (New York: National Urban League, 1961).

Of the active publishers operating during the earlier period, three (7 percent) published titles intended to change the political, social, and cultural attitudes of Black Americans by advancing specific

Black ideologies. *The Philosophy and Opinions of Marcus Garvey*, volume 1, compiled and edited by Amy Jacques Garvey (New York: Universal Publishing House, 1923) and *Guide to Racial Greatness*, by Sutton E. Griggs (Memphis: National Public Welfare League, 1923) were among two of the titles embodying this publishing objective. From 1960 to 1974 six (16 percent) publishers released titles reflecting of this publishing objective. Notable among these titles were: *Dope: An Agent of Chemical Warfare*, by Herman B. Ferguson (New York: The East, 1972); and *Islam and Pan-Africanism*, by Agadem L. Diara (Detroit: Agascha Productions, 1973).

Each of the religious publishers active in both periods issued titles to assist clergy and laymen in their understanding and performance of the doctrines and procedures of specific Afro-American religious denominations. These titles included such works as disciplines, denominational manuals, hymnals, and Sunday school instructional manuals.

Between 1960 and 1974 a larger percentage of publishers released titles in five of the eight publishing objectives than had publishers of the earlier period, indicative of greater diversity in the publishing objectives of more publishers in the later period. In the earlier period, although publishers released titles reflective of all eight objectives, a greater percentage of these publishers issued titles illustrative of fewer publishing objectives than publishers that were active between 1960 and 1974.

After 1960 the growth of Black book publishing did accelerate in the number of publishers, with the greatest number coming into existence from 1960 through 1974—more than in any previous period in the twentieth century. The composition of the Black book-publishing sector of the American book-publishing industry changed after 1960. Previously the sector had been dominated by institutional publishers. After 1960 commercial book publishers predominated, due largely to the rising economic and educational levels of Black Americans, which enabled them to support a commercial book-publishing market.

Publishers after 1960 did exhibit greater diversity in their book-publishing activities than publishers active from 1900 to 1959. All of the categories of publishers, except one, after 1960 released more titles than publishers in these same categories had issued before 1960. Five of the seven categories of publishers in the later period published titles in more literary genres than did publishers active in the same categories in the earlier period. And, finally, a greater percentage of publishers after 1960 published titles illustrative of more publishing objectives than had publishers who operated from 1900 to 1959.

NOTES

1. See Appendix A, Graphs 1-8.
2. See Appendix A, Table 1.

7

Vendors or Victims of the American Book-Publishing Industry: Problems Encountered by Black Book Publishers, 1960–1974

INTRODUCTION

Although the years from 1960 through 1974 constituted a period of accelerated growth in the Black book-publishing sector of the American book-publishing industry, several of the sector's executives reported in the periodical literature on problems experienced during these years. These problems were related to acquiring capital, to the lack of expertise in book publishing, and to the neglect of books published by Black book publishers by the major white reviewing media.

To explore the nature and extent of these problems, the executives with twenty-six of the thirty-seven book-publishing enterprises active from 1960 through 1974 were interviewed. These interviews were designed to elicit from the executives information about their experiences with these problems.

ACQUIRING CAPITAL

The publishing executives interviewed employed three methods of acquiring capital. They were: (1) applying to financial institutions for loans; (2) seeking grants from foundations; and (3) soliciting funds from friends of the corporation or members of the organization.

Twelve of the twenty-six executives reported that they had applied to financial institutions for loans for their book-publishing enterprises.[1] These executives were associated with one cultural organization, five religious publishers, and six commercial book-publishing firms.

The twelve executives applied for loans for various reasons.[2] Often one executive applied to several institutions for different reasons. Five executives with commercial book-publishing firms and one executive with a cultural organization made loan applications to financial institutions to start their book-publishing enterprises. Six executives with commercial book-publishing firms and five religious book-publishing executives submitted loan applications to financial institutions to publish new titles or new editions. One executive with a commercial book-publishing firm and five executives with religious publishers applied for loans to publish new printings of titles already published.

Eleven of the executives applied to white-owned banks, while seven applied to Black-owned banks. Seven reported that they had applied to both white-owned and Black-owned banks. One executive made application to a Black savings and loan institution.[3]

Seven of the eleven executives who applied to white-owned banks were granted loans.[4] Five of these executives were with religious publishers and two were associated with commercial book-publishing firms. The same five religious publishing executives also reported that they obtained loans from Black-owned banks, however, the two commercial book-publishing firms that applied to Black-owned banks had their loan applications rejected. The commercial book-publishing executive who applied to a Black savings and loan institution was not given a loan. Consequently, only seven of the twelve publishing executives who applied to financial institutions for loans were successful in obtaining loans.

Commercial book-publishing firms were less successful than religious publishers. Of the six executives with these firms who reported that they had applied for loans only two received them. They related that they had been granted loans from white-owned banks. None of the six executives who applied to Black-owned banks reported that they had been successful in obtaining loans from these institutions.

Cultural organizations were least successful. The executive with the only cultural organization who applied to a white-owned bank for a loan did not receive it.

Undoubtedly, there were several reasons why the religious publishers were more successful in securing loans. Among them were: the long life spans of these publishers; their captive buying audi-

ences, which guaranteed sales, thus giving them a low-risk profile to bankers; and the financial support of their denominations. The executives with the two commercial book-publishing
firms obtaining loans attributed their success to specific reasons.
One executive related that his firm had been awarded a contract by
a state board of education to publish a second printing of a title that
the firm had published originally. During the interview with bank
loan officers he presented this contract and, according to him, this
was the deciding factor in his firm receiving the loan. The other
executive's firm had published a few titles that sold very well. Sales
records for these titles were attached to his loan application. The
successful sale of these titles, he believed, was a key factor in his
firm's receiving the loan.

The five executives who did not receive loans cited reasons why
they thought they were not successful. These reasons were generally related to insufficient personal collateral or the short length of
time their firms had been in business. None of the five executives
indicated that they thought their loan applications were rejected by
white-owned banks because of race per se. But undoubtedly it
appeared that it was very important to prepare a convincing case
for the strength of the firm applying for a loan. Where this was
done, loans were granted. Making such a case, however, may have
been particularly difficult for Black book publishers, which were
almost always small firms and in many instances new to the business of book publishing.

Eleven executives applied to foundations for grants.[5] These executives represented four cultural and professional organizations
and institutions, one university press, two civil rights organizations, and four commercial book publishing firms.

Ten of the executives who applied to foundations were successful
in receiving grants. Only one executive, representing a cultural
organization, reportedly applied for a grant and did not receive it.

By comparison, executives were obviously more successful in obtaining grants from foundations than they had been in acquiring
loans from financial institutions. All of the executives with commercial book-publishing firms, for instance, who applied to foundations for grants received them. However, only two of the six executives in this category who made loan applications to financial
institutions received them.

Twenty of the executives stated that they solicited funds in some way from friends and members of their firms or organizations to start or expand their book-publishing activities. These executives represented five cultural and professional organizations and institutions, ten commercial book-publishing firms, and five religious publishers. This method of raising capital took three forms. Executives with civil rights, cultural, and professional organizations and institutions noted that they generally taxed their memberships directly or indirectly to acquire the funds to underwrite their book publishing activities. Commercial book-publishing executives raised capital by selling stock to friends who became members of their corporations. Religious publishers had capital provided for them by denominational officials who budgeted a certain percentage of the denomination's membership-giving for publishing.

An overwhelming majority of executives, twenty-four, subscribed to the view that the problem of acquiring capital could be resolved or aided by Black book publishers participating in various copublishing ventures among themselves.[6] The most frequently mentioned ventures included joining distribution cooperatives on the national level, joint purchasing of materials and services by groups of local publishers from suppliers and tradesmen located in the same city or geographical area, and joint publication of certain kinds of titles by two or more publishers.

By contrast, only one executive voiced the opinion that the problem could be helped by Black book publishers participating in copublishing ventures with large, established, white book publishers. This executive suggested such copublishing activities as the distribution of a Black book publisher's titles by a large white book publisher having an established distribution mechanism; or the selling of paperback rights of titles to white paperback publishers at a price that would realize a profit for the Black publisher. Similarly, only a single executive believed that one way to aid the problem would be for Black book publishers to merge with established white publishing firms, thus giving them access to the capital, expertise in book publishing, and the distribution mechanism which many of these firms enjoyed. This executive, however, did emphasize that if a merger occurred, participating Black publishers should take steps to insure their own identity.

The twenty-six publishing executives were also polled on the merit of a proposal initiated by the Council on Interracial Books for Children in 1971 to establish a minority publishing fund. Capital for this fund was to have been contributed by foundations and established white publishing firms. From it, minority publishers would have been allowed to make low-interest loans for their book publishing activities.[7] A slight majority, fourteen, of the executives did not think that such a fund would have been a good solution to the problem. Most of these dissenting executives openly stated that they did not believe in subsidy publishing of any kind, because such an arrangement might influence the editorial content of the books published. However, a sizeable number of the executives, twelve, agreed that such a fund would have been a possible solution to the problem.

Various publishers had adopted some of the aforementioned solutions. Three commercial book-publishing firms, based in the same city, were engaged in joint purchasing of supplies and joint contracting with a local printer. Two commercial book-publishing firms reported that their books were being distributed by large, established, white publishing firms. And a group of publishers had joined together to form a national cooperative distribution program.

In summary, Black publishers who engaged in book publishing from 1960 through 1974 were very successful in acquiring capital from foundations in the forms of grants. However, this is not the major channel for obtaining capital for growth and development of most business enterprises in the American society. This method of acquiring capital is philanthropy. It is not the function of philanthropy to support on a sustaining basis profit-making businesses. And book publishing, even though embarked upon by many non-profit organizations and institutions, is in the strict sense a business, seeking in most instances to make a profit like other businesses.

Notwithstanding the success of many Black publishers in their efforts to raise capital from friends and members of their firms and organizations, this method of acquiring capital, although used by many large corporations and organizations, should not be the mainspring of Black book publishing. Black Americans, who were prominently involved in these solicitations, comprised, along with Chicanos, native Americans and Appalachian whites, one of the most undercapitalized minorities in the American society.

The major avenue traveled by most American businesses in their quest for capital is through the country's financial institutions. Capital is made available to these businesses by financial institutions in the form of loans, lines of credit, and mortgages. Indeed, this avenue has been the mainstay of American business enterprise. But it was on this thoroughfare of American free enterprise that Black book publishers between 1960 and 1974 experienced the least success. Hence, it can be concluded that Black book publishers, as evidenced by the sample of executives interviewed, did experience a measurable degree of difficulty in acquiring capital from financial institutions, both Black-owned and white-owned, which unquestionably inhibited and even discouraged to some degree the growth and development of Black book publishing from 1960 through 1974.

EXPERTISE IN BOOK PUBLISHING

The twenty-six executives reported various levels of experience and expertise in book publishing. Some executives had worked in book publishing for a number of years before they assumed the positions they held in 1974 and they demonstrated great expertise in the field. By contrast, other executives had moved into book publishing from such diverse vocational areas as computer science and engineering, but, nevertheless, demonstrated a high degree of professional expertise in operating their book-publishing enterprises. Still other executives who had worked in fields related to book publishing showed little working knowledge of the management aspects of book publishing.

Professional Backgrounds

Nine of the twenty-six executives had professional experience in book publishing prior to assuming the positions they held in 1974. These executives had worked in such positions as executive editors, marketing analysts, advertising managers, and production managers.[8] The largest concentration of these executives, four, were associated with religious publishing houses. Three were with commercial book publishers; one headed a cultural organization's publishing program; and another directed a university press.

The largest number of executives, eleven, had previously held positions in various aspects of publishing, excluding book publishing, or had followed some vocational pursuit that involved extensive skill in the use of books. The positions more often cited by this group of executives were journalists, free-lance writers, librarians, and teachers. Six of these executives were with commercial book-publishing houses; five directed the publishing programs of cultural and civil rights organizations; and one headed the book-publishing division of a periodical publisher.

Six of the executives had previously been employed in positions that did not involve book publishing or any marginally related field. Among some of these former positions reported were computer programmer, engineer, and vocational counselor.

Administrative Frameworks and Techniques
Developed by the Publishing Executives

A book-publishing executive's knowledge and expertise of the administrative aspects of book publishing are often reflected in the decisions he makes relative to the publication of a single title. Generally, the experienced executive has developed a well-defined administrative framework for the acquisition of manuscripts, the weeding out of unpublishable, unsolicited manuscripts, the editorial and production management of manuscripts; the promotional management of titles; and the marketing of management of titles.

Acquisition of Manuscripts. The majority of executives reported that they employed more than one method to generate new manuscripts.[9] The two most frequently cited methods were soliciting manuscripts through contacts with elementary and secondary school teachers, college professors, and other persons in academia; and soliciting manuscripts through contacts with authors previously published by them. Slightly over one-third of the executives used literary agents, editors, and other professional literary contacts to acquire manuscripts. All of the executives indicated, however, that they accepted unsolicited manuscripts but varied in the procedure which they had established to weed them out.

Weeding Out Unpublishable, Unsolicited Manuscripts. In *Book Publishing, What It Is, What It Does* (New York: Bowker, 1974) John P. Dessauer, the frequently quoted authority on book publishing, describes the procedure used by most established book publishers to weed out unpublishable, unsolicited manuscripts.

> In houses where unsolicited manuscripts are welcome they are often given a first reading by a junior staff member who prepares a report which together with the manuscript is reviewed by a staff editor. Such a report addresses itself to the significance of the work, its subject matter, the quality of writing and its market potential and recommends either further consideration or rejection. The staff editor on the basis of the report and his own examination of the manuscript will decide whether the material should be declined or further examination is warranted.[10]

Twenty-one of the executives had developed a procedure similar although not as expansive as Dessauer's description of this procedure. The following response of Dudley Randall, president of Broadside Press, was typical of the descriptions given by these executives.[11] "The manuscripts are first read by the assistant editor. And she rejects most of them and sends them back. Those she thinks are of merit she turns over to me."[12] The responses of five executives gave little evidence that they had any systematic procedure for weeding out unpublishable, unsolicited manuscripts. These executives were associated primarily with Black cultural and professional organizations and institutions, where book publishing was an adjunct activity to the main programs of these bodies.

Editorial and Production Management. In most established publishing houses a manuscript advances through definite editing and production stages before it becomes a book. These stages are: (1) preliminary editing by the editor; (2) consultations between the author and editor, who might recommend changes in editorial style or content; (3) copy editing; (4) proofreading of the galleys by the author; (5) book designing; and (6) bookmaking or book manufacturing. Often these stages occur simultaneously and require a high level of administrative skill and broad knowledge of book publishing on the part of the executive to effectively coordinate them to keep costs within a planned budget and to make deadlines to realize an established publication date.

The responses of fourteen of the executives revealed that they possessed a good working knowledge of book publishing and had developed sufficient administrative skills to guide effectively a manuscript through the various stages of editorial and production management. The following recollection of Doris E. Saunders, formerly director of the Book Division of Chicago's Johnson Publishing Company, of her management of Lerone Bennet, Jr.'s, *The Shaping of Black America* (1975), although more detailed than most of the responses of the other thirteen executives, was similar to their descriptions in the content and level of sophistication.

> Well, let us take *The Shaping of Black America*. That manuscript came from Mr. Bennett about May of last year [1974] and it was on 8½"-by-11" paper. It was double-spaced and it was typed with adequate margins. My first job was to read it. I had read the articles in *Ebony Magazine* that preceded it, so that it wasn't all new, but Mr. Bennett had rewritten much of it. So the first step was to read it. When you read it you get some idea of the flow. The author had already put it into chapters, so that it is not your job, at least that was not the job I had with this book. My job with this book was to make a decision in terms of the kind of book I wanted it to be. And then I had to meet with the artists, who in this case was Mr. Hunter [Norman Hunter] who was going to be the designer. Let him get some idea of the feel so that he would, also, have an idea of what kind of type to recommend. Then I called the book manufacturer and asked them to come over and I talked to them about the book. Told them what kind of feeling I wanted to have. I wanted a book that had an obvious feel of quality. I wanted a book that could reflect a people. I wanted it to do more than just be another book. Mr. Bennett had written a number of books on Black history. This one had to be different. I couldn't come out and say: "This book is covering the same period of time that *Before the Mayflower* did so you should buy it and pay $15.95

for it, when you have already got *Before the Mayflower* at
$6.95." I had to give to the consumer something that was
going to make him buy what, as far as he knows was the same
book, and pay twice as much for it. So I had to get a format in
my own mind that would help me do that.

Fortunately, Mr. Bennett and Charles White [the celebrated
Afro-American artist] were good friends. We were members
of a group called the Black Academy of Arts and Letters. We
talked at one point about Charles illustrating a Bennett book.
This seemed to be the ideal time for that. So then the problem
was to talk to Mr. Johnson, to sell him on the idea of the book
being illustrated. We had not illustrated, other than with
photographs, a book before of this nature. When he [Mr.
Johnson] agreed that we could at least enter into a discussion
about it, we invited Mr. White to meet with Mr. Bennett and
myself to talk about it to see whether the artist could conceive
of the book in the same way that we did and whether he felt
that he could do illustrations that would stand by themselves
and yet would complement the book.

We made tear sheets of the *Ebony* article, because we
couldn't give him at that point the manuscript. And we sent
him back to California to come up with some ideas.

He did. He came back with an idea of what he could do.
How it would be able to fit into the kinds of things we were
saying in *The Shaping of Black America*, and yet would stand
by themselves as works of art.

We negotiated a price. Mr. Johnson agreed on the price. So
we commissioned him [Mr. White]; signed a contract for him
to do the work for us.

Meanwhile the author is still writing, not adding, but
rewriting in terms of going back changing words and changing phrases. Working with the book designer, we have established that we like this type. But until we see it on a page, we
really don't know. So we ask the typesetter, which is another
person we have to deal with and another group of people, we
asked the typesetter to type in that type. We get these pages
back. We are not really sure. We let the author look at them.
He is not really convinced that this is the type that he likes so
we open the spacing. Instead of 12 point on a 14 point, we

make it 12 to 15. This gives them a little more space on each line. We get that reset. So it's a constant thing going back and forth. It's trial and error. "Do you like it? or don't you?" Sort of trying to judge just to get something that finally feels good to him. Then when it feels good to the artist. Then when it feels good to all three. Then you give it to the publishers and say: "Does it feel good to you? Do you like it?"

The paper, we had to get two or three different kinds of paper. We made the decision finally to print that book in brown ink. But we couldn't print the book in black type and have the illustrations in sepia. And if we did the illustrations in black, then they would lose all the qualities that the artist had put into the originals. So how do you get the original qualities of the illustrations to be maintained and get the type so that it is a good readable type? Well, we did it in the darkest brown that they had. It's almost black. And we used a paper that has a lot of opacity. So all of these things are what went on.[13]

The largest number of these executives, five, headed religious publishing houses. Four were with commercial book-publishing firms and two were associated with Black civil rights and political organizations.[14] One executive was associated with a cultural institution and another with a university press.

Ten of the executives provided descriptions which revealed that they had limited knowledge of book publishing and had developed very few administrative skills for guiding a manuscript through the stages of editing and production. Most of these executives had little or no familiarity with such aspects of book publishing as book design, book manufacturing, and various typesetting or printing processes. Some of them demonstrated in their responses that they hadn't developed sufficient administrative skills to coordinate simultaneously various stages of editorial and production management. These executives were evenly divided between two categories: cultural and professional organizations and commercial book-publishing firms.

The descriptions presented by two of the executives revealed that they had no administrative skills and an insufficient amount of knowledge about book publishing to guide a manuscript through the various stages of editing and book production. These executives related that they simply edited the manuscripts and contracted a printer and binder to make other decisions about the book's production. One of these executives was with a cultural organization and the other was a commercial book publisher.

Promotional Management. Most new books receive little advertising. Dessauer views this fact as an indication of the poor distribution system which characterizes the entire book-publishing industry in the United States today.

> Given the fact that most books are not adequately represented in bookstores and cannot be expected to sell in sufficient quantity to warrant the expense of national or cooperative advertising, it is hardly surprising that most books are simply not advertised to any great extent. This is less a sign of the publisher's unwillingness to support his book or his lack of responsibility toward his author than it is an indication of the failures of the entire book distribution system to which we have repeatedly referred. Advertising is to total distribution what grease and oil are to an engine: necessary lubricants which will make the engine function more smoothly and successfully. If the engine lacks power, is antiquated, and in bad need of overhauling, pumping more oil into it or greasing it more will do little to improve its performance.[15]

In spite of this observation, the twenty-six publishing executives reported various techniques which they used to promote new titles.[16]

The majority of the twenty-six publishing executives used more than one promotional technique to diffuse knowledge about the titles they published. Most of them used direct mail advertising to the consumer as a promotional technique. Lists for these mailings were generally developed from former customers, membership lists (in the case of institutional publishers), and lists which were bought. Seventeen of the executives reported that they advertised new titles in newspapers, and eleven executives related that they advertised their titles in national trade journals. Only two of the executives indicated that they used radio and television. This type of promotion generally took the form of an author appearance on a talk show or spot announcements.

Ten of the executives used other promotional techniques. Among some of them were autograph parties; newsletters; public poetry readings and lectures; book fairs; and exhibits at conferences, workshops and conventions.

Marketing Management. Most of the publishing executives used several channels for the distribution of new titles.[17] The largest number, twenty-four, used direct mail sales to the consumer. Fifteen executives distributed their books through bookstores. Only nine used national wholesalers to distribute their books. These were generally the larger publishers, such as: the Book Division of Johnson Publishing Company; Broadside Press; the Third Press; Howard University Press; and Third World Press. Five of the executives reported that they employed salesmen to distribute their books.

To summarize, because only a minority of the executives, nine, had relatively strong backgrounds in book publishing before they assumed the positions in book publishing that they held in 1974, it would seem that the development of Black book publishing between 1960 and 1974 would have been hampered. However, despite this lack of experience in book publishing among Black Americans, a majority of the twenty-six publishing executives interviewed demonstrated an adequate degree of administrative skills and knowledge in several key areas of book publishing. For instance: twenty-one of the executives had developed a systematic process for weeding out unpublishable manuscripts; fourteen of the executives had developed administrative skills and an adequate knowledge of book publishing to guide their manuscripts through the various stages of editorial and production management; the majority of executives used at least two techniques to promote their books; and a majority of the executives employed at least two of the regular channels to distribute their books. Hence, it can be concluded that the Black book-publishing sector of the American book-publishing industry, by and large, was not generally inhibited by a lack of experience and expertise among Black-Americans in book publishing. However, in one key area, the administrative skills and knowledge of book publishing needed to effectively guide a manuscript through the various stages of editorial and production management, a significant number of publishing executives in the sector, twelve, were hampered by a lack of skills and knowledge.

Undoubtedly, as their experience in book publishing broadens, the administrative skills and knowledge of these executives in this area will increase or they will leave the business.

BOOK REVIEWING BY THE MAJOR
WHITE REVIEWING MEDIA

In 1974, publishers in the United States issued 30,574 new titles.[18] Only a relatively small percentage of these titles, however, were reviewed. For example, the most comprehensive source of book review excerpts in the United States, the *Book Review Digest* which covers book reviews from seventy book reviewing sources, reported that it carried excerpts of book reviews of six thousand new titles in 1974.[19] Thus, based on this report, it can be estimated that approximately 19.6 percent of all new titles published in the United States in 1974 were reviewed. An even smaller percentage of new titles, consequently, were reviewed by the major white-owned book reviewing media. This segment of the book reviewing media is defined as periodicals, newspapers, and services that review a substantial number of new titles regularly and/or enjoy nationwide circulation among librarians and other professionals involved in book selection. The following book reviewing periodicals, newspapers, and services, representative of the major white-owned book reviewing media, were selected for this study: *New York Review of Books; Library Journal; New York Times Book Review; A.L.A. Booklist and Subscription Books Bulletin; Kirkus Book Reviews; School Library Journal; Atlantic Monthly; Harper's; Saturday Review/World; Choice; Time; Newsweek;* and the *New Yorker.*

Have the major white-owned reviewing media neglected reviewing books published by Black book publishers? What has been the fortune or misfortune of Black book-publishing executives in their efforts to get their books reviewed by this very influential segment of the book reviewing media? The twenty-six executives were queried about their attempts to have their books reviewed by the fourteen selected reviewing periodicals, newspapers, and services.

Nineteen of the twenty-six executives reported that they sent books to book reviewing media.[20] The majority of executives in every category of publishers, with the exception of religious publishers, sent review copies to the book reviewing media. Only one religious publisher sent review copies.

Nineteen of the publishing executives reported that they had sent review copies to each of the major, fourteen, white-owned reviewing periodicals or reviewing services.[21] The largest number of executives, fifteen, sent review copies to *Library Journal* and the *New York Times Book Review*. Eleven of the executives sent review copies to *ALA Booklist*. Ten of the executives reportedly sent review copies to the *New York Review of Books, Kirkus Book Reviewing Service*, and *School Library Journal*. Less than 50 percent of the executives reported that they had sent review copies to any one of the remaining eight book reviewing periodicals.

The greater number of publishing executives, twelve, reported that the review copies they sent to *Library Journal* had been reviewed. To a lesser extent publishing executives reported that they were able to get their books reviewed in the following book reviewing periodicals and book reviewing services: *New York Review of Books; New York Times Book Review; ALA Booklist; Kirkus Book Reviewing Services; School Library Journal; Saturday Review/World; Choice; Time;* and the *New Republic.* None of the executives reported that the review copies sent to the following book reviewing periodicals had been reviewed: *Atlantic Monthly; Harper's; Newsweek;* and the *New Yorker.*

Publishing executives enjoyed the greatest success in getting their books reviewed by the library-oriented periodicals.[22] In *Choice,* 86 percent of the publishing executives who sent review copies were successful in getting them reviewed. Twelve, or 80 percent, of the publishing executives who sent review copies to *Library Journal* reported that their books were reviewed.

The non-library-oriented book reviewing media were consistently less responsive to reviewing books sent to them by publishing executives than were the library-oriented book reviewing media. The *New York Times Book Review,* considered by one authority of book publishing as the leading medium in the field of book reviewing, only reviewed books sent by 47 percent of the executives.[23] The *New Republic* reviewed books sent by only 38 percent of the executives. And *Kirkus Book Reviewing Service* reviewed books sent by a mere 30 percent of the executives. With seven of the fourteen reviewing periodicals and book reviewing services, less than 20 percent of the publishing executives who sent books were able to get them reviewed. And four of these reviewing periodicals did not review any of the titles sent to them by the executives.

Consequently, one segment of the major white-owned book reviewing media, as evidenced by the responses of the nineteen executives, consistently accepted and reviewed books published by Black book publishers, and, thus, did encourage the development of Black book publishing between 1960 and 1974. Library-oriented book reviewing periodicals and book reviewing services reviewed books sent to them by 58 percent of the publishing executives. This relatively high percentage is the result of the pro-Black activism in the library-oriented media today and traditionally.

On the other hand, major non-library-oriented white-owned book reviewing media, although reviewing books sent to them by a small percentage of publishing executives, for the most part did not review the books sent to them by Black book publishers. Consequently, they did not encourage the development of Black book publishing between 1960 and 1974.

NOTES

1. See Appendix B, Table 2: Book Publishers Applying for Financial Assistance.

2. See Appendix B, Table 3: Purpose of Application for Financial Assistance.

3. See Appendix B, Table 4: Institutions Applied to for Financial Assistance.

4. See Appendix B, Table 5: Institutions Giving Loans to Black Book Publishers.

5. See Appendix B, Table 6: Publishers Applying for Grants from Foundations.

6. See Appendix B, Table 7: Executive Solutions to Acquiring Capital for Growth and Development.

7. Bradford Chambers, an interview held at the Council on Interracial Books for Children, New York, N.Y., 25 November 1975.

8. See Appendix B, Table 8: Prior Vocational and Professional Pursuits of Book-Publishing Executives.

9. See Appendix B, Table 9: Contacts Used by Publishers to Generate the Flow of Manuscripts.

10. John P. Dessauer, *Book Publishing: What It Is, What It Does* (New York: Bowker, 1974), p. 31.

11. See Appendix B, Table 10: Methods for Weeding Out Unpublishable Manuscripts.

12. Dudley Randall, an interview held at Broadside Press, Detroit, Michigan, 7 November 1975.

13. Doris Saunders, an interview held at Johnson Publishing Company, Chicago, Illinois, 4 March 1975.

14. See Appendix B, Table 11: Professional Competence of Publishing Executives.

15. Dessauer, *Book Publishing: What It Is, What It Does,* p. 141.

16. See Appendix B, Table 12: Promotional Techniques Employed by Publishing Executives.

17. See Appendix B, Table 13: Channels of Distribution Used by Book Publishers.

18. U.S., Department of Commerce, *Statistical Abstract of the United States, 1976,* 97th annual ed. (Washington, D.C.: Government Printing Office, 1976), p. 543.

19. *Literary Market Place,* 1975–76 ed. (New York: Bowker, 1975).

20. See Appendix B, Table 14: Book-Publishing Executives Regularly Sending Titles for Review.

21. See Appendix B, Table 15: Publishers Sending Review Copies to Selected Major White Reviewing Media.

22. See Appendix B, Table 16: Publisher Success in Receiving Reviews from Major White Reviewing Media.

23. Dessauer, *Book Publishing, What It Is, What It Does,* p. 134.

8

Testifiers to Times of Entrenchment and Singers of a Bright New Future: Black Book Publishers Speak in 1981

As the last years of the 1970s were ending and the 1980s were unfolding, some of the same forces which were active in the Black community in previous decades were still exercising positive influences on the demand in the market for books about Black Americans. For example, the number of Blacks in institutions of higher learning continued to rise through the 1970s from 345,000 in 1970 to 601,000 in 1978 with expectations of increasing in the 1980s. The median money income of Black households steadily climbed in the 1970s from $5,537 in 1970 to $8,422 in 1977, with the trend predicted to continue into the 1980s.[1] However, during these same years some ominous developments were taking place inside as well as outside of the Black community that were having, and would have in the near future, negative effects in the market environment of Black book publishing. The high unemployment rate among Blacks and other minorities twenty years of age and older leaped from an astounding 10.7 percent for males and 12.7 percent for females in August, 1977, to a crippling 12.3 percent for males and 13.5 percent for females in August, 1981. This rise in unemployment severely limited the purchasing power of a large segment of Blacks for all goods, including books.[2] The sharp increase in the open market interest rates, which soared from 5.43 percent in July, 1977, to a record 17.10 percent in July, 1981, adversely affected all businesses, especially small business enterprises like Black commercial book-publishing firms seeking loans.[3] The federal government's decisions to drastically reduce funding of such library programs as Title 4B of the Elementary and Secondary School Act (school libraries), Titles IIA and IIC of the Higher Education Act (college and research libraries), Title I of the Library Services and Construction Act (public libraries) and other book-related educational and cultural programs is resulting in a sizeable loss in the demand for books, including books about Black Americans.[4] And, finally, the wave of neoconservativism in the attitudes of white Americans about Black Americans sweeping across the country in the early 1980s is having a negative influence on the demand by white Americans for books about Black Americana and Africana and, in the words of one sophisticated observer, even threatens the gains already made in Black equality in the country.

> These are difficult and discouraging times for Afro-Americans. A tide of conservatism or "neoconservative" white opinion has arrested the progress toward racial equality that began in the 1950s and threatens to roll back some of the gains already made. The Reagan Administration has cut back on programs to relieve black poverty that were inadequate to begin with and the Justice Department is switching sides on desegregation cases in an effort to take the government out of the business of enforcing integration.[5]

Against this bittersweet backdrop of the fortunes and misfortunes in the market environment, how is Black book publishing faring in the 1980s? What are Black book-publishing executives saying about the publishing enterprises in 1981?

A sampling of Black book-publishing executives discussed their publishing enterprises, the problems of raising capital, getting their books reviewed by the white reviewing media, and the general status of Black book publishing in 1981. Their observations were reported in the current literature or in questionnaires that were sent to them in the fall of 1981. Together their comments constitute an insightful and diversified appraisal of the state of Black book publishing in 1981.

Third Press International. Appearing on a symposium, "Minorities in Publishing," sponsored by Harper and Row Publishers, in early 1981, Dr. Joseph Okpaku, president of the New York City-based firm, spoke very positively about the current state of Black book publishing, despite the troubled economy. Addressing his remarks to the question, "Are Black publishers filling the void of books authored by Blacks?" Dr. Okpaku answered without reservations in the affirmative, but declared that Black book publishing must internationalize its scope to command resources to make publishing profitable. Eighty percent of his firm's sales, he noted, was to African countries. His firm has developed the Nigeria/U.S. Consolidated Book Procurement and Distribution Program to give Black book publishers international distribution. "The world is a different place than it was 10 years ago," Dr. Okpaku observed and pointed out that Third World publishers are today economically independent of Western companies.[6]

Turning to another aspect of Black book publishing, the willingness of Black authors to publish with Black book publishers, the Nigerian-born publisher asserted, "Blacks must learn to assume responsibility for their own culture. If you don't control the means of production, you're being controlled in what you say." This successful publisher's optimism about the future of Black book publishing was articulated in this charge to Black book publishers: "Stay in Black publishing; it will work. . . . We need to set up our own institutions."[7]

One of the most active Black book publishers in the United States, Third Press International (formerly known as the Third Press, Joseph Okpaku Publishing Company) issued a host of titles in the late 1970s and early 1980s. Foremost among some of them have been: *Family Planning as Preventive Psychiatry*, by Samuel O. Okpaku (1980), a study of the beliefs, attitudes, and practices of community mental health practitioners; *Camwood on the Leaves and Before the Blackout: Two Short Plays*, by Wole Soyinka (1980), the popular Nigerian playwright; and *Repetitions—Poems on Many Subjects*, by Judge Bruce McC. Wright (1980), a collection of poems by the controversial New York judge on the rights of the accused, with a focus on the racial attitudes of arresting officers.

Third World Press. Chicago's Third World Press, headed by poet Haki R. Madhubuti, like Third Press International, continues, notwithstanding the current economic crunch, to be an active book publisher. The firm has, in the words of Madhubuti, ". . . Changed management—We are more business-like."[8]

Third World Press's current catalog showcases several unique new titles for adults and children. *Cultural Unity of Black Africa*, by Cheikh Anta Diop (1980), is a well-documented treatise in which the erudite Black Africanist reestablishes Egypt as an integral part of the Black past. Haki R. Madhubuti's *Enemies—The Clash of Races* (1980) is a book of essays presenting an in-depth analysis of Black politics, education, communication, and economics and their relationships to the twenty-first century. Among the new titles for the younger readers are *How They Made Biriyani*, by Mari Evans (1981), a family-centered story illustrating the values of a family working together, and *I Want to Be*, by Dexter and Patricia Oliver (1980), a multipurpose alphabet reader.

Despite the success of his firm, Madhubuti views the prospects of financial institutions making loans for Black book-publishing firms with skepticism. Consequently he does not think that the chances of Black book publishers acquiring loans are any better in 1981 than they were in 1974. He indirectly accuses banks and financial institutions of racial redlining when it comes to financing Black book publishing. "Most banks and lending institutions don't think Black people read."[9]

The neglect by the major white reviewing media of books published by Black publishers, a problem experienced by many Black book publishers in 1974, has not, in Madhubuti's opinion, improved in 1981. Book reviewing by the major white reviewing media he sees as a racial-financial conspiracy. "Publishing and reviewing are businesses. That means Money and self-interest are one. White money and white self-interests are seldom at odds."[10]

Broadside Press. Poet Dudley Randall, former owner of Detroit's Broadside Press, agrees with Haki Madhubuti that the major white reviewing media continue to neglect books published by Black publishers. But Randall also interprets it as a problem shared by all small presses. "Small presses are still not reviewed by the major white reviewing media."[11]

In 1974 Broadside Press under Randall's management was one of the most prolific Black commercial book-publishing firms in the United States. Late in 1975, Broadside Press stopped publishing books and in 1977 the firm was sold, because, as Randall reports, of financial reasons. "I owed the printer. Had to economize and pay debts. I sold Broadside Press to an Episcopal church, Alexander Crummell Memorial Center in Highland Park, a suburb within Detroit in 1977. It is now called Broadside/Crummell Press. I still retain a certain proportion of the press, and I am Editorial Consultant."[12] Undoubtedly, Randall's unfortunate experience as a small Black businessman caught in the vise of the inflationary national economy of the late 1970s gives him insight into today's economic climate. Randall believes that the ability of Black pub- lishers to get loans from financial institutions has not improved since 1974. In 1981, given the present economic situation, Randall proclaims: "Times are worse than ever, economically."[13]

The Book Division of Johnson Publishing Company. Like Dudley Randall, Doris E. Saunders, formerly director of the Book Division of Johnson Publishing Company and presently consultant for book publishing to the same company, believes that the present economy is a factor hampering the success of Black book publishers in ac- quiring capital from financial institutions. But Ms. Saunders, also, cites other reasons.

> The entire economy has moved in a direction of 180° from the premise which existed ten years ago. Blacks are not "in" and if they can hold on to even the vestiages of participation in "mainstream" activities such as publishing, radio, television ownership, etc., they will do well. These are not optimistic times, I fear.[14]

Since 1976 the Book Division of Johnson Publishing Company has limited its book publications to about one title per year. *Black Society*, by Gerri Major and Doris Saunders was released in 1976. This scrupulously researched social history of prominent Black families, illustrated with many rare photographs, is a classic in Black history. In 1978 *Du Bois: A Pictorial Biography*, by Shirley Graham Du Bois appeared. Lerone Bennett, Jr.'s, *Wade in the Water*, a book of engaging interpretative commentaries on signifi- cant events in Black history, was published in 1979. And in 1981 *I*

Wouldn't Take Nothing for My Journey, by Chicago physician Leonidas Berry, a geneological history of a Black family from the early 1800s to the present, was released. But why was the Book Division's annual list so severely cut after 1976? Saunders answered:

> The shift in public attitude towards Blacks in general—Black culture in particular—meant a decline in the audience in terms of schools, libraries, general bookstores, etc.
>
> The Black book buying market has always been limited. Television and other forms of mass entertainment have not made for more book buyers unless it is accompanied by Hollywood type promotion, i.e., *Roots*. Johnson Publishing Company, utilizing all of its media know-how, still had relatively slight success, even with its "Best" author—Lerone Bennett, Jr., in the later publications, such as *Wade in the Water*. Commitment to publishing, even though there was no possibility of breaking even on the print order undertaken, has to be the raison d'etre for Johnson's continuation in the field—even at the scaled-down rate of one title per year. They are still high-quality books, produced with top manufacturing standards.[15]

Saunders agrees with other publishing executives that the major white reviewing media continue to neglect reviewing books published by Black book publishers. In fact she thinks that they have become worse. "I think they no longer feel the national imperative to give even lip service to the recognition of Black writers, and certainly not Black publishers."[16]

Lotus Press. A more prolific publisher in recent years has been Detroit's Lotus Press, publishing twenty-seven new titles between 1975 and early 1981 and releasing seven additional titles in late 1981. Publishing mostly poetry, some of Lotus Press's new titles in 1981 were *Songs and Dances*, by Philip M. Royster; Dudley Randall's *A Litany of Friends; Poems Selected and New; Cardinal Points and Other Poems*, by Eugene Haun; *Heartland: Selected Poems*, by Ron Welburn; and *Lock This Man Up*, by David L. Rice.

In 1980 Lotus Press incorporated as a nonprofit literary and educational organization and became a tax-exempt organization. This new status will allow this publisher to seek funds from a vareity of sources, as Dr. Naomi Andrews optimistically surmises. "As a nonprofit tax-exempt corporation, we can now solicit contributions (tax exempt) and apply for grants from state and federal agencies."[17]

Dr. Andrews, like other Black book publishers, is critical of the major white reviewing media's neglect of titles published by Black book publishers, but also extends her criticism to the small press reviewers.

> Not only do I feel that the *major* white reviewing media has not been responsive, but the *small* press reviewing media has not been more responsive either. Many white reviewers seem to feel automatically that they cannot deal with Black American literature and immediately assign it to black reviewers, if they are on the staff, or ignore it. They tend to relegate it to some outer sphere of expression, as if it were written in some foreign language to which white reviewers do not have the key. They seem not to be able or willing to deal with it as just *literature*. Some few white reviewers, whose commitment to black literature has already been established (such as Joe Wiexlman at *Black American Literature Forum*), or such nonconformists as Daniel Berrigan may be counted on to respond with understanding and perception, but in general, white reviewers ignore what is being written by black authors. I do not see any improvement in the picture between 1974 and the present. The Black press must still look towards its own Black critics to evaluate what is being done.[18]

Afro Am Publishing Company. In contrast to Lotus Press, Chicago's Afro Am Publishing Company ceased publishing books in 1975. Eugene Winslow, the firm's new president, explained why. "The investment required to produce and promote a single title is more than a small publisher can afford, particularly when it may take several years for the sale of a book to return the investment." Although no longer a book publisher, Afro Am Publishing Company is still in the book business from another angle. "The single most important development was our change from a publishing operation to a catalog jobber, or distributor, of Black/integrated educational materials for grades kindergarten through high school. We discontinued direct selling (via salesmen) and participation in convention shows."[19]

The prospects of acquiring capital from financial institutions by Black book publishers in 1981 are much more unlikely than they were, Winslow believes, in 1974.

> I do not feel that Black-American book publishers can acquire any amount of capital presently or in the near future because: (1) government (SBA) loans are not, and never have been available for printers, publishers or distributors limiting their operations to a single ethnic or minority group; (2) commercial banks are unwilling to make loans to small/minority businesses without the SBA guarantee; and (3) Black publishing is too high a risk venture to attract capital, especially in the present climate of high interest rates.[20]

Free Lance Press. Another Black publisher that is no longer active is Free Lance Press. Former Coeditor Casper LeRoy Jordan explains why Free Lance Press stopped publishing in 1980. "Free Lance was a two-man operation and because of personal and professional duties its closing was forced after thirty years."[21] From 1975 through 1980 Free Lance Press published no books. It did, however, release four issues of *Free Lance Magazine* before it folded in 1980.

DuSable Museum of African American History. On the other hand, Chicago's expanding DuSable Museum of African American History, under the dynamic leadership of Dr. Margaret Burroughs, continues, although on a restricted basis, to be an active book publisher. Dr. Burroughs, obviously referring to the state of the economy, states that the museum's book publishing program is "limited due to finances."[22]

Since 1975, this publisher has released about six books in the areas of Black history and poetry. Two of these titles were Charles Dawson's *ABCs of Great Negroes* (1976), a collective biography for young readers, and *Man Born of Woman*, by Milton Glaseve, (1977), a volume of poetry.

The Townsend Press/Sunday School Publishing Board of the National Baptist Convention, U.S.A., Inc. Undaunted, like most Black religious book publishers, by the troubled economy, the Townsend Press/Sunday School Publishing Board continued in 1981 to be one of the strongest Black book publishers in the United States. Since 1975, this religious publisher has released thirty-six titles. Examples of some of these new monographs have been *A Story of Christian Activism*, by Dr. J. H. Jackson, president of the National Baptist Convention, U.S.A., Inc., and pastor of Chicago's historic Olivet Baptist Church (1980); *Prairie Voices*, by Kenny Jackson, a literary anthology (1980); and *Annual Sunday School Commentary*, by the editorial division (1981). The Sunday School Publishing Board, in the optimistic assessment of S. E. Grinstead, its public relations director, is expanding. "We have installed new machinery and increased the number of employees."[23]

To summarize, as the 1980s evolve Black book publishers are reacting differently to the positive and negative factors in their market environment. Some commercial firms, like Afro Am Publishers and Broadside Press, have ceased book publishing, due largely to financial constraints triggered by the inflationary economy, while other commercial publishers such as Third Press International and Third World Press are keeping afloat and forging new frontiers, despite the economy. Representative of cultural organizational publishers, Chicago's DuSable Museum of African American History, although restricting its book publishing because of finances, is still an active book publisher; while Free Lance Press, for reasons unrelated to any market factors, has folded. However, Lotus Press with its newly acquired status as a cultural/educational organization is flourishing, with plans for future expansion. By contrast the Book Division of Johnson Publishing Company, pointing to the perilous economy and the neoconservative attitudes among white Americans about Blacks, has cut back severely on its book-publishing program. However, Howard University Press is thriving.[24] And religious publishers, as evidenced by the Townsend

Press/Sunday School Board of the National Baptist Convention, U.S.A., undoubtedly will continue in the 1980s, with their captive audiences and denominational funding, to be the most viable of Black book publishers.

Hence, it can be concluded that, despite problems related to acquiring capital and getting their books reviewed by the major white reviewing media, coupled with negative factors in the market environment, Black book publishers are continuing in the 1980s to be a productive segment in the American book-publishing industry.

NOTES

1. U.S., Department of Commerce, Bureau of the Census, *Statistical Abstract of the United States,* 100th ed. (Washington, D.C.: Government Printing Office, 1979), pp. 161, 458.

2. "A-10. Unemployed Persons by Marital Status, Race, Age and Sex," *Employment and Earnings* 24 (September 1977): 28; 28 (September 1981): 16.

3. "Finance-Banking," *Survey of Current Business* 57 (August 1977): 5–18; 61 (September 1981): 5–15.

4. Marilyn Killebrew Gell, "Washington Update: The Blue Book," *Library Journal* 106 (May 15, 1981): 1010–11.

5. George M. Frederickson. "Two Steps Forward, One Step Back." *New Republic* 492 (December 16, 1981): 33.

6. Wendy Smith, "Two H. & R. Symposiums Look at Blacks in Book Publishing," *Publishers Weekly* 219 (March 20, 1981): 13–16.

7. Ibid., p. 16.

8. Haki R. Madhubuti to the author, September 22, 1981.

9. Ibid.

10. Ibid.

11. Dudley Randall to the author, September 14, 1981.

12. Ibid.

13. Ibid.

14. Doris E. Saunders to the author, September 14, 1981.

15. Ibid.

16. Ibid.

17. Dr. Naomi Andrews to the author, September 16, 1981.

18. Ibid.

19. Eugene Winslow to the author, September 17, 1981.

20. Ibid.
21. Casper LeRoy Jordan to the author, October 7, 1981.
22. Dr. Margaret Burroughs to the author, September 15, 1981.
23. S. E. Grinstead, Sr., to the author, December 1, 1981.
24. One of the most significant projects initiated by Howard University Press has been Howard University Press's Book Publishing Institute, a first in Black book-publishing history. Begun in the summer of 1980 with $61,000 seed money from Time, Inc., this institute is a six-week workshop which enrolls, with full or partial scholarships, individuals interested in careers in book publishing. The sessions are conducted by representatives from several established book-publishing houses. In 1980 nineteen applicants were enrolled. Fifteen applicants, provided with scholarships by ten publishers, were participants in the institute in the summer of 1981. Howard Fields, "Publishers Back Howard's Book Institute, Now Two," *Publishers Weekly* 220 (July 31, 1981): 14.

An attempt was made to query at least one publisher in each category. The category of college and university publisher is not represented, because Howard University Press, the only active Black university press in the United States today, did not respond to the two follow-up questionnaires that the author sent. In 1981, however, Howard University Press, as evidenced by advertisements and book reviews in various journals on titles that it released, is still an active publisher. Some of the titles are: *The Wayward and the Seeking: A Collection of Writings by Jean Toomer*, edited by Darwin T. Turner (1980) (reviewed by J. Corene Clam in *Journal of Negro History* 66 [Spring 1981]: 55–56); *A Knot in the Thread: The Life and Work of Jacques Roumain* (1980) (reviewed by Wendell P. Holbrook in *Journal of Negro History* 66 [Summer 1981]: 153–155); and *The Changing Mood in America: Eroding Commitment?* by Faustine Jones (1977) (advertised in *Journal of Negro Education* 50 [Winter 1981]: 93).

9

A Chance to Speak for Ourselves: A Concluding Commentary on the Growth and Development of Black Book Publishing, 1817–1981

INTRODUCTION

This study has attempted to survey the growth and development of Black book publishing in the United States from 1817 through 1981. The book-publishing activities of nineteenth-century publishers were presented in the light of emerging Black institutions. An effort was made to record the growth of Black book publishing from 1900 to 1960 by discussing forces within and outside the Black community that influenced its growth; by identifying Black book publishers that flourished during the period; by classifying these publishers according to type; by discussing their objectives; and by citing titles illustrative of these objectives. In treating publishers that existed between 1961 and 1974, the focus of the study was broadened to include the problems they experienced. And, finally, the state of Black book publishing in 1981 was explored through observations and comments by representative publishing executives.

Throughout the study several conclusions have been drawn about specific aspects of Black book publishing. In this chapter general conclusions about the overall development of the Black book publishing in the United States will be made relative to: (1) the major forces that influenced its growth and development; (2) the changing publishing objectives of Black book publishers over the last 164 years; and (3) the future development of Black book publishing.

MAJOR FORCES THAT INFLUENCED THE GROWTH AND DEVELOPMENT OF BLACK BOOK PUBLISHING, 1817–1981

Forces Outside the Black Community

Between 1817 and 1981 several forces outside the Black community have influenced directly or indirectly the growth and development of Black book publishing in the United States. These forces have been both negative and positive in nature and have changed over the years.

Nineteenth Century. Outside the Black community in the last years of the eighteenth century and the entire nineteenth century, the forces of blatant segregation and discrimination practiced against Blacks by the majority of white Americans in their institutions gave birth to a number of Black institutions. Some of these institutions became book publishers while others aided in the development of Black book publishing. For example, two of the Black religious denominations founded in the early years of the nineteenth century were established because of discriminatory practices against Blacks by leaders and communicants in white churches. These two Black religious denominations, the African Methodist Episcopal Church and the African Methodist Episcopal Zion Church, organized their own publishing houses, which were pioneering ventures in the history of Black book publishing. In the last decade of the century the American Baptist Publication Society, by its decision to exclude Black Baptist writers from its list of contributors, precipitated the establishment by Black Baptists of the National Baptist Publishing Board in 1896, which quickly became one of the leading Black book-publishing houses in the United States.

By contrast, leaders of the liberal white community during the nineteenth century aided, and sometimes initiated, the founding and development of Black institutions that became book publishers. Notable among these were such educational institutions as Fisk University, Hampton Institute, Howard University, Atlanta University, and Tuskegee Institute.

1900–1959. As the nineteenth century matured and the twentieth century dawned, other forces were at work outside the Black community that influenced the growth of Black book publishing. The white racist-inspired writings of popular and astute white writers and historians, claiming the inferiority of the Black American's mental and moral capacities, appeared and prompted the founding of a host of Black book publishers who sought through their publications to repudiate these claims. Among some of these publishing enterprises were the American Negro Academy, the Orion Publishing Company, the Negro Yearbook Publishing Company, and J. A. Rogers Publications.

During these years positive forces from the liberal white community were also operative and directly supported the development of Black book publishing. Liberal white Americans aided in the formation of the NAACP and the National Urban League that eventually became major Black book publishers. Dr. Robert E. Park, the prominent white sociologist working at Tuskegee, cofounded the Negro Yearbook Publishing Company. And in 1943, white members of the American Communist Party organized with Black Americans the Negro Publication Society of America, which was an active book publisher before 1959.

1960–1974. During this later period, a greater array of more positive forces outside the Black community tended to influence the development of Black book publishing. White-owned banks, although denying loans to some Black book publishers, did grant loans to all of the Black religious publishers who applied. The library-oriented segment of the major white book reviewing media was very responsive to reviewing books sent to them by Black book publishing executives, although the majority of nonlibrary-oriented book reviewing media reviewed very few books sent to them by Black book-publishing executives. White philanthropic foundations were very generous in their support of Black book publishing during these years: 91 percent of the publishing executives who applied to these foundations for grants were successful in receiving them. And, finally, the Council on Interracial Books for Children was, indeed, a major positive influence. Through the efforts of its chairman, Bradford Chambers, the existence and plight of Black and minority book publishers were brought to the attention of the publishing world in articles which Chambers authored in *Publishers Weekly* in the late 1960s and early 1970s.

1981. In the opening years of the 1980s five major developments outside the Black community are having a negative affect on Black book publishing: (1) the inflationary economy; (2) the severe cut in funding by the federal government of many book-related educational and cultural programs; (3) the high unemployment rate among Blacks; (4) the exorbitant interest rates; and (5) the neoconservative attitudes of white Americans towards Blacks which is sweeping the country. These developments have already caused some publishers to fold and others to limit their publishing activities.

Other developments, however, are occurring which are encouraging. In early 1981 Harper and Row, Publishers, sponsored a well-attended symposium on Blacks in book publishing. And for two years, beginning in 1980, several white book-publishing houses have cosponsored, both financially and with personnel, with Howard University Press a six-week institute on book publishing at Howard University for Blacks interested in careers in book publishing.

Forces Within the Black Community

Within the Black community from 1817 through 1981 many forces existed supportive of Black book publishing. Some of these forces contributed directly to its growth while others did so indirectly.

Nineteenth Century. In the nineteenth century the establishment of Black institutions by Black Americans greatly influenced the growth of Black book publishing. Many of these institutions became active book publishers, such as the previously mentioned religious denominations, newspaper and periodical publishers, and cultural organizations. The library and literary societies begun in the 1820s and 1830s laid the foundation for developing a demand in the marketplace among Black Americans for books about Black Americana. Black educational institutions in which Blacks played a major role in their founding, such as Tuskegee Institute and Atlanta University, became book publishers. And, finally, Black banks, founded late in the century, provided financial aid to Black book publishers.

1900-1959. During these years, forces within the Black community that encouraged the development of Black book publishing included: the pioneering and extensive research conducted on the Black American by several Black universities and civil rights organizations; and the leadership provided by the intellectual segment of the Black community characterized by such men as Sutton E. Griggs, Carter G. Woodson, W.E.B. Du Bois, J. A. Rogers, and Monroe Work. The efforts of these institutions and individuals were augmented by the constantly rising literacy rate and educational level among Black Americans; the growing momentum of the civil rights movement; the migration of Black Americans from rural areas to urban communities; the rising economic status of Black Americans; the increasing numbers of Black Americans employed in professional and technical pursuits; the awakening interest of Black Americans in their past; and the increasing participation of Black Americans in the nation's political, intellectual, and recreational life.

1960-1974. Between 1960 and 1974 the aforementioned forces continued with greater momentum. Added to their presence was the rising numbers of Black Americans enrolled in institutions of higher learning and the growing Black student movement which demanded and succeeded in getting more Black studies courses taught in Black and white universities.

1981. In the throes of many negative factors in the market environment of the 1980s, the most significant forces in support of Black book publishing within the Black community are the ingenuity and business acumen of Black book-publishing executives. For instance, Dr. Joseph Okpaku, president of Third Press International, through the Nigeria/U.S. Consolidated Book Procurement and Distribution Program is providing international markets for Black book publishers. The visionary executives of the Howard University Press, recognizing the need for formal training among Blacks in book publishing, are providing training through Howard's book-publishing institute. And foremost are those many self-sacrificing Black publishing executives whose acute business sense and devotion to Black book publishing have guided them in keeping their book-publishing enterprises afloat in troubled economic and social times.

THE CHANGING PUBLISHING OBJECTIVES
OF BLACK BOOK PUBLISHERS,
1817-1981

The publishing objectives of Black book publishers changed over
the 164 years from 1817 to 1981. These changing objectives
reflected the evolving social, political, economic, educational, and
cultural status of Black Americans.

The religious and academic publishers, which dominated the
sector in the nineteenth century, developed publishing programs
with publishing objectives that were intentionally narrow. These
pioneering publishers produced books almost exclusively for
adults. Religious publishers released titles to realize objectives
related to fulfilling some religious purpose, whereas academic publishers, for the most part, issued titles for the instruction of students
at a particular institution or for publicizing an institution's program in an effort to raise money from Northern philanthropists. In
the last years of the century, however, the Atlanta University Press
established a new trend in Black book publishing by bringing out
the Atlanta University Publications, which documented the social,
economic, and political conditions of Black Americans.

As the first decades of the twentieth century unfolded, the status
of Black Americans in every facet of American life reached new
dimensions. Consequently, the publishing objectives of Black book
publishers were broadened. More publishers issued books for
children as well as adults. Publishers released books to vindicate
the Black American, portray his plight in the American experience,
and to document little-known aspects of Black history and culture.

The trend of expanding their publishing objectives by Black book
publishers continued as the century matured. In the 1960s and
1970s Black publishers issued books advancing Black ideologies
and exploring subjects unrelated to Black Americana or Africana.
Thus, as the 1980s begin, we find two trends in publishing objectives developing among Black book publishers; on the one hand, a
number of publishers are releasing titles only on Black Ameri-
cana/Africana, incorporating the aforementioned publishing objectives; on the other hand, some Black book publishers are publishing books on Black Americana/Africana with the traditional
publishing objectives, but are also including books on a variety of

subjects unrelated to Black Americana/Africana, having as their publishing objectives the advancement of some aspect or ideology inherent in these unrelated subjects. Hence, we see in these latter publishers an attempt to move into the mainstream of American book publishing.

THE FUTURE DEVELOPMENT OF BLACK BOOK PUBLISHING

What is the future of Black book publishing? Will the problems, cited previously in this study, that Black book publishers experienced continue to inhibit and discourage the development of Black book publishing in the United States?

The Acquisition of Capital

As fledgling business enterprises, Black book publishers had difficulty securing capital in the form of long-term loans from financial institutions. Because they were small and new, these publishers presented a high-risk profile, as do most small businesses, to bank loan officers. In addition, there is the possibility, but not proven in this study, that there may have been some racial component in the bankers' decisions. The evidence presented, however, showed that banks, both white-owned and Black-owned, did not treat Black book publishers in a way that was obviously unfair, but neither did they give them special treatment. It is interesting to note that this was true of Black-owned banks, which were developed specifically to support Black businesses, as well as white-owned banks. The religious publishers, because of their longer publishing histories and captive audiences, were able, reportedly, to secure loans from white-owned as well as Black-owned banks. It, therefore, can be hoped that as newer book-publishing enterprises are in business longer and develop a market for the books they publish, they, like the religious publishers, will be in a better position to present a low-risk profile to bank loan officers. If so, they should experience, in the future, fewer problems of acquiring capital from financial institutions.

Lack of Administrative Skills and Knowledge
of Book Publishing

Another impediment to the success of these publishers was the lack of experience. Although the publishers were more knowledgeable than may have been anticipated, a number of publishers did show a lack of familiarity in some key aspects of publishing. Undoubtedly, this will be improved with experience. These executives, as they publish more titles, will develop more efficient administrative skills and a greater knowledge of book publishing, or else they will cease to exist as publishers.

The Neglect by the Major White Reviewing
Media of Books Published by Black
Book Publishers

Although no evidence was, or could be, presented to show that the nonlibrary sector of the major white book reviewing media improperly rejected books sent to them by Black book-publishing executives for review, there was evidence to show that a large number of these executives did send books to media in this sector and, for whatever reasons, they were not reviewed. The problem is a very complex one. No doubt reviews of their books by major white reviewing periodicals and services would greatly assist the Black book publisher. But, on the other hand, those media are by nature very restrictive, reviewing only a minute fraction of the items sent to them. In many cases, the Black book publisher is small and lacks the contacts that would help him get his books reviewed. This difficulty he shares with all small book publishers. The library-oriented book reviewing media have self-consciously taken upon themselves a role of assisting minority groups in their choice of books to review. This role is not shared by the nonlibrary media, although one may prefer it to be. Certainly this sector of the reviewing media, like the library-oriented reviewing sector, should give greater exposure to books about the nation's largest minority; Black book publishers often release titles depicting unique aspects of the Black American and African experience.

Conclusion

Black book publishing in the United States will continue to grow, despite many negative forces in its market environment. Its growth to a large measure will depend on the ingenuity and devotion of Black book-publishing executives and the expanding market of book-buying Black Americans, which is growing as a result of the rapidly rising educaitonal level of Blacks. As this trend continues, the Black book-publishing segment of the American book-publishing industry will, like the Black recording segment of the American recording industry, command a greater share of the Black business market.

As one looks at the growth and development of Black book publishing over the last 164 years, it is apparent that Black book publishers have, indeed, through their publishing efforts made a significant contribution to the development of American book publishing. They have stood at the forefront with Black publishers in other media in the production and distribution of knowledge about Black Americans.

And, finally, one must look with profound respect at Black book publishers in the United States today. Many of them, although operating commercial firms, did not enter book publishing with the expectation of making a profit, but rather to publish books documenting and portraying the Black American and African experience and to open publishing opportunities for Black writers. They often hold full-time positions in other professions, but sacrifice their time, money, and energy to publish books that they believe will enrich American culture.

Selected Characteristics of Black-Owned Book Publishing, 1900–1974

Data for the graphs and tabulations in this Appendix are based on information obtained through personal interviews with publishing executives as well as an examination of published and unpublished documents and literature related to Black-owned book publishing.

Graph 1
Black Commercial Publishers: Title Output, 1900–1974

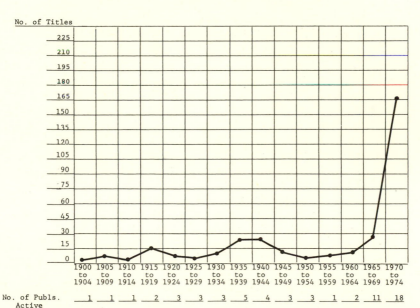

No. of Titles

	1900 to 1904	1905 to 1909	1910 to 1914	1915 to 1919	1920 to 1924	1925 to 1929	1930 to 1934	1935 to 1939	1940 to 1944	1945 to 1949	1950 to 1954	1955 to 1959	1960 to 1964	1965 to 1969	1970 to 1974
No. of Publs. Active	1	1	1	2	3	3	3	5	4	3	3	1	2	11	18

Graph 2
Black Civil Rights Organizations: Title Output, 1900–1974

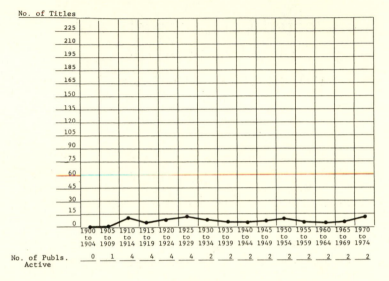

No. of Titles

| No. of Publs. Active | 0 | 1 | 4 | 4 | 4 | 4 | 2 | 2 | 2 | 2 | 2 | 2 | 2 | 2 | 2 |

Graph 3
Black Periodical Publishers: Title Output, 1900–1974

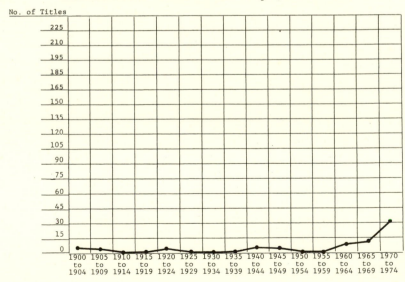

No. of Titles

| No. of Publs. Active | 2 | 2 | 0 | 0 | 1 | 0 | 0 | 0 | 2 | 2 | 1 | 1 | 1 | 1 | 1 |

Graph 4
Black Cultural and Professional Organizations: Title Output, 1900–1974

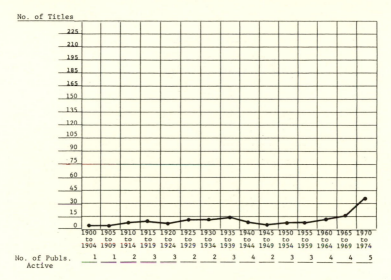

No. of Titles

No. of Publs. Active: 1 1 2 3 3 2 2 3 4 2 3 3 4 4 5

Graph 5
Black Newspaper Publishers: Title Output, 1900–1974

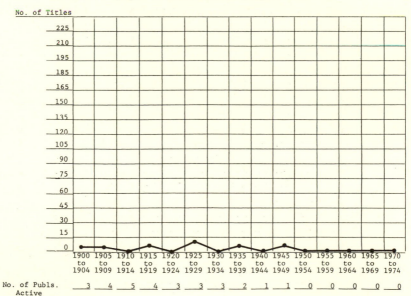

No. of Titles

No. of Publs. Active: 3 4 5 4 3 3 3 2 1 1 0 0 0 0 0

Graph 6
Black Religious Publishers: Title Output, 1900-1974

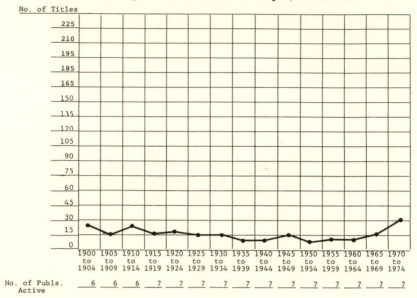

No. of Titles

No. of Publs. Active   6   6   6   7   7   7   7   7   7   7   7   7   7   7   7

Graph 7
Black Colleges and Universities: Title Output, 1900-1974

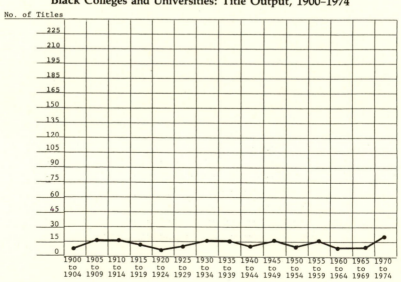

No. of Titles

No. of Publs. Active   4   4   5   6   6   6   6   7   5   3   2   2   1   1   1

Graph 8
Sixty-six Black Publishers: Title Output, 1900–1974

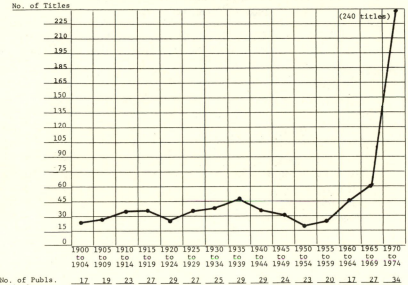

No. of Titles

(240 titles)

No. of Publs. Active: 17 19 23 27 29 27 25 29 29 24 23 20 17 27 34

Table 1
A Comparison of the Number of Publishers Issuing Titles in Nineteen Literary Genres During 1900–1960 and 1961–1974

	CULTURAL ORGANIZATIONS AND INSTITUTIONS		UNIVERSITY PRESSES	
Adult Nonfiction				
1. Textbooks	(1)	2	(2)	0
2. Poetry	(1)	0	(1)	1
3. Social, political, historical, artistic, literary, economic, scientific treatises	(7)	5	(6)	1
4. Biography, autobiography	(1)	1	(0)	1
5. Reference books	(1)	2	(5)	1
6. Other nonfiction (speeches, annual reports, travel, cookbooks, songbooks, etc.)			(4)	1
Adult Fiction				
7. Novels	(0)	1	(0)	1
8. Other fiction (short story, anthologies, novelettes)	(0)	0	(0)	1
Juvenile Nonfiction				
9. Textbooks	(0)	1	(0)	0
10. Folktales	(0)	1	(0)	0
11. Readers	(0)	2	(0)	0
12. Poetry	(0)	0	(0)	0
13. Biography, autobiography	(0)	0	(0)	0
14. Reference books	(0)	0	(1)	0
15. Other nonfiction (monographs on (various subjects)	(0)	2	(0)	0
Juvenile Fiction				
16. Novels	(0)	0	(0)	0
17. Story books	(0)	1	(0)	0
18. Picture books	(0)	1	(0)	0
19. Other fiction	(0)	0	(0)	0
No. of Lit. Genres	(5)	11	(6)	7

Note: Numbers in parentheses represent the number of publishers publishing titles in each genre 1900–1960. Numbers without parentheses are figures for 1961–

Table 1—*Continued*

CIVIL RIGHTS ORGANIZATIONS		COMMERCIAL BOOK PUBLISHERS		PERIODICAL PUBLISHERS	
(1)	0	(1)	1	(0)	1
(0)	0	(2)	9	(0)	1
(4)	2	(6)	15	(0)	1
(2)	0	(3)	5	(0)	1
(1)	2	(2)	6	(0)	1
(2)	2	(0)	4	(2)	1
(0)	0	(2)	4	(1)	1
(0)	0	(0)	2	(1)	0
(0)	0	(0)	3	(0)	0
(0)	0	(0)	2	(0)	1
(0)	0	(0)	3	(0)	0
(0)	0	(0)	3	(0)	1
(1)	0	(2)	3	(1)	1
(0)	0	(0)	3	(0)	0
(0)	0	(1)	4	(0)	0
(1)	0	(0)	0	(0)	0
(0)	0	(0)	1	(0)	1
(0)	0	(0)	0	(0)	1
(0)	0	(0)	0	(0)	0
(7)	3	(9)	16	(4)	12

1974. "No. of Lit. Genres" represents the number of literary genres in which titles were released, not total of publishers.

Table 1—*Continued*

	RELIGIOUS PUBLISHERS		NEWSPAPER PUBLISHERS	
Adult Nonfiction				
1. Textbooks	(0)	0	(0)	0
2. Poetry	(3)	0	(2)	0
3. Social, political, historical, artistic, literary, economic, scientific treatises	(4)	2	(5)	0
4. Biography, autobiography	(2)	1	(1)	0
5. Reference books	(0)	0	(1)	0
6. Other nonfiction (speeches, annual reports, travel, cookbooks, song-books, etc.)	(3)	1	(0)	0
Adult Fiction				
7. Novels	(2)	0	(1)	0
8. Other fiction (short story, anthologies, novelettes)	(0)	0	(0)	0
Juvenile Nonfiction				
9. Textbooks	(0)	1	(0)	0
10. Folktales	(0)	0	(0)	0
11. Readers	(0)	1	(0)	0
12. Poetry	(0)	0	(0)	0
13. Biography, autobiography	(0)	1	(0)	0
14. Reference books	(0)	0	(0)	0
15. Other nonfiction (monographs on (various subjects)	(0)	0	(0)	0
Juvenile Fiction				
16. Novels	(0)	0	(0)	0
17. Story books	(0)	1	(0)	0
18. Picture books	(0?	0	(0)	0
19. Other fiction	(0)	0	(0)	0
No. of Lit. Genres	(6)	7	(5)	0

Statistics on Specific Problems Reported by Black Book–Publishing Executives, 1961–1974

Data for tables in Appendix B are based on personal interviews with the publishing executives.

Table 2
Book Publishers Applying for Financial Assistance

NATURE OF PUBLISHER	NO. OF APPLICANTS[a]	PERCENTAGE OF GROUP[b]
Black cultural and professional organizations and institutions	1	16.6
Black colleges and universities	0	0.0
Black civil rights, political, and social welfare organizations	0	0.0
Black commercial publishers— published only books	6	27.3
Black periodical publishers— also published books	0	0.0
Black religious publishers	5	100.0
Total	12	

[a]Publishers interviewed constitute 46% of extant publishing enterprises, 1960–1974.
[b]Proportion of publishers within each category that applied for financial aid.

Table 3
Purpose of Application for Financial Assistance

NATURE OF PUBLISHER[a]	INAUGURATE FIRM OR BOOK-PUBLISHING UNIT	PUBLISH NEW TITLES OR NEW EDITIONS	PUBLISH NEW PRINTINGS
Black cultural and professional organizations and institutions	1	0	0
Black colleges and universities	0	0	0
Black civil rights, political, and social welfare organizaitons	0	0	0
Black commercial publishers— published only books	5	6	1
Black periodical publishers— also published books	0	0	0
Black religious publishers	0	5	5
Total	6	11	6

[a]Twelve book publishers applied for assistance.

Table 4

Institutions Applied to for Financial Assistance

NATURE OF PUBLISHER[a]	WHITE-OWNED BANKS	BLACK-OWNED BANKS	BLACK-OWNED SAVINGS & LOAN INSTS
Black cultural and professional organizations and institutions	1	0	0
Black colleges and universities	0	0	0
Black civil rights, political, and social welfare organizations	0	0	0
Black commercial publishers— published only books	5	2	1
Black periodical publishers— also published books	0	0	0
Black religious publishers	5	5	0
Total	11	7	1

[a]Of the twleve publishers involved, some applied to more than one type of financial institution.

Table 5
Institutions Giving Loans to Black Book Publishers

NATURE OF PUBLISHER	WHITE-OWNED BANKS	BLACK-OWNED BANKS
Black cultural and professional organizations and institutions	0	0
Black colleges and universities	0	0
Black civil rights, political, and social welfare organizations	0	0
Black commercial publishers— published only books	2	0
Black periodical publishers— also published books	0	0
Black religious publishers	5	5
Total Receiving Loans	7	5
Total applying	11	7
Percentage of publishers receiving loans	64.0	71.0
Percentage of all publishers receiving loans	58.3	41.6

Table 6
Publishers Applying for Grants from Foundations

NATURE OF PUBLISHER[a]	APPLIED	RECEIVED TWO OR MORE GRANTS	DID NOT RECEIVE A GRANT
Black cultural and professional organizations and institutions	4	3	1
Black colleges and universities	1	1	0
Black civil rights, political, and social welfare organizations	2	2	0
Black commercial publishers—published only books	4	4	0
Black periodical publishers—also published books	0		
Black religious publishers	0		
Total	11	10	1
(Percentage)	(100)	(91)	(9)

[a]Several publishers applied for and received more than one grant.

Table 7
Executives' Solutions to Acquiring Capital
for Growth and Development

TYPE OF SOLUTION	NUMBER OF EXECUTIVES	PERCENTAGE OF TOTAL
Black publishers should participate in co-publishing ventures among themselves	24	92.4
Black publishers should participate in co-publishing ventures with large white publishers	1	3.8
Black publishers should merge with large white publishing firms	1	3.8

Table 8
Prior Vocational and Professional Pursuits of
Book-Publishing Executives

EXECUTIVE'S AFFILIATION	EXPERIENCE IN BOOK PUBLISHING	EXPERIENCE RELATED TO BOOK PUBLISHING	EXPERIENCE UNRELATED TO BOOK PUBLISHING
Black cultural and professional organizations and institutions	1	2	4
Black colleges and universities	1	0	0
Black civil rights, political, and social welfare organizations	0	2	0
Black commercial publishers—published only books	3	6	1
Black periodical publishers—also published books	0	1	0
Black religious publishers	4	0	1
Total	9	11	6
(Percentage of total)	(34.6)	(42.3)	(23.1)

Table 9
Contacts Used by Publishers to Generate the Flow
of Manuscripts

NATURE OF PUBLISHER	CONTACTS WITH LITERARY PROFESSIONALS	ACADEMIC CONTACTS ACADEMIA	CONTACTS WITH PREVIOUS AUTHORS	OTHER CONTACTS
Black cultural and professional organizations and institutions	1	3	5	2
Black colleges and universities	1	1	1	1
Black civil rights, political, and social welfare organizations	0	2	1	0
Black commercial book publishers	6	9	8	7
Black periodical publishers	1	0	1	0
Black religious publishers	0	4	2	0
Total	9	19	18	10
(Percentage of total)	(35)	(73)	(69)	(38)

Table 10
Publishers' Methods for Weeding Out Manuscripts

NATURE OF PUBLISHER	HAD SYSTEMATIC PROCEDURE	HAD NO SYSTEMATIC PROCEDURE
Black cultural and professional organizations and institutions	3	4
Black colleges and universities	1	0
Black civil rights, political, and social welfare organizations	2	0
Black commercial book publishers	9	1
Black periodical publishers	1	0
Black religious publishers	5	0
Total	21	5
(Percentage of total)	(81)	(19)

Table 11
Professional Competence of Publishing Executives

EXECUTIVE'S AFFILIATION	ADEQUATE DEGREE OF ADMINISTRA-TIVE SKILLS & KNOWLEDGE	LIMITED DEGREE OF ADMINISTRA-TIVE SKILLS & KNOWLEDGE	VERY LOW DEGREE OF ADMINISTRA-TIVE SKILLS & KNOWLEDGE
Black cultural and professional organizations and institutions	1	5	1
Black colleges and universities	1	0	0
Black civil rights, politican, and social welfare organizations	2	0	0
Black commercial publishers— published only books	4	5	1
Black periodical publishers— also published books	1	0	0
Black religious publishers	5	0	0
Total	14	10	2
(Percentage of total)	(54)	(38)	(8)

NOTE: The twenty-six executives were evaluated in terms of their description of methods used in editing a manuscript and their knowledge of book design and bookmaking.

Table 12
Promotional Techniques Employed by Publishing Executives

EXECUTIVE'S AFFILIATION	ADVERTISING IN NATIONAL BOOK TRADE JOURNALS	DIRECT MAIL ADVERTISING	ADVERTISING IN NEWSPAPERS	ADVERTISING ON RADIO OR TELEVISION	OTHER TECHNIQUES
Black cultural and professional organizations and institutions	2	6	4	0	3
Black colleges and universities	1	1	1	1	1
Black civil rights, political, and social welfare organizations	0	2	2	0	2
Black commercial book publishers	6	8	4	0	4
Black periodical publishers	1	1	1	1	0
Black religious publishers	1	5	5	0	0
Total	11	23	17	2	10
(Percentage of total)	(42)	(88)	(65)	(7)	(38)

Table 13
Channels of Distribution Used by Book Publishers

NATURE OF PUBLISHER	DIRECT SALES TO BOOKSTORES	NATIONAL WHOLESALERS	COMPANY SALESMEN	DIRECT MAIL SALES TO CONSUMER	OTHER METHODS
Black cultural and professional organizations and institutions	6	1	2	7	1
Black colleges and universities	1	1	1	1	1
Black civil rights, political, and social welfare organizations	0	0	0	2	0
Black commercial book publishers	4	5	1	8	2
Black periodical publishers	1	1	2	1	0
Black religious publishers	3	1	0	5	4
Total	15	9	5	24	8
(Percentage of total number of publishers)	(58)	(35)	(19)	(92)	(15)

Table 14
Book-Publishing Executives Regularly Sending
Titles for Review
(N = 26)

EXECUTIVES AFFILIATION	NUMBER	PERCENTAGE
Black cultural and professional organizations and institutions	5	19
Black colleges and universities	1	4
Black civil rights, political, and social welfare organizations	1	4
Black commercial book publishers	10	39
Black periodical publishers	1	4
Black religious publishers	1	4
Total	19	74

NOTE: The Black religious publisher reportedly sent review copies of books that it published to the book reviewing media: the Townsend Press, a division of the Sunday School Publishing Board of the National Baptist Convention, U.S.A.

Table 15
Publishers Sending Review Copies to Selected
Major White Reviewing Media

BOOK REVIEWING PERIODICAL OR SERVICE	NO. OF PUBS. SENDING COPIES	NO. OF PUBS. REPORTING COPIES REVIEWED	NO. OF PUBS. REPORTING COPIES NOT REVIEWED
Booklist (ALA)	11	8	3
Atlantic Monthly	7	0	7
Choice	7	6	1
Harpers	7	0	7
Kirkus Reviews	10	3	7
Library Journal	15	12	3
New Republic	8	3	5
Newsweek	5	0	5
New Yorker	6	0	6
New York Review of Books	10	1	9
New York Times Book Review	15	7	8
Saturday Review/ World	8	1	7
School Library Journal	10	6	4
Time	5	1	4

Table 16
Publisher Success in Receiving Reviews
from Major White Reviewing Media
(in percentages)

BOOK REVIEWING PERIODICAL OR SERVICE	PUBLISHER SUCCESS IN GETTING REVIEWS
Booklist (ALA)	73
Atlantic Monthly	0
Choice	86
Harpers	0
Kirkus Reviews	30
Library Journal	80
New Republic	38
Newsweek	0
New Yorker	0
New York Review of Books	10
New York Times Book Review	47
Saturday Review/World	11
School Library Journal	60
Time	20

NOTE: Nineteen Black publishers sent review copies to each of the fourteen white reviewing periodicals or services.

Profiles of the Sixty-six Black Publishers and Two Printers Identified as Engaging in Black-Owned Book Publishing, 1817–1981

Profiles of each publisher or printer in this directory include information relative to seven items. They are: (1) dates of existence; (2) major officers with dates of tenure; (3) major publications citing author, title, and publication date for books and titles for periodicals with opening and closing dates; (4) type of business structure; (5) categories of books published; (6) types of editions published; and (7) publishing objectives.

Profiles are arranged alphabetically by name of the publisher or printer. Publishers who were still active in 1981 are identified by an asterisk.

1. THE A.M.E. BOOK CONCERN,
Philadelphia, Pennsylvania (1817–1835),
Brooklyn, New York (1835–1848),
Pittsburgh, Pennsylvania (1848–1852),
Philadelphia, Pennsylvania (1852–1952)

(1) Dates of existence: 1817–1952 (operations temporarily ceased in 1952 by the General Conference of the A.M.E. Church; (2) Major officers: none appointed after 1952; (3) Major publications: (A) periodicals (selected): *Church Magazine*, 1841–1849; the *Christian Recorder* (published as the *Christian Herald*, 1848–1852), 1852–   ; the *African Methodist Episcopal Church Review*, 1888–1927; (B) books: (i) pre-1900: (a) religious titles (selected): *Book of Discipline* (1817); *Hymn Book* (1818); *The Doctrine and Discipline of the A.M.E. Church*, by Richard Allen (bp) and Jacob Tapisco (1819); *My Recollections of the A.M.E. Ministers; or, Forty Years Experiences in the A.M.E. Church*, by Alexander Wayman (bp) (1881);

Genesis Re-read; or, The Latest Conclusions of the Physical Science View-ed in Their Relation to the Mosaic Record, by Theophilus Gould Stewart (1885); *The Genius and Theory of Methodist Polity; or, The Machinery of Methodism* (1885); *Digest of Christian Theology Designed for the Use of Beginners in the Study of Theological Science,* by James Crawford Embry (1890); *Our Father's House and Family, Past, Present and Future,* by James Crawford Embry (1893); *The Land of Promise; or, The Bible Land and Its Revelation,* by Daniel P. Seaton (1895); *The Color of Solomon—What? My Beloved Is White and Ruddy,* by Benjamin T. Tanner (bp) (1895); (b) secular titles (selected): *Memories of Mrs. Rebecca Steward,* by Theophilus Gould Stewart (1877); *The Negro and the White Man,* by Wesley J. Gaines (1897); (ii) post-1900: (a) religious titles (selected): *A Manual of the A.M.E. Church,* by Benjamin T. Tanner (bp) (1901); *The African Methodist Episcopal Hymn and Tune Book, Adapted to the Doctrines and Usage of the Church.* 5th ed. (1904); *Sanctified Dollars, How We Get Them, and Use Them,* by Solomon P. Hood (1908); *Fifty-two Suggestive Sermons Syllabi,* by Levi J. Coppin (bp) (1910); *The Ideal Christian Ministry,* by R. William Frickland (1910); *A.M.E. Church Liturgy* (1911); *Fifty Years of Religious Progress,* by Levi J. Coppin (bp) (1913); *A.M.E. Church Ecclesiastical Judicial Practice,* by William H. H. Butler (1914); *Hymnal, Adapted to the Doctrines and Usages of the African Methodist Episcopal Church.* 6th ed. (1915); *Centennial Encyclopedia of the African Methodist Episcopal Church,* ed. by Richard Robert Wright, Jr. (bp) (1916); *Studies Upon Important Themes in Religion and Expositions of Difficult Passages of the Scriptures,* by George Washington Henderson (1917); *Turner's Catechism,* by Henry McNeil Turner (bp) (1917); *Bishop Richard Allen and His Spirit,* by Daniel Minort Baxter (1923); *From Slavery to the Bishopric in the A.M.E. Church,* by William Henry Harrison Heard (bp) (1924); *Who's Who in the General Conference,* by Richard Robert Wright (bp) (1924); *Back to Methodism,* by Daniel Minort Baxter (1926); *African Methodist Episcopal Church Yearbook* (1930); *Rt. Rev. Richard Allen,* by Richard Allen (bp) (1933); *Daniel Alexander Payne, Christian Educator,* by Josephus Coan (1935); *History of the A.M.E. Church in Florida,* by Charles Sumner Long (1939); *Vital Facts Concerning the A.M.E. Church, Its Origin, Doctrines, Government, Usages, Policy, Progress,* by James H. Smith (1941); *The Doctrine and Discipline of the African Methodist Episcopal Church.* 27th rev. ed. (1940); *African Methodist Episcopal Church Liturgy,* ed. W. K. Hopes (1947); *Encyclopedia of the African Methodist Episcopal Church,* ed., Richard Robert Wright (bp). 2d rev. ed. (1947); (b) secular titles (selected): *The Seven Kingdoms: A Book of Travel, History, Information and Entertainment,* by Moses Buckingham Salter (1902); *Are the White People of the South the Negroes' Best Friends? or, The Only Just Human Methods of Solving Race Problems,* by Joseph Elias

Hayne (1903); *The Place of the Negro in American History*, by R. William Fickland (1905); *Fifty Years of Freedom; or, From Cabin to Congress; A Drama in Five Acts*, by Katherine Davis Tillman (1909); *Out of the Briars: An Autobiography and Sketch of the Twenty-Ninth Regiment*, by Alexander H. Newton (1910); *Evolution of Life*, by Algernon B. Jackson (1911); *Who's Who in Philadelphia*, ed. Charles Frederich White (1912); *The Negro in Pennsylvania: A Study in Economic History*, by Richard Robert Wright (bp) (1912); *The Question before Congress: A Consideration of the Debates and Final Action by Congress upon Various Phases of the Race Question in the United States*, by George Washington Mitchell (1918); *The Resentment: A Novel*, by Mary Etta Spencer (1921); *Daddy's Love and Other Poems*, by Irvin W. Underhill (1930); (4) Type of business structure: nonprofit corporation; (5) Books published in the following categories: (i) religious books: (a) adult nonfiction: textbooks on general religion; commentaries; treatises and yearbooks on Afro-American religion; denominational handbooks; histories; encyclopedias; commentaries; treatises; hymnals; autobiographies and biographies; (ii) secular books: (a) adult nonfiction: general biographical works on Afro-Americana; social commentaries and treatises on Afro-Americana; Afro-American poetry and drama; general histories on Afro-Americana and Africana; (b) adult fiction: novels; (6) Types of editions published other than first editions: revised editions; (7) Publishing objectives related to publishing books to: (a) document various aspects of the Afro-American and African experience; (b) assist clergy and laymen in their understanding and performance of the doctrines, procedures, and history of the A.M.E. Church.

2. *THE A.M.E. SUNDAY SCHOOL UNION AND PUBLISHING HOUSE, Bloomington, Illinois (1884-1886), Nashville, Tennessee (1886-   )

(1) Dates of existence: 1884–   ; (2) Major officers: Rev. Andrew White, Executive Secretary, 1974–   ; (3) Major publications: (A) periodicals (selected): *The Scholar's Quarterly*, 1885–   ; *The Teacher's Quarterly*, 1886–   ; (B) books (selected): (i) pre-1900; (a) religious books: *Recollections of Seventy-Years*, by Daniel A. Payne (bp) (1888); *Sermons Delivered before the General Conference of the A.M.E. Church, Indianapolis, Indiana, May, 1888*, by Daniel A. Payne (bp) (1888); *History of the A.M.E. Church*, by Daniel A. Payne (bp) (1891); *Life and Labors of Rev. John Early*, ed. George A. Singleton (1894); (b) secular books:

Poor Ben: A Story of Real Life, by Lucretia H. Coleman (1890); *School Days at Wilberforce*, by Reverdy C. Ransom (bp) (1892); *Glimpses of Africa, West and Southwest Coast*, by Charles S. Smith (1895); (ii) post-1900: (a) religious books: *The Life and Times of Rt. Rev. H. B. Parks, Presiding Bishop of the Twelfth Episcopal District of the African Methodist Episcopal Church*, by T. W. Haigler (1909); *The Heroism of the Rev. Richard Allen*, by Isaiah H. Welch (1910); *Centennial Retrospect History of the A.M.E. Church*, by John T. Jenifer (1916); *Episcopal Address*, by Joseph S. Flipper (1920); *Sunday School Problems*, by William Henry Shackelford (1925); *Sunday, The Christian Sabbath*, by Timothy D. Scott (1928); *The Dogmas and Precepts of the Fathers*, by Monroe H. Davis (1948); *The Pilgrimage of Harriet Ransom's Son*, by Reverdy C. Ransom (bp) (1950); *Preface to the History of the A.M.E. Church*, by Reverdy C. Ransom (bp) (1950); *Richard Allen and Present Day Social Problems*, by Howard D. Gregg (1959); *The Bishops of the A.M.E. Church*, by Richard Robert Wright (bp) (1963); *Know Your Church Manual*, by Andrew White (1965); *You and Your Church*, by Andrew White (1969); *A Layman Looks with Love at Her Church*, by Dorothy Hoover (1970); (b) secular books: *The Negro at Mount Bayou*, by Aurelius P. Hood (1910); *A Knowledge of History Is Conducive to Racial Solidarity and Other Writings*, by Charles V. Roman (1911); *Lack of Cooperation*, by James W. T. Brooks (1917); *The Spirit of Freedom and Justice: Orations and Speeches*, by Reverdy C. Ransom (bp) (1926); *Of Men and Arms*, by John Gregg (bp) (1945); (4) Type of business structure: nonprofit corporation; (5) Books published in the following categories: (i) religious books: (a) adult nonfiction: general commentaries on religion, denominational sermons, denominational hand-books, denominational textbooks, denominational histories, denominational biographies and autobiographies; (ii) secular books: (a) adult non-fiction: history and travel books on Afro-Americana and Africana; social commentaries of Afro-Americana; (6) Types of editions published other than first editions: revised editions; (7) Publishing objectives related to publishing books to: (a) document various aspects of Afro-Americana and Africana and (b) assist clergy and laymen in their understanding and performance of the doctrines, procedures, and history of the A.M.E. Church.

3. *A.M.E. ZION PUBLISHING HOUSE,
New York, N.Y. (1841–1894),
Charlotte, North Carolina (1894–   )

(1) Dates of existence: 1841–   ; (2) Major officers: Lem Long, Interim Manager, 1974–   ; Dr. Robert Pyant, Ass't. Manager, 1974–   ; (3)

Major publications: (selected): (A) newspapers and periodicals: *Star of Zion*, 1876–   ; *A.M.E. Zion Quarterly Review*, 1888–   ; (B) books (i) pre-1900: (a) religious books: *The Doctrines and Discipline of the African Methodist Episcopal Church*. Revised and published quadrennially following each general quadrennial conference (1872–1972); *The Graded Catechism for the Use of the A.M.E. Zion Church*, by John Jamison Moore (bp) (1889); *The Children's Catechism*, by Robert R. Morris (1892); *Hymnbook*, ed. by B. F. Wheeler (1892); *The Minister's Handbook*, by Robert R. Morris (1892); *New Hymn and Tune Book of the African Methodist Episcopal Zion Church* (1892); *One Hundred Years of the African Methodist Episcopal Zion Church; or, The Centennial of African Methodism*, by James Walker Hood (1895); *Zion's Historical Catechism*, ed. Cicero Richardson Harris (1898); *My Silver Anniversary with a Few Papers Appended*, by William Moore (1899); (b) secular books: none identified; (ii) post-1900: (a) religious books: *Historical Catechism of the A.M.E. Zion Church; For Use of Families and Sunday Schools*, by Cicero Richardson Harris (1922); *The Anthology of Zion Methodism*, by William H. Davenport (1925); *Daily Helps: Book of Birthday Horoscopes, Dictionary on Thoughts, Biblical Standpoints, True Facts and Daily Helps and Interpretation of Dreams; also, a Few Borrowed Ideas*, by Lawrence S. King (1925); *Membership in Zion Methodism; the Meaning of Membership in the A.M.E. Zion Church*, by William H. Davenport (1936); *The A.M.E. Zion Hymnal* (1947); *Zion's Historical Catechism* (rev. ed. 1972); *The African Methodist Episcopal Zion Church: Reality of the Black Church*, by William J. Walls (bp) (1974); (4) Type of business structure: nonprofit organization; (5) Books published in the following categories: (i) religious books: (a) adult nonfiction: general commentaries on religion, denominational handbooks, histories, hymnals, disciplines, biographies and autobiographies; (b) juvenile nonfiction: handbooks and textbooks; (6) Types of editions published other than first editions: revised editions; (7) Publishing objectives related to publishing books to: assist clergy and laymen in their understanding and performance of the doctrines, procedures, and history of the A.M.E. Zion Church.

4. *AFRO AM PUBLISHING COMPANY, INC., Chicago, Illinois

(1) Dates of existence: 1963–   ; (2) Major officers: David Ross, President, 1963–   ; Eugene Winslow, Vice-President, 1963–   ; (3) Major publications: (A) books: *Great Negroes, Past and Present*, by Russell Adams (1st ed., 1963) (2d ed., 1964) (3d ed., 1969); *The Meeting: A Play*, by Peggy Osborn (1968); *Colors Around Me*, by Vivian Church

(1972); (B) multimedia materials (selected): *Black ABCs: Study Prints*
(1972); *Colors Around Me Duplicating Masters* (1972); *Negroes in Our
History; A Portfolio of Display Prints* (1972); (4) Type of business
structure: private closed corporation; (5) Books published in the following
categories: (a) adult nonfiction: collective biography; (b) juvenile nonfiction: coloring books; plays; collective biography; (6) Types of editions
published other than first editions: revised editions; (7) Publishing
objectives related to publishing books to: (a) document various aspects of
Afro-Americana and Africana; and (b) to assist students and teachers in
learning and teaching Afro-Americana and Africana.

5. *AFRO-AMERICAN PUBLISHING COMPANY, Baltimore, Maryland

(1) Dates of existence: 1892–   ; (2) Major officers: John H. Murphy, III,
President, 1967–   ; (3) Major publications (selected): (A) newspapers:
the *Afro-American*, Baltimore, 1892–   ; the *Afro-American* (Richmond,
Va., ed.) 1938–   ; the *Afro-American* (Capital ed., Washington, D.C.),
1933–   ; (B) books: *The White Man's Failure in Government*, by Harvey
Elijah Johnson (1900); *The Ethiopian's Place in History, and His
Contribution to the World's Civilization. . . .*, by John William Norris
(1916); *This is Our War, Too*, by the Baltimore Afro-American Staff
(1945); *Baltimore, America's 5th Largest Negro Market*, by the Baltimore
Afro-American Staff (1946); (4) Type of business structure: private
corporation; (5) Books published in the following categories: (a) adult
nonfiction: political, social, and historical commentaries; (6) Types of
editions published other than first editions: none; (7) Publishing objectives
related to publishing books to: document various aspects of Afro-
Americana and Africana.

6. *AGASCHA PRODUCTIONS, Detroit, Michigan

(1) Dates of existence: 1970–   ; (2) Major officers: Agadem L. Diara,
President; Schavi Mali Diara, Executive Editor; (3) Major publications
(selected): books: *Hey, Let a Revolutionary Brother and Sister In*, by
Agadem Diara and Schavi Diara (1970); *Bridge From Hell*, by Richard E.
Bibbins (1972); *Growing Together*, by Schavi Diara (1973); *Islam and Pan
Africanism*, by Agadem Diara (1973); *Solo in Black*, by Freddie Robinson
(1974); *Thoughts from the Asylum*, by Ulysses Marshall (1974); (4) Type of
business structure: partnership; (5) Books published in the following categories: (a) adult nonfiction: political and social commentaries; poetry; (6)

Types of editions published other than first editions: revised editions; (7) Publishing objectives related to publishing books to: (a) portray some aspect of the Afro-American and African experience; (b) change the political, social, and cultural attitudes of Afro-Americans by advancing specific Black ideologies.

7. *ALKEBU-LAN BOOKS ASSOCIATION OF THE ALKEBU-LAN FOUNDATION, Inc., New York, N.Y.

(1) Dates of existence: 1970–   ; (2) Major officers: Dr. Yosef ben-Jochannan, Chairman of the Board of Directors; Mary Fugate, Secretary to the Board of Directors; James Brade, Esq., Attorney; George Simmonds, President; (3) Major publications books (selected): *African Origins of the Major Western Religions*, by Yosef ben-Jochannan (1970); *Black Man of the Nile*, by Yosef ben-Jochannan (1970) (rev. ed., 1972); Africa: Mother of Western Civilization, by Yosef ben-Jochannan (1971); *The Black Man's North and East Africa*, by Yosef ben-Johannan and George E. Simmonds (1972); *The Black Man's Religion*, by Yosef ben-Jochannan (1974); (4) Type of business structure: nonprofit organization; (5) Books published in the following categories: adult nonfiction: historical commentaries and treatises; (6) Types of editions published other than first editions: revised editions; (7) Publishing objectives related to publishing books to: (a) document various aspects of Afro-Americana and Africana; and (b) change the political, social, and cultural attitudes of Afro-Americans by advancing specific Black ideologies.

8. THE AMERICAN NEGRO ACADEMY, Washington, D.C.

(1) Dates of existence: 1897–1924; (2) Major officers: Alexander Crummell, founder; among its presidents who were elected annually were: W.E.B. Du Bois and A. A. Schomburg; (3) Major publications: (A) pamphlets: *Occasional Papers, 1–10* (1897–1904), *12–17* (1904–1914), *20–22* (1916–1924); (B) books: *Occasional Papers No. 11* (1905); *Occasional Papers 18–19* (1915); and *The Negro in American History*, by John W. Cromwell (1914); (4) Type of business structure: nonprofit organization; (5) Books published in the following categories: adult nonfiction: social, political, historical, and artistic commentaries; (6) Types of editions published other than first editions: none (7) Publishing objectives related to publishing books to: (a) document various aspects of Afro-Americana; and (b) defend the Afro-American against racist-inspired writings.

9. *ASSOCIATED PUBLISHERS, INC.,
Washington, D.C.

(1) Dates of existence: 1921–   ; (2) Major officers: John W. Davis, President (1974); Louis Mehlinger, Esq., Treasurer (1974); Arnett Lindsay, Secretary (1974); (3) Major publications: books (selected): *The History of the Negro Church*, by Carter G. Woodson (1921); *The Negro in Tennessee, 1865–1880*, by A. A. Taylor (1924); *Fugitives of the Pearl*, by John H. Paynter (1930); *Plays and Pageants for the Life of the Negro*, by Willis Richardson (1930); *Women Builders*, by Sadie Iola Daniel (1931); *Richard Allen, Apostle of Freedom*, by Charles Wesley (1935); *Negro History in Thirteen Plays*, by Willis Richardson (1935); *The Picture–Poetry Book*, by Gertrude P. McBrown (1935); *Negro Musicians and Their Music*, by Maud Cuney Hare (1936); *The Child's Story of the Negro*, by Jane D. Shackleford (1938); *Negro Art, Music, and Rhyme for Young Folk*, by Helen Whiting (1938); *Echos from the Hills*, by Bessie Woodson (1939); *The First Negro Medical Society*, by William Cobb (1939); *The Negro in Sports*, by Edwin Henderson (1939); *The Negro in Drama*, by Frederick W. Bond (1940); *The Economic History of Liberia*, by George W. Brown (1941); *Word Pictures of the Great*, by Elsie P. Derricotte (1941); *The Land of Cotton and Other Plays*, by Randolph Edmonds (1942): *The Negro in English Romantic Thought*, by Eva B. Dykes (1942); *Five French Negro Authors*, by Mercer Cook (1943); *Gladiola Garden*, by Effie Lee Newsome (1944); *My Happy Days*, by Jane D. Shackleford (1944); *Creole Voices*, by Armand Lanusse (1945); *Distinguished Negroes Abroad*, by Beatrice J. Fleming (1945); *The Pastor's Voice*, by Walter Henderson (1945); *Negro Makers of History*, by Carter G. Woodson, rev. by Charles H. Wesley, (5th ed., 1958); *The Story of the Negro Retold*, by Carter G. Woodson, rev. by Charles H. Wesley (4th ed., 1959); (4) Type of business structure: private closed corporation; (5) Books published in the following categories: (a) adult nonfiction: social, political, literary, and historical commentaries, and plays; (b) adult fiction: novels; (c) juvenile nonfiction: poetry, picture books, textbooks, histories; (d) juvenile fiction: story books; (6) Types of editions published other than first editions: revised editions and reprint editions; (7) Publishing objectives related to publishing books to: (a) document various aspects of Afro-Americana and Africana; (b) portray some aspect of the Afro-American or African experience; (c) assist students and teachers in learning and teaching specific nonreligious academic subjects.

10. ASSOCIATES IN NEGRO FOLK EDUCATION,
Washington, D.C.

(1) Dates of existence: 1935–1940; (2) Major officers: Alain Leroy Locke, Founder and Owner, Robert E. Martin, Assistant Editor; (3) Major

publications: (books): *Adult Education among Negroes*, by Ira DeAugustine Reid (1935) (Bronze Booklet, no. 1); *The Negro and His Music*, by Alain Leroy Locke (1936) (Bronze Booklet no. 2); *Negro Art Past and Present*, by Alain Leroy Locke (1936) (Bronze Booklet, no. 3); *A World View of Race*, by Ralph J. Bunche (1936) (Bronze Booklet, no. 4); *The Negro and Economic Reconstruction*, by T. Arnold Hill (1937) (Bronze Booklet, no. 5); *The Negro in American Fiction*, by Sterling Brown (1937) (Bronze Booklet, no. 6); *Negro Poetry and Drama*, by Sterling Brown (1937) (Bronze Booklet, no. 7); *The Negro in Art*, by Alain Leroy Locke (1940); (4) Type of business structure: proprietorship; (5) Books published in the following categories: adult nonfiction: social, artistic, political, and literary commentaries; (6) Types of editions published other than first editions: none; (7) Publishing objectives related to publishing books to document various aspects of Afro-Americana and Africana.

11. THE ASSOCIATION FOR THE STUDY OF AFRO-AMERICAN LIFE AND HISTORY, Washington, D.C.

(1) Dates of existence: 1915–   ; (2) Major officers: J. Rupert Picott, Executive Director, 1974–   ; (3) Major publications: (A) periodicals: *Journal of Negro History*, 1916–   ; *Negro History Bulletin*, 1937–   ; (B) books (selected): *A Century of Negro Migration*, by Carter G. Woodson (1918); *Slavery in Kentucky*, by Ivan Eugene McDougle (1918); *The Company of Royal Adventurers Traders Into Africa*, by George F. Zook (1919); *The Education of the Negro Prior to 1861*, by Carter G. Woodson (1919); *Paul Cuffee*, by Henry Noble Sherwood (1923); *Free Negro Owners of Slaves in the United States in 1830*, by Carter G. Woodson (1924); *The Negro in South Carolina during the Reconstruction*, by Carter G. Woodson (1924); *Free Negro Heads of Families in the United States in 1830*, by Carter G. Woodson (1925); *The Mind of the Negro as Reflected in Letters Written during the Crisis, 1800–1860*, ed. Carter G. Woodson (1926); *The Negro in the Reconstruction of Virginia*, by A. A. Taylor (1926); *A Sidelight on Anglo-American Relations, 1839–1858*, by Frank J. Klingberg (1927); *Anti-Slavery Sentiment in American Literature*, by Lorenzo Dow Turner (1929); *The Negro as a Business Man*, by J. H. Harmon, Arnett G. Lindsay, and Carter G. Woodson (1929); *Extracts from the Records of the African Companies*, by Ruth A. Fisher (1930?); *The Rural Negro*, by Carter G. Woodson (1930); *The Negro Professional and the Community*, by Carter G. Woodson (1934); *The African Background; or, Handbook for the Study of the Negro*, by Carter G. Woodson (1936); *Controversy over the Distribution of Abolition Literature*, by W. Sherman Savage (1938); *Negro Casualties in the Civil War*, by Herbert Aptheker

(1939); (4) Type of business structure: nonprofit organization; (5) Books published in the following categories: adult nonfiction: historical commentaries; (6) Types of editions published other than first editions: none; (7) Publishing objectives related to publishing books to document various aspects of Afro-Americana or Africana.

12. ATLANTA UNIVERSITY PRESS,
Atlanta, Georgia

(1) Dates of existence: 1888-1936? (2) Major officers: early superintendents of the Printing Department, which functioned as the University Press: Arthur Shumway, 1888-1889; W. A. Stearns, 1889-189?; (3) Major publications (selected): (A) periodicals: *Bulletin of Atlanta University*, eight times a year, 1888-1910, quarterly, 1910-1926, bimonthly, 1926-1929, quarterly, 1929-   ; *The Scroll*, weekly, 1895-1896, monthly, 1896-1929; *The Crimson and Gray*, monthly, 1910-1915, quarterly, 1915-1932?; (B) catalogues: *The General Catalogue of Atlanta University* (semicentennial publication) (1918); *The General Catalogue of Atlanta University, 1867-1929*, comp. Myron W. Adams (2d ed., 1929); (C) books: Atlanta University Publications: no. 1 - *Mortality among Negroes in Cities* (1896); no. 2 - *Social and Physical Conditions of Negroes in Cities* (1897); no. 3 - *Some Efforts of American Negroes for Their Own Social Betterment* (1898); no. 4 - *The Negro in Business* (1899); no. 5 - *The College-Bred Negro* (1900); no. 6 - *The Negro Common School* (1901); no. 7 - *The Negro Artisan* (1902); no. 8 - *The Negro Church* (1903); no. 9 -*Some Notes on Negro Crime Particularly in Georgia* (1904); no. 10 - *A Selected Bibliography of the Negro American* (1905); no. 11 -*Health and Physique of the American Negro* (1906); no. 12 - *Economic Cooperation among Negro Americans* (1907); no. 13 -*The Negro Family* (1908); no. 14 -*Efforts for Social Betterment Among Negro Americans* (1909); no. 15 - *The College-Bred Negro American* (1910); no. 16 - *The Common School and the Negro American* (1912); no. 17 - *The Negro Artisan* (1912); No. 18 -*Morals and Manners among Negro Americans* (1914); no. 19 - *Economic Cooperation among Negroes in Georgia* (1917); no. 20 - Selected Discussions of Negro Problems (1916); *A History of Atlanta University* by Myron W. Adams (1930); *Madame de Duras Ourika, Followed by Delphine Gay's Poem Ourika*, ed. Mercer Cook and Guichard Parris (Atlanta University French Series) (1936); (4) Type of business structure: a nonprofit organization; (5) Books published in the following categories: adult nonfiction: social, political, economic, and educational commentaries; textbooks; (6) Types of editions published other than first editions: none: (7) Publishing objectives related to publishing books related to: (a)

document various aspects of Afro-Americana; (b) assist students and teachers in learning and teaching specific, nonreligious academic subjects.

13. *BALAMP PUBLISHING COMPANY, Detroit, Michigan

(1) Dates of existence: 1971–   ; (2) Major officers: James J. Jay, owner; (3) Major publications: (A) books: *Negroes in Science: Natural Science Doctorates, 1876-1969*, by James M. Jay (1971); *The Academic Department or Division Chairman: A Complex Role*, ed. James Brann and Thomas Emmet (1972); *Black American Scholars—A Study of Their Beginnings*, by Horace Mann Bond (1972); *My World of Reality: The Autobiography of Hildrus A. Poindexter*, by Hildrus A. Poindexter (1973); (4) Type of business structure: proprietorship; (5) Books published in the following categories: adult nonfiction: biographies, autobiographies, educational commentaries; (6) Type of editions published other than first editions: none; (7) Publishing objectives related to publishing books to: (a) document various aspects of Afro-Americana; (b) enlighten individuals on subjects unrelated to Afro-Americana and Africana.

14. BI-MONTHLY NEGRO BOOK CLUB, Columbus, Ohio

(1) Dates of existence: 1936?–1936?; (2) Major officers: not available; (3) Major publications: (A) books: *Greater Need Below*, by O'Wendell Shaw (1936); (4) Type of business structure: not enough information available to determine; (5) Books published in the following categories: adult fiction: novels; (6) Types of editions published other than first editions: none; (7) Publishing objectives related to publishing books to portray some aspect of the Afro-American experience.

15. *BLACK ACADEMY PRESS, INC., Buffalo, New York (1970-1973), Bloomfield, New Jersey (1973–   )

(1) Dates of existence, 1970–   ; (2) Major officers: Sebastian Okechukwu Mezu, President; (3) Major publications (selected): (A) periodicals: *Black Academy Review*, a quarterly, 1970–   ; (B) books: *Black Leaders of the Centuries*, ed. Sebastian Okechukwu Mezu and Ram Desai (1970); *The Tropical Dawn*, by Sebastian Okechukwu Mezu (2d rev. ed., 1970); *The American Image of Africa: Myth and Reality*, by Felix N. Okoye (1971); *Ibo Market Literature*, ed. Sebastian Okechukwu M. (1971);

Modern Black Literature, ed. Sebastian Okechukwu Mezu (1971); *Topics in Afro-American Studies,* ed. Henry J. Richards (1971); *Black Academy Cookbook: A Collection of Authentic African Recipes,* by Odincheza Oka (1972); *African Students in Alien Cultures,* by Amechi Anumoye (1974); (4) Type of business structure: private corporation; (5) Books published in the following categories: adult nonfiction, collective biography, literary, social, and political commentaries; poetry; cookbooks; (6) Types of editions published other than first editions: revised editions; (7) Publishing objectives related to publishing books to: (a) document various aspects of Afro-Americana and Africana; (b) portray some aspect of the African experience.

16. BLACK STAR PUBLISHERS,
Detroit, Michigan†

(1) Dates of existence: 1970?–1974?; (2) Major officers: not available; (3) Major publications (selected): (A) periodicals: *Inner-City Voice,* a monthly, 1970–1974?; (B) books: *The Political Thought of James Forman,* by James Forman (1970); (4) Type of business structure: not enough information available; (5) Books published in the following categories: adult nonfiction: political commentaries; (6) Types of editions published other than first editions: none; (7) Publishing objectives related to publishing books to: (a) document various aspects of Afro-Americana; (b) change the political, social, and cultural attitudes of Afro-Americans by advancing specific Black ideologies.

---

†Several inquiries were sent to Black Star Publishers in an effort to obtain information about its operations, but no replies were forthcoming. This information was gleaned from secondary sources.

17. *BLYDEN PUBLISHING COMPANY, INC.,
New York, N. Y.

(1) Dates of existence: 1967–   ; (2) Major officers: A. Faulkner Watts, President; (3) Major publications: (A) books: *Africa in the Curriculum: A Resource Bulletin and Guide for Teachers,* by Beryle Banfield (1968); *Black Focus on Multicultural Education,* by Beryle Banfield (1979); *Haiti through Its Holidays,* by Eleanor Wong Telemaque (1980); *Out of the Somali World,* by Abdillahi Ahmed Wied (1981); (4) Type of business structure: private corporation; (5) Books published in the following categories: adult nonfiction: teacher's handbooks; travel books; (6) Types of editions published other than first editions: none; (7) Publishing objectives related to

publishing books to: (a) document various aspects of Afro-Americana and Africana; (b) assist students and teachers in learning and teaching specific nonreligious academic subjects.

18. THE BLYDEN SOCIETY, New York, N.Y.

(1) Dates of existence: 1935–1940; (2) Major officers; Willis Huggins, President; (3) Major publications: (A) books: *An Introduction to African Civilization, with Main Currents in Ethiopian History*, by Willis Huggins and John G. Jackson (1939); (4) Type of business structure: nonprofit organization; (5) Books published in the following categories: adult nonfiction: historical commentaries; (6) Types of editions published other than first editions: none; (7) Publishing objectives related to publishing books to document various aspects of Africana.

19. BROADSIDE PRESS, Detroit, Michigan

(1) Dates of existence: 1966–1977†; (2) Major officers: Dudley Randall, owner; Melba J. Boyd, Assistant Editor; (3) Major publications (selected): (A) books: *Poem Counterpoem*, by Margaret Danner (1966); *Think Black*, by Haki R. Madhubuti (Don L. Lee) (1967); *Black Judgement*, by Nikki Giovanni (1968); *Black Pride*, by Haki R. Madhubuti (Don L. Lee) (1968); *For Malcolm: Poems on the Life and Death of Malcolm X*, ed. Dudley Randall and Margaret Burroughs (2d ed., 1969); *Poems from Prison*, by Etheridge Knight (1969); *Black Feeling, Black Talk*, by Nikki Giovanni (1970); *Don't Cry, Scream*, by Haki R. Madhubuti (1970); *Frank: A Picture Story*, by Gwendolyn Thompson (1970); *Impressions of African Art*, by Margaret Danner (1970); *My Blackness Is the Beauty of This Land*, by Lance Jeffers (1970); *Panther Mann*, by James Emanuel (1970); *Prophets for a New Day*, by Margaret Walker (1970); *Re-Creation*, by Nikki Giovanni (1970); *Riot*, by Gwendolyn Brooks (1970); *We A BaddDDD People*, Sonia Sanchez (1970); *We Walk the Way of the World*, by Haki R. Madhubuti (1970); *Aloneness*, by Gwendolyn Brooks (1971); *Black Wisdom*, by Frenchy Hodges (1971); *A Broadside Treasury*, ed. Gwendolyn Brooks (1971); *Directionscore: Selected New Poems*, by Haki R. Madhubuti (1971); *Dynamite Voices: Black Poets of the 1960s*, by Haki R. Madhubuti (1971); *Family Pictures*, by Gwendolyn Brooks (1971); *From Plan to Planet—Life Studies: The Need for Afrikan Minds and Institutions*, by Haki R. Madhubuti (1971); *Jump Bad: A New Chicago Anthology*, ed.

---

†This publisher is now known as Broadside/Crummell Press, and it is located in Highland Park, Michigan.

Gwendolyn Brooks (1971); *A Safari of African Cooking*, by Bill Odarty (1971); *Against the Blues*, by Alvin Aubert (1972); *The Broadside Annual*, ed. Jill Witherspoon Boyer, (1st ed., 1972) (2d ed., 1973) (3d ed., 1974); *Cities and Disasters*, by Dudley Randall (1972); *Claude McKay: The Black Poet at War*, by Addison Gayle (1972); *Enough to Die For*, by Habte Wolde (1972); *Holy Ghosts*, by Ahmed Alhamisi (1972); *Report from Part One: An Autobiography*, by Gwendolyn Brooks (1972); *St. Nigger*, by C. E. Cannon (1972); *We Don't Need No Music*, by Pearl Lomax (1972); *Billy Sand and Other Poems*, by Etheridge Knight (1973); *Black Words*, by Arthur Boze (1973); *East 110th Street*, by Jose-Angel Figueroa (1973); *From a Land Where Other People Live*, by Audre Lorde (1973); *Gabriel*, by George Barlow (1973); *Judith's Blues*, by Judy Simmons (1973); *October Journey*, by Margaret Walker (1973); *Singing Sadness Happy*, by Lyn Levy (1973); *Windy Place*, by Henry Blakely (1973); *And Then the Harvest: Three Television Plays*, by Regina O'Neal (1974); *Betcha Ain't: Poems from Attica*, ed. Celes Tisdale (1974); *Bloodwhispers/Blacksongs*, by Gene Drafts (1974); *A Blues Book from Blue Black Magical Women*, by Sonia Sanchez (1974); *Book of Life*, by Haki R. Madhubuti (1974); *Broadside Authors and Artists: An Illustrated Biographical Directory*, ed. Leaonead P. Bailey (1974); *For the African Woman, Part I*, by Malaika Wangara (1974); *The Last Ride of Wild Bill*, by Sterling Brown (1974); *Phillis Wheatley*, by William H. Robinson (1974); *Tengo*, by Nicolas Guillen (1974; *Who Is Chauncey Spencer?*, by Chauncey E. Spencer (1974); (4) Type of business structure: proprietorship; (5) Books published in the following categories: (a) adult nonfiction: plays, poetry, autobiographies, collective biographies, literary criticism; (b) juvenile nonfiction: picture books, poetry, juvenile fiction: storybooks; (6) Types of editions published other than first editions; none; (7) Publishing objectives related to publishing books to: (a) document various aspects of Afro-Americana; (b) portray some aspect of the Afro-American or African experience.

20. BUCKINGHAM LEARNING CORPORATION, New York, N.Y.

(1) Dates of existence: 1968–1973?; (2) Major officers: Oswald White, President; (3) Major publications (selected): (A) books: *Dear Dr. King*, ed. Oswald White (1968); (B) learning sets: *No. 1, Black Civil Rights Leaders* (1969); (4) Type of business structure: private corporation; (5) Books published in the following categories: (a) juvenile nonfiction: social commentaries; (b) adult nonfiction: teacher's handbooks; (6) Types of editions published other than first editions: none; (7) Publishing objectives related to publishing books to: (a) document various aspects of Afro-Americana; (b) to assist students and teachers in learning and teaching specific nonreligious academic subjects.

21. *THE C.M.E. PUBLISHING HOUSE,
Jackson, Tennessee (1870–1972),
Memphis, Tennessee (1972–   )

(1) Dates of existence: 1870–   ; (2) Major officers: M.C. Pettigrew, Publishing Agent: Torrance Toney, Administrative Assistant; (3) Major publications (selected): (A) periodicals, *Christian Index*, 1867–   ; † (B) books: (i) pre-1900:‡ *Discipline of the Colored Methodist Episcopal Church*, by the General Conference (n.d.); *The Doctrines of Christ and His Church*, by R. T. Brown (n.d.); *Handbook of Church Government of the Colored Methodist Episcopal Church*, by F. M. Hamilton (n.d.); *Historical Sketch of Israel Metropolitan C.M.E. Church*, by S. L. Nichols (1888); *The History of the Colored Methodist Episcopal Church of America*, by C. H. Phillips (1898); *Pastor's Memorandum Book*, by I. H. Anderson (n.d.); *Plain Account of the Colored Methodist Episcopal Church*, by F. M. Hamilton (n.d.); (ii) post-1900: *The History of the Colored Methodist Episcopal Church of America*, by C. H. Phillips (2d ed., 1900); *Songs of Love and Mercy*, comp. F. M. Hamilton and L. H. Holsey (bp) (1904); *The History of the Colored Methodist Episcopal Church America, Book One and Two*, by C. H. Phillips (3d ed., 1925); *The Doctrines and Discipline of the Colored Methodist Episcopal Church*, by the Colored Methodist Episcopal Church (rev. ed., 1934); *History of the Women's Missionary Society in the Colored Methodist Episcopal Church*, by Sara Jane McAfee (1934); *The Passion Week*, by Augustus Ceasar Bailey (1935); *The Religious Educational Opportunity of the Local Church*, by B. Julian Smith (1936); *Christian Education in the C.M.E. Church: A Handbook for Workers in Christian Education*, by the General Board of Education of the C.M.E. Church (1961); *Christian Methodist Episcopal Church through the Years*, by E.W.F. Harris and H. M. Craig (rev. ed., 1965); *The Challenge to Become Involved*, by H. C. Bunton (1967); *The C.M.E. Primer: Our Heritage*, by C. D. Coleman (1970); *From Miles to Johnson: One Hundred Years*, by M. C. Pettigrew (1970); (4) Type of business structure: nonprofit organization; (5) Books published in the following categories: (a) adult

---

†The *Christian Index* began publication in 1867 in the interest of the *Colored Methodist Episcopal Church*. It was edited by Dr. Samuel Watson. In 1870, at the First General Conference, it was adopted as the official organ of the Colored Methodist Episcopal Church.

‡All pre-1900 titles with no publication date (n.d.) were cited as being published before 1898 in the following work: *The History of the Colored Methodist Episcopal Church in America*, by C. H. Phillips (Jackson, Tenn.: Publishing House of the C.M.E. Church, 1898), pp. 237–38.

nonfiction: denominational hymnals, doctrines and disciplines, histories, handbooks; (b) juvenile nonfiction: histories and textbooks; (6) Types of editions published other than first editions: revised editions; (7) Publishing objectives related to publishing books to assist clergy and laymen, adult and juvenile, in their understanding and performance of the doctrines, procedures, and history of the Christian Methodist Episcopal Church.

22. *CHURCH OF GOD IN CHRIST PUBLISHING HOUSE, Memphis, Tennessee

(1) Dates of existence: 1907–   ; (2) Major officers: Elder Roy L. H. Wimbush, Editor and Chairperson; (3) Major publications (selected): (A) periodicals: *The Whole Truth*, 1895;† (B) books: *Yearbook of the Church of God in Christ* (1932–   ); *History and Formative Years of the Church of God in Christ with Excerpts from the Life and Works of Its Founder—Bishop C. H. Mason*, by J. O. Patterson (bp), Germain R. Ross, and Julia Mason Atkins (1969); *Here Am I, Send Me*, by Frances Burnett Kelly and Germain R. Ross (1970); *The National Church Directory* (1974); *The National Church Discipline* (1974); (4) Type of business structure: nonprofit organization; (5) Books published in the following categories: (a) adult nonfiction: denominational handbooks, biographies, histories, yearbooks; (b) juvenile nonfiction: textbooks; (6) Types of editions published other than first editions: revised editions; (7) Publishing objectives related to publishing books to assist clergy and laymen, adult and juvenile, in their understanding and performance of the doctrines, procedures, and history of the Church of God in Christ.

---

†The Church of God in Christ was organized in Argenta, Arkansas, in 1895, but it was reorganized in 1907 by C. H. Mason in Memphis. In that same year Bishop Mason appointed a book agent and thus founded the Church of God in Christ Publishing House. In that year, also, *The Whole Truth's* place of publication was transferred from Argenta, Ark. to Memphis, Tenn.

23. THE ROBERT W. COLEMAN PUBLISHING COMPANY, Baltimore, Maryland

(1) Dates of existence: 1913–1927; (2) Major officers: Robert W. Coleman, founder and owner; (3) Major publications: *The First Colored Professional,*

Clerical, Skilled, and Business Directory of Baltimore City, ed. Robert W. Coleman (1st ed., 1913) (2d ed., 1914) (3d ed., 1915) (4th ed., 1916) (5th ed., 1917); *The First Colored Professional, Clerical, Skilled, and Business Directory of Baltimore City, With Washington, D.C., and Annapolis, Maryland, Annex*, ed. Robert W. Coleman (6th ed. 1918) (7th ed., 1919) (8th ed., 1920) (9th ed., 1921) (10th ed., 1922) (11th ed., 1923) (12th ed., 1924) (13th ed., 1925) (14th ed., 1927) (15th ed., 1927); (4) Type of business structure: proprietorship; (5) Books published in the following categories: adult nonfiction: biographical business directories; (6) Types of editions published other than first editions: revised editions; (7) Publishing objectives related to publishing books to document various aspects of Afro-Americana.

24. THE COLORED COOPERATIVE PUBLISHING COMPANY, Boston, Massachusetts

(1) Dates of existence: 1900–1904; (2) Major officers: Walter W. Wallace, President; Jesse Watkins, Secretary and Assistant Editor; Harper S. Fortune, Treasurer; and Walter A. Johnson, Vice President; (3) Major publications: (A) periodicals: *The Colored American Magazine*, 1900–1904;† (B) books: *Contending Forces*, by Pauline Hopkins (1900); (4) Type of business structure: public cooperative; (5) Books published in the following categories: adult fiction: a novel; (6) Types of editions published other than first editions: none; (7) Publishing objectives related to publishing books to portray some aspect of the Afro-American experience.

25. *COMMONSENSE BOOKS, A DIVISION OF BLACK HOPE FOUNDATION, INC., Toledo, Ohio

(1) Dates of existence: 1955–   ; (2) Major officers: Don Benn Owens, Jr., founder and President; Ethel Esther Owens, Secretary and Treasurer; Carl Martin, Director; (3) Major publications (selected): (A) pamphlets: *The Most Controversial American/and Why the Negro Race Lacks Unity*, by Don Benn Ownes (1963); (B) books: *I Am a Black Hooded Klansman*, by Don Benn Owens, Jr. (1970); *Dark Valor: The Man History Forgot*, by Don

---

†*The Colored American Magazine* was purchased by the Moore Publishing Company in 1904. From 1904 to 1909 it was published by this company in New York City.

Benn Owens, Jr. (1970); *You Can Become a Selling Writer Within 30 Short Days*, by Don Benn Owens, Jr. (1974); (4) Type of business structure: non-profit organization; (5) Books published in the following categories: (a) adult nonfiction: handbook; (b) adult fiction: novels; (6) Types of editions published other than first editions: revised editions; (7) Publishing objectives related to publishing books to: (a) portray some aspect of the Afro-American experience; (b) enlighten individuals on subjects unrelated to Afro-Americana and Africana.

26. THE DABNEY PUBLISHING COMPANY,
Cincinnati, Ohio

(1) Dates of existence: 1907–1952; (2) Major officers: Wendell P. Dabney, Editor and Publisher; (3) Major publications: (A) newspapers: the *Union*, 1907–1952; (B) books: *Cincinnati's Colored Citizens*, by Wendell P. Dabney (1926); *Chisum's Pilgrimage and Others*, by Wendell P. Dabney (1927); *The Life of Maggi L. Walker*, by Wendell P. Dabney (1927); (4) Type of business structure: proprietorship; (5) Books published in the following categories: adult nonfiction; histories; biographies, and political commentaries; (6) Types of editions published other than first editions: none; (7) Publishing objectives related to publishing books to: (a) document various aspects of Afro-Americana; (b) defend the Afro-American against racist-inspired writings.

27. DRUM AND SPEAR PRESS, INC.,
Washington, D.C.

(1) Dates of existence: 1969?–1974?; (2) Major officers: Carolyn Carter, Director, 1969?–1974?; Anne Forrester Holloway, Assistant Director, 1969?–1974?; Judy Richardson, Executive Director, 1969?–1974?; (3) Major publications (selected): *The History of the Pan African Revolt*, by C. L. R. James (1969); *The Book of African Names*, by Chief Ofuntoki (1970) (African Heritage Series); *Children of Africa: A Coloring Book* (1970); *Enemy of the Sun: Poems of Palestinian Resistance*, ed. Naseer Auru and Edmund Ghareed (1970) (Poets of Liberation Series); *Speaking Swahili: Kusema Kiswahili*, by Bernard K. Muganda (1970); (4) Type of business structure: private corporation; (5) Books published in the following categories: (a) adult nonfiction: histories, handbook; textbook; poetry; (b) juvenile nonfiction: coloring book; (6) Types of editions published other than first editions: reprint editions; (7) Publishing objectives related to publishing books to: (a) document various aspects of Afro-Americana and

Africana; (b) assist teachers and students in teaching and learning specific nonreligious academic subjects; (c) enlighten individuals on subjects unrelated to Afro-Americana or Africana.

28. THE DU BOIS AND DILL PUBLISHING COMPANY, New York, N.Y.

(1) Dates of existence: 1919–1921; (2) Major officers: W.E.B. Du Bois and Augustus Granville Dill, co-owners and publishers; Jesse Redmon Fauset, Editor; (3) Major publications: (A) periodicals: *The Brownies' Book*, a monthly magazine for children (1920–1921); (B) books: *Unsung Heroes*, by Elizabeth Haynes (1921); (4) Type of business structure: partnership; (5) Books published in the following categories: juvenile non-fiction: collective biography; (6) Types of editions published other than first editions: none; (7) Publishing objectives related to publishing books to document for children various aspects of Afro-Americana.

29. *THE DUSABLE MUSEUM OF AFRICAN AMERICAN HISTORY, Chicago, Illinois

(1) Dates of existence: 1961–   ; (2) Major officers: Margaret Burroughs, Executive Director; Eugene Feldman, Director of Research and Publications; (3) Major publications (selected): *Figures in Negro History*, ed. Eugene Feldman (1965); *Whip Me, Walk Me, Pudding and Other Tales; or, Riley Rabbit and His Fabulous Friends*, by Margaret Burroughs (1966); *What Shall I Tell My Children Who Are Black*, by Margaret Burroughs (1968); *Black Power in Old Alabama; The Life and Stirring Times of James T. Rapier*, by Eugene Feldman (1968); *Figures in Black History*, by Eugene Feldman (rev. ed., 1970); *No Place Is Big Enough to House My Soul*, by Helen Burleson Frederick (1970); *My Name Is Arnold*, by Essie Branch (1972); *House My Soul*, by Marion Black (1977); *Man Born of a Black Woman*, by Milton Glaseve (1977); (4) Type of business structure: nonprofit corporation; (5) Books published in the following categories: (a) adult nonfiction: histories, biographies, collective biographies, poetry; (b) juvenile nonfiction: folktales, readers; (6) Types of editions published other than first editions: revised editions; (7) Publishing objectives related to publishing books to: (a) document various aspects of Afro-Americana or Africana; (b) portray some aspect of the Afro-American or African experience; (c) assist students and teachers in learning and teaching specific nonreligious academic subjects.

30. *THE EAST, Brooklyn, New York

(1) Dates of existence: 1970–   ; (2) Major officers: Kasisi Jitu Weusi, Director; Akim Boami, Adm. Ass't; (3) Major publications (selected): (A) periodicals: *Black News*, 1970   ; (B) books: *The Weusi Alphabet*, by Kasisi Jitu Weusi (1970); *Dope: An Agent of Chemical Warfare*, by Herman B. Ferguson (1972); *A Message from a Black Teacher*, by Kasisi Jitu Weusi (1972); *Shaka the Great, King of the Zulus*, by G. K. Osei (1972); *Three Speeches by Minister Louis Farrakhan*, by Louis Farrakhan (1972); *African Names—Why? Which? Where?* (1973); *The Young Black Poets of Brooklyn*, ed. Yusef Kman (1973); *Think Black: A Coloring Book*, (1974); *Yesterday, Today and Tomorrow* (1974); (4) Type of business structure: nonprofit corporation; (5) Books published in the following categories: (a) adult nonfiction: social and political commentaries, poetry, handbooks, textbooks; (b) juvenile nonfiction: textbooks, readers, coloring books; (c) juvenile fiction: storybooks; (6) Types of editions published other than first editions: revised editions; (7) Publishing objectives related to publishing books to: (a) document various aspects of Afro-American or African experience; (b) assist students and teachers in learning and teaching specific nonreligious academic subjects; (c) change the political, social, and cultural attitudes of Afro-Americans by advancing specific Black ideologies.

31. *EMERSON HALL PUBLISHERS, INC., New York, N.Y.

(1) Dates of existence: 1969–   ; (2) Major officers: Alfred E. Prettyman, President; (3) Major publications (selected): *What Students Want*, ed. James D. Williams (1971); *The Mind Game: Witchdoctors and Psychiatrists*, by E. Fuller Torrey (1972); *Possible Reality: A Design for High Academic Achievement for Inner-City Students*, by Kenneth B. Clark (1972); *Race in Literature and Society*, by Rebecca Barton (1972); *Strength of Black Families*, by Robert B. Hill (1972); *New Days, A Book of Poems*, by June Jordan (1973); *No*, by Clarence Major (1973); *Why Blacks Kill Blacks*, by Alvin Poussaint (1973); (4) Type of business structure: private corporation; (5) Books published in the following categories: (a) adult nonfiction: social, educational, literary, and psychological commentaries; poetry; (b) adult fiction: novels; (6) Types of editions published other than first editions: none; (7) Publishing objectives related to publishing books to: (a) document various aspects of Afro-Americana or Africana; (b) portray some aspect of the Afro-American experience.

32. *ENERGY BLACK SOUTH PRESS,
DeRidder, Louisiana (Deepsouth Office),
Washington, D.C. (Upsouth Office)

(1) Dates of existence: 1972–   ; (2) Major officers: Ahmos Zu Bolton, III, Editor; (3) Major publications: *Hodo One* (1972); *Hodo Two* (1973); *Hodo Three* (1974); (4) Type of business structure: proprietorship: (5) Books published in the following categories: adult nonfiction: poetry; (6) Types of editions published other than first editions: revised editions; (7) Publishing objectives related to publishing books to portray some aspect of the Afro-American experience.

33. FISK UNIVERSITY PRESS, Nashville, Tennessee

(1) Dates of existence: 1915–1949; (2) Major officers: the overseeing of the university's publications was the responsibility of various administrative officers over the years; (3) Major publications: *Folk Song of the American Negro*, by John W. Work (1915); *Differential Mortality in Tennessee, 1917–1928*, by Elbright Sibley (1930); *The Free Negro Family*, by E. Franklin Frazier (Social Science Series) (1932); *History of Ancient Mexico*, by Fray Bernadino de Sahagun, trans. Fanny Bandelier (1932); *An Outline for a Sourcebook on the Negro*, by Charles S. Johnson (1932); *The Economic Status of Negroes*, by Charles S. Johnson (1933); *People versus Property*, by Herman Long and Charles S. Johnson (1947); *Build a Future*, by Charlie S. Johnson (1949); (4) Type of business structure: nonprofit organization; (5) Books published in the following categories: adult nonfiction: social, economic, historical commentaries: (6) Types of editions published other than first editions: none; (7) Publishing objectives related to publishing books to: (a) document various aspects of Afro-Americana; (b) enlighten individuals on subjects unrelated to Afro-Americana or Africana.

34. FORTUNE AND PETERSON PUBLISHING
COMPANY, New York, N.Y.

(1) Dates of existence: 1887–1905; (2) Major officers: T. Thomas Fortune and Jerome Peterson, Publishers and Editors; (3) Major publications: (A) newspapers: *New York Age*, (1887–1905); (B) books: *Dreams of Life*, by Thomas Fortune (1905); (4) Type of business structure: partnership; (5) Books published in the following categories: adult nonfiction; poetry; (6) Types of editions published other than first editions: none; (7) Publishing objectives related to publishing books to enlighten individuals on subjects unrelated to Afro-Americana or Africana.

35. FREE LANCE PRESS, Cleveland, Ohio

(1) Dates of existence: 1950–1980; (2) Major officers: Casper L. Jordan and Russell Atkins, Coeditors; (3) Major publications (selected): (A) periodicals: *Free-lance*, 1950–   ; (B) books; *Perchance to Dream, Othello*, by Conrad Kent Rivers (1959); *Phenomena*, by Russell Atkins (1961); *These Black Bodies and This Sunburn Face* (1962); *Purgatory and Carousels: A Poetic Autobiography*, by Jau Billera (1963); *Two by Atkins: The Abortionist and the Corpse, Two Poetic Dramas to be Set to Music*, by Russell Atkins (1963); *Permit Me Voyage*, by Adelaide Simon (1964); *Dusk at Selma*, by Conrad Kent Rivers (1965); *North American Book of the Dead*, by D. A. Levy (1965); *The Mantu Poets of Cleveland*, by Russell Atkins (1968); *The Nail*, by Russell Atkins (1970); *Maleficium*, by Russell Atkins (1971); (4) Type of business structure: nonprofit organization; (5) Books published in the following categories: adult nonfiction: poetry, drama, and literary criticism; (6) Types of editions published other than first editions: none; (7) Publishing objectives related to publishing books to: (a) portray some aspect of the Afro-American experience; (b) enlighten individuals on subjects unrelated to Afro-Americana or Africana.

36. *THE GUIDE PUBLISHING COMPANY, Norfolk, Virginia

(1) Dates of existence: 1911–   ; (2) Major officers: Plummer B. Young, Jr., owner and Publisher; (3) Major publications: (A) newspapers: *Journal and Guide* (Norfolk), 1911–   ; (B) books (selected): *Random Rhymes*, by John Riley Dungee (1929); *A History of the Virginia State Teachers Association*, by Luther Porter Jackson (1937); *The African Society Becomes Emanuel African Methodist Episcopal Church, Portsmouth, Virginia*, by Charles E. Stewart (1944); (4) Type of business structure: private corporation; (5) Books published in the following categories: adult nonfiction: poetry, histories; (6) Types of editions published other than first editions: none; (7) Publishing objectives related to publishing books to document various aspects of Afro-Americana.

37. HAMPTON INSTITUTE PRESS, Hampton, Virginia

(1) Dates of existence: 1871–1940; (2) Major officers: the overseeing of the university's publications was the responsibility of various administrative officers over the years; (3) Major publications (selected): (A) periodicals:

Southern Workman, 1872–1939; (B) books: (i) pre-1900: *Economic Crumbs, or Plain Talks for the People About Labor, Capital, Money, Tariff, Etc.*, by T. T. Bryce (1879); *Mixed Races: Their Environment, Temperament, Heredity, and Phrenology*, by John S. Sampson (1881); *Emancipation: Its Course and Progress From 1481 B.C. to A.D. 1875*, by Joseph T. Wilson (1882); *Visitors' Handbook of Old Point Comfort, Va., and Vicinity*, by Charles Betts (3d ed., 1883); *Tuskegee Normal and Industrial School for Training Colored Teachers*, ed. Helen Ludlow (1884); *Richard Armstrong*, by Mary Armstrong (1887); *Hampton Negro Conference* (1888); *On Habits and Manners: Written Originally for the Students of Hampton N. & A. Institute*, by Mary Frances Armstrong (rev. ed., 1888); *Cabin and Plantation Songs as Sung by Hampton Students*, comp. and arr. Thomas P. Fenner (2d ed. 1891); *Hampton Hymnal and School Service* (1892); *Twenty-two Years of the Hampton Normal and Agricultural Institute at Hampton, Virginia: Records of Negro and Indian Graduates and Ex-Students*, by E. A. Hobbs and A. E. Cleveland (1893); (ii) post-1900: *What Hampton Graduates Are Doing* (1905); *The History of African Methodism in Virginia; or, Four Decades in the Old Dominion*, by Israel Lafayette Butts (1908); *The Hampton Arithmetic*, by Flora F. Low (1909); *Religious Folk Songs of the Negro as Sung at Hampton Institute*, ed. Robert N. Dett (6th rev. ed., 1927); *Virginia's Contribution to Negro Leadership: Biographies of Outstanding Negroes Born in Virginia*, ed. William Cooper (1936); *Sonnets for the Weaker Sex, as Well as Certain Other Poems*, by Arland C. Hampton (1939); *Hampton Institute Conference on the Participation of the Negro in National Defense* (1940); (4) Type of business structure: nonprofit institution; (5) Books: publishing in the following categories: adult nonfiction: travel books, poetry, textbooks, songbooks, collective biographies, histories, conference proceedings; (6) Types of editions published other than first editions: revised editions; (7) Publishing objectives related to publishing books to: (a) document various aspects of Afro-Americana; (b) portray some aspect of the Afro-American experience; (c) assist students and teachers in learning and teaching specific nonreligious academic subjects; (d) enlighten individuals on subjects unrelated to Afro-Americana; (e) publicize the programs and philosophy of Hampton Institute.

38. *HOWARD UNIVERSITY PRESS,
Washington, D.C.

(1) Dates of existence: Officially authorized, initially, by the Board of Trustees of Howard University, February 7, 1919, although books were

published before that year using the "Howard University Press" imprint. Officially authorized again by the Board of Trustees of Howard University and organized as a business unit within the university with a staff and a systematic publishing program, June, 1972; (2) Major officers: Charles Harris, Executive Director, 1972-   ; (3) Major publications (selected): (A) periodicals: *Journal of Negro Education*, 1931-   ; *Journal of Religious Thought*, 1944-   ; (B) books using the "Howard University Press" imprint prior to 1919: *The History of Howard University*, by William Weston Patton (1896); *Esther Burr's Journal*, by Jeremiah E. Rankin (1901); *Commercial College Studies of Negroes in Business* (1914); (C) books using the "Howard University Press" imprint between 1919-1972: *The Founding of the School of Medicine of Howard University, 1868-1873*, by Walter Dyson (Howard Studies in History, no. 10, 1929); *History of Alpha Phi Alpha*, by Charles Wesley (1929); *The Housing of Negroes in Washington, D.C.: A Study in Human Ecology*, by William H. Jones (1929); *Journal of Negro Education Yearbook, nos. 1-40* (1931-1972); *The Negro in the Americas*, ed. Charles Wesley (1940); *Howard University; The Capstone of Negro Education*, by Walter Dyson (1941); *Trust and Non-Self-Governing Territories*, ed. Merze Tate (1948); *The New Negro Thirty Years Afterwards*, ed. Rayford Logan (1955); *Wellsprings of Life and Other Addresses*, ed. Daniel Grafton Hill (1956); *A Catalogue of the African Collection in the Moorland Foundation of Howard University*, comp. Dorothy B. Porter (1958); (D) books published by the newly organized Howard University Press between 1972 and 1981: *Aiiieeeee! An Anthology of Asian-American Writers*, ed. Frank Chin, Jeffrey Chan, Lawson Inada, Shawn Wong (1974); *Bid the Vassal Soar*, by Merle A. Richmond (1974); *Black Engineers in the United States—A Directory*, ed. James K. Ho (1974); *From the Dark Tower: Afro-American Writers, 1900 to 1960*, by Arthur P. Davis (1974); *Hoodo Hollerin' Bebop Ghosts*, by Larry Neal (1974); *How Europe Underdeveloped Africa*, by Walter Rodney (1974); *Pillars in Ethiopian History: The William Leo Hansberry African History Notebook*, vol. 1, ed. Joseph E. Harris (1974); *A Poetic Equation: Conversations between Nikki Giovanni and Margaret Walker* (1974); *Quality Education for All Americans*, by William F. Brazziel (1974); *Reluctant Reformers*, by Robert Allen (1974); *Saw the House in Half*, by Oliver Jackman (1974); *The Short Fiction of Charles W. Chestnutt*, by Sylvia Lyons Render (1974); *Song of Mumu*, by Lindsay Barrett (1974); *The Dilemma of Access: Minorities in Two-Year Colleges*, by Michael A. Olivas (1979); *Versatile Guardian: Research in Naval History*, ed. Richard A. Von Doenhoff (1979); *Clio Was a Woman: Studies in the History of American Women*; ed. Mabel E. Deutrich and Virginia C. Purdy (1980); *A Knot in The*

Thread: The Life and Work of Jacques Roumain (1980); *Profile of the Negro in Dentistry*, ed. Foster Kidd (1980); *A Study on the Historiography of the British West Indies*, by Elsa V. Goveia (1981); (4) Type of business structure: nonprofit organization; (5) Books published in the following categories: (a) adult nonfiction: poetry; histories, social, political, educational, and literary commentaries; biographical directories; bibliographies; conference procedings; (b) adult fiction: novels; (7) Publishing objectives related to publishing books to: (a) document various aspects of Afro-Americana and Africana; (b) portray some aspect of the Afro-American or African experience; (c) enlighten individuals on subjects unrelated to Afro-Americana or Africana.

39. THE IOWA STATE BYSTANDER PUBLISHING COMPANY, Des Moines, Iowa

(1) Dates of existence: 1894–1974; (2) Major officers: Raymond Ray, Editor; (3) Major publications: (A) newspapers: *Iowa State Bystander*, 1894–1974; (B) books: *History and Views of Colored Officers Training Camp for 1917 at Fort Des Moines*, by John Lay Thompson (1917); *The History of the Order of the Eastern Star among Colored People*, by Sue M. Wilson Brown (1925); (4) Type of business structure: proprietorship; (5) Books published in the following categories: adult nonfiction: histories and social commentaries; (6) Types of editions published other than first editions: none; (7) publishing objectives related to publishing books to document various aspects of Afro-Americana.

40. *JOHNSON PUBLISHING COMPANY, INC. (formerly known as the NEGRO DIGEST PUBLISHING COMPANY, 1942–1949)—THE BOOK DIVISION, Chicago, Illinois

(1) Dates of existence, 1942–   ; (Book Division established in 1961); (2) Major officers: John H. Johnson, Publisher; Doris E. Saunders, Head, Book Division; (3) Major publications (selected): (A) periodicals: *Negro Digest/Black World*, 1942–1951; 1961–1976; *Ebony*, 1945–   ; *Jet*, 1951–   ; *Ebony, Jr.*, 1973–   ; (B) books: *The Best of Negro Humor*, ed. John H. Johnson and Ben Burns (published under the imprint "Negro Digest Publishing Co.) (1942); *Burn, Killer, Burn*, by Paul Crump (1962); *Before the Mayflower*, by Lerone Bennett, Jr. (1st ed., 1962) (2d ed., 1963) (3d ed., 1966) (4th ed., 1969); *The Ebony Cookbook*, by Freda Deknight (1st ed., 1962) (2d ed., 1973); *The Day They Marched*, ed. Doris E.

Saunders (1963); *Negro First in Sports*, by Andrew S.N. Young (1963); *Sonny Liston, the Champ Nobody Wanted*, by Andrew S.N. Young (1963); *Color Me Brown*, by Lucille Giles (1964); *The Negro Mood, and Other Essays*, by Lerone Bennett, Jr. (1964); *The Negro Politician*, by Edward T. Clayton (1964); *What Manner of Man: A Biography of Martin Luther King, Jr.*, by Lerone Bennett, Jr. (1964); *Confrontation: Black and White*, by Lerone Bennett, Jr. (1965); *The Negro Handbook*, ed. Doris E. Saunders (1966); *Black Power, U.S.A.: The Human Side of Reconstruction, 1867–1877*, by Lerone Bennett, Jr. (1967); *Martin Luther King, Jr.: An Ebony Picture Biography*, by the editors of *Ebony* (1968); *Pioneers in Protest*, by Lerone Bennett, Jr. (1969); *Autobiography of a Fugitive Negro*, by Samuel Ringgold Ward (Foreword by Vincent Harding) (Ebony Classics Series) (1970); *Black and White: Land, Labor and Politics in the South*, by T. Thomas Fortune (Foreword by John H. Bracey) (Ebony Classics Series) (1970); *Black Power, Gary Style*, by Alex Poinsett (1970); *The Underground Railroad*, by William Still (Foreword by Benjamin Quarles) (Ebony Classics Series) (1970); *The Black Revolution*, by the editors of *Ebony* (1970); *The Ebony Book of Black Achievement*, by Margaret Peters (1970); *Men of Mark*, by William J. Simmons (Foreword by Lerone Bennett, Jr.) (Ebony Classics Series) (1970); *My Bondage and My Freedom*, by Frederick Douglass (Forward by Lerone Bennett, Jr.) (Ebony Classics Series) (1970); *To Gwen with Love*, ed. Patricia Brown, Don L. Lee, and Francis Ward (1971); *Pictorial History of Black America*, by the editors of *Ebony* (1971–1973); *The Integrated Cookbook*, by Mary Jackson and Lelie Wishart (1972); *Names of Africa*, by Oganna Chuks-Onji (1972); *Soul of Christmas*, by Helen King (1972); *Challenge of Blackness*, by Lerone Bennett, Jr. (1973); *The Ebony Success Library*, by the editors of *Ebony* (1973); *Lil'l Tuffy and His ABC's*, by Jean P. Smith (Ebony Jr. Book) (1973); *What Color Are You?*, by Darwin Walton (Ebony Jr. Book) (1974); *Color Me Brown*, by Lucille Giles (rev. ed., 1974); *The Ebony Handbook*, ed. the editors of *Ebony* (1974); *The Legend of Africania*, by Dorothy Robinson (Ebony Jr. Book) (1974); *Wade in the Water: Great Moments in Black American History*, by Lerone Bennett, Jr. (1979); *I Wouldn't Take Nothin for My Journey*, by Leonidas Berry (1981); (4) Type of business structure: private corporation; (5) Books published in the following categories: (a) adult nonfiction: poetry, histories, cookbooks, pictorial commentaries, biographies, social and political commentaries, handbooks, collective biographies, encyclopedias, literary anthologies; (b) adult fiction: a novel; (c) juvenile fiction: storybooks; (d) juvenile nonfiction: coloring books, folktales; (6) Types of editions published other than first editions: revised editions and reprint editions: (7) Publishing objectives related to publishing books to: (a) document various aspects of Afro-Americana and Africana; (b) portray some aspect of the Afro-American or African experience.

41. *LOTUS PRESS, Detroit, Michigan

(1) Dates of existence: 1972–   ; (2) Major officers: Naomi Andrews, Associate Editor and Publisher; Leonard Andrews, Associate Editor and Publisher; (3) Major publications (selected): (A) books: *Pink Ladies in the Afternoon: New Poems, 1965–1971*, by Naomi Cornelia (Long) Madgett (1972): (B) portfolios: *Deep Rivers: A Portfolio: 20 Contemporary Black American Poets* (with teacher's guide), by Naomi Cornelia (Long) Madgett (1972); *Grandsire*, by Lance Jeffers (1979); *A Chisel in the Dark*, by James A. Emanuel (1980); *Cardinal Paints and Other Poems*, by Eugene Haun (1981); *Heartland: Selected Poems*, by Ron Welburn (1981); *A Litany of Friends: Poems Selected and New*, by Dudley Randall (1981); *Phantom Nightengale*, by Naomi (Long) Madgett (1981); *Song for Anninho*, by Gayl Jones (1981); *Songs and Dances*, by Phillip M. Royster (1981); (4) Type of business structure: partnership; (5) Books published in the following categories: (a) adult nonfiction: poetry, teacher's guides; (b) juvenile nonfiction: poetry; (6) Types of editions published other than first editions: none; (7) Publishing objectives related to publishing books to portray some aspect of the Afro-American experience.

42. McGIRT PUBLISHING COMPANY, Philadelphia, Pennsylvania

(1) Dates of existence: 1903–1907; (2) Major officers: James Ephraim McGirt, owner and Publisher; (3) Major publications: (A) periodicals: *McGirt's Magazine*, 1903–1907; (B) books: *The Triumphs of Ephraim*, by James Ephraim McGirt (1907); (4) Type of business structure: public corporation; (5) Books published in the following categories: adult fiction: short stories; (6) Types of editions published other than first editions: none; (7) Publishing objectives related to publishing to portray some aspect of the Afro-American experience.

43. A. WENDELL MALLIET & COMPANY, New York, N.Y.

(1) Dates of existence: 1938?–1952?; (2) Major officers: A. Wendell Malliet, founder and owner; (3) Major publications (selected): *The Life of*

Abraham Lincoln, by James Henry Hubert (1939); *Counter-Clockwise*, by John M. Lee (1940); *An Economic Detour*, by Merah Steven Stuart (1940); *British and Axis Aids in Africa*, by Kingsley Ozuomba Mbadiwe (1942); *Harlem, the War, and Other Addresses*, by John Howard Johnson (1942); *The Negro Handbook*, ed. Florence Murray (1942); *A Traipsin' Heart*, by Mildred Martin Hall (1943); *We Who Would Die*, by Henry Binga Dismond (1943); *Rhymes of the Times*, by J. Farley Ragland (1946); *The First Night*, by Emil Michael Rasmussen (1947); *Freedom's Soldiers and Other Poems*, by Richardo Weeks (1947); *The Challenge of Negro Leadership*, by Julius J. Adams (1949); (4) Type of business structure: proprietorship; (5) Books published in the following categories: (a) adult nonfiction: poetry, social, political, and historical commentaries, handbooks, speeches; (b) adult fiction: novels; (6) Types of editions published other than first editions: none; (7) Publishing objectives related to publishing books to: (a) document various aspects of Afro-Americana and Africana; (b) portray specific aspects of the Afro-American and African experience.

44. *MUHAMMAD'S TEMPLE NO. 2,
PUBLICATIONS DEPARTMENT,
Chicago, Illinois

(1) Dates of existence: 1956–   ; (2) Major officers: Wallace Muhammad, Publisher, 1974–   ; Herbert Muhammad, National Publications Director, 1974; (3) Major publications (selected): (A) newspapers: *Muhammad Speaks*, 1960–   ; (B) books: *The Supreme Wisdom to the So-Called Negroes' Problem*, by Elijah Muhammad (rev. ed., 1957); *Muhammad's Children: A First Grade Reader*, by Christine Johnson (1963); *Message to the Blackman in America*, in Elijah Muhammad (1965); *How to Eat to Live*, by Elijah Muhammad (1967); *The Fall of America*, by Elijah Muhammad (1974); *How to Eat to Live*, by Elijah Muhammad (2d ed., 1974); *Muslim Accomplishments*, by Elijah Muhammad (1974); (4) Type of business structure; nonprofit organization;(5) Books published in the following categories: (a) adult nonfiction: sociopolitical-religious commentaries, nutrition commentaries; religious commentaries; histories; (b) juvenile nonfiction: readers; (6) Types of editions published other than first editions: revised editions; (7) Publishing objectives related to publishing books to: (a) assist clergy and laymen, adult and juvenile, in their understanding and performance of the doctrines, procedures, and history of the Nation of Islam; (b) document various aspects of Afro-Americana and Africana; (c) publicize the programs and philosophies of the Nation of Islam; (c) change the political, social, and cultural attitudes of Afro-

Americans by advancing the Black ideologies associated with the Nation of Islam.

45. *MURRAY BROTHERS PRINTING COMPANY, Washington, D.C.

(1) Dates of existence: 1908–   ; (2) Major officers: Freeman Murray, President; George M. Lee, Vice-President; Ethel Murray, Treasurer; Norma M. Jorgensen, Secretary; (3) Major publications: served as a job printer for Afro-American authors who published the following selected books privately: *Fireside Musings*, by Walter Todd (1908); *Gathered Treasures*, by Walter Todd (1st ed., 1912); . . . *Emancipation and the Freed in American Sculpture: A Study in Interpretation*, by Freeman Henry Morris Murray (1916); *A Little Sunshine*, by Walter E. Todd (1917); *As It Is; or, the Conditions under Which the Race Problem Challenges the White Man's Solution*, by Mamie Jordan Carver (1919); *Gems of the Soul*, by Harry Wilson Patterson (1935); *The John Brown Reader*, by William C. Hueston (1949); (4) Type of business structure: private corporation; (5) Job printing done for Afro-American authors who privately published books in the following categories: (a) adult nonfiction: poetry; art and history and criticism; social, historical, and political commentaries; (6) Types of editions in which the firm served as a job printer other than first editions: revised editions; (7) Publishing objectives reflected in the books which the firm served as a job printer were related to publishing books to: (a) document various aspects of Afro-Americana and Africana; (b)portray some aspect of Afro-Americana or Africana.

46. *THE NATIONAL ASSOCIATION FOR THE ADVANCEMENT OF COLORED PEOPLE (also known as THE CRISIS PUBLISHING COMPANY), New York, N.Y.

(1) Dates of existence: 1910–   ; (2) Major officers: Benjamin Hooks, Executive Secretary, 1977–   ; Warren Marr, Editor, *Crisis Magazine*, 1972–   ; (3) Major publications (selected): (A) periodicals: *Crisis Magazine*, 1910–   ; (B) pamphlets: *How the National Association for the Advancement of Colored People Began*, by Mary White Ovington (1914); *Stop That Bully* (1950); *The Fantastic Case of the Trenton Six* (1951); *NAACP Acclaimed by Distinguished Americans* (rev. ed., 1951); *Guideposts to Freedom* (1953); *Urban Renewal or Urban Removal?* (1959); *The President's Civil Rights Program* (1963); *Let's March to the Voters'*

Registration Desk (1964); (C) books: *A Child's Story of Dunbar*, by Julia L. Henderson (1913); *Hazel*, by Mary White Ovington (1913); *Norris Wright Cuney*, by Maude Cuney Hare (1913); *Prince Hall and His Followers*, by George Williamson Crawford (1914); *Thirty Years of Lynching in the United States, 1889-1918* (1919); *Place: America* (a theatre piece), by Thomas Richardson (1939); *The Negro Wage-earner and Apprenticeship Training Program* (1960); *Emancipation's Unfinished Business: 54th Annual Convention Souvenir Program Book* (1963); *In Freedom's Vanguard, NAACP Report for 1963; A New Birth of Freedom: NAACP Report for 1964* (1965); (4) Type of business structure: nonprofit organization; (5) Books published in the following categories: (a) adult nonfiction: plays; political and social commentaries; biographies; annual reports; (b) adult fiction: novels; (c) juvenile nonfiction: biographies; (6) Types of editions published other than first editions: serial editions; (7) Publishing objectives related to publishing books to: (a) document various aspects of Afro-Americana; (b) portray some aspect of Afro-Americana; (c) publicize the programs and philosophy of the National Association for the Advancement of Colored People.

47. *THE NATIONAL BAPTIST PUBLISHING BOARD (also known as THE BOYD PUBLISHING COMPANY), Nashville, Tennessee

(1) Dates of existence: 1896–   ; (2) Major officers: T. B. Boyd III, Secretary-Treasurer, 1979–   ; (3) Major publications (selected): (A) periodicals: *National Baptist Union-Review*, 1899–   ; (B) books: (i) pre-1900: (a) religious works: *Pulpit and Platform Efforts: Sanctifications vs. Fanaticism*, by James Henry Eason (1899); (b) secular works: none identified; (ii) post-1900: (a) religious works: *Baptist Pastor's Guide and Parliamentary Rules*, by Richard Henry Boyd (1900); *The Beacon Lights of Tennessee Baptists*, by Allen D. Hurt (1900); *Golden Gems: A Song Book for the Church Choir, The Pew, and Sunday School* (1901?); *Sermons, Addresses, and Reminiscences and Important Correspondence*, by E. C. Morris (1901); *Up the Ladder in Foreign Missions*, by Lewis Garnett Jordan (1901); *Life of Charles T. Walker, D. C. (The Black Surgeon), Pastor of Mt. Olive Church, New York City*, by Silas Floyd (1902); *The National Baptist Hymnal*, ed. R. H. Boyd and William Rossburgh (3d ed., 1903); *Theological Kernels*, by Jacob T. Brown (1903); *Once a Methodist, Now a Baptist—Why?*, by Eugene Carter (1905); *The Blighted Life of Methuselah*, by Henry Roger Williams (1908); *God's Promise to His People*, by William C. Current (1908); *Christianity Under the Searchlight*, by George Wylie Clinton (1909); *Preacher's Text and Topic Book with One Hundred Ordination Questions*, by H. M. Williams

(1909); *Sermons and Sermonetts*, by J. P. Robinson (1909); *Twenty Years in Public Life, 1890–1910*, by Thomas O. Fuller (1910); *An Outline of Baptist History*, by N. H. Pius (1911); *History of Louisiana Negro Baptists, 1804–1914*, by William Hicks (1915); *Selected Sermons*, by Andrew Stokes, Jr. (1920); *A Story of the National Baptist Publishing Board: The Why, How, When, Where, and By Whom It was Established*, by Richard Henry Boyd (rev. and enl. ed. with Appendix by Rev. C. H. Clark and David E. Over, 1924); *God and the Negro*, by Alonzo P. B. Holly (1937); *Sermons Outlined*, by S.W.R. Cole (9th ed., 1940); *Pilate's Judgement Hall and Other Messages as Delivered in Broadcast Services of the New Light Baptist Church*, by P. S. Wilkinson (1948); (b) secular works: *Laboratory Methods of Histology and Bacteriology*, by John H. Holman (1903); *The Nations from a New Point of View*, by Harvey E. Johnson (1903); *Out of Darkness; or, Diabolism and Destiny*, by John Wesley Grant (1909); *The Separate or "Jim Crow" Car Laws; or, Legislative Enactments of Fourteen Southern States: A Reply in Compliance with a Resolution of the National Baptist Convention*, by Archard H. Boyd (1909); *Sentimental and Comical Poems*, by James H. Thomas (1913); *The Harp Ethiopia*, by Maurice Corbett (1914); *Thoughts of Idle Hours*, by Myra Viola Wilds (1915); *Finger Prints: American Custom vs. American Ideals*, by Samuel R.H. Reed (1921); (4) Type of business structure: nonprofit private corporation as chartered under the laws of the State of Tennessee on August 15, 1898; (5) Books published in the following categories: (a) religious works: (i) adult nonfiction: denominational hymnals, histories, law commentaries, biographies, handbooks, commentaries, textbooks; (ii) juvenile nonfiction: denominational textbooks; (b) secular works: (i) adult nonfiction: social commentaries, poetry, textbooks; (ii) adult fiction: novels; (6) Types of editions published other than first editions; revised editions; (7) Publishing objectives related to publishing books to: (a) document various aspects of Afro-American or African experience; (b) assist clergy and laymen, adult and juvenile, in their understanding and performance of the doctrines, procedures, and history of the Afro-American Baptist denomination; (c) defend the Afro-American against racist-inspired writings; (d) assist students and teachers in learning and teaching specific nonreligious academic subjects.

48. *NATIONAL DENTAL ASSOCIATION,
Charlottesville, Virginia

(1) Dates of existence: 1913–   ; (2) Major officers: Ellard N. Jackson, Director and Executive Secretary in 1974; (3) Major publications: (A) periodicals: *Bulletin of the National Dental Association*, 1941–   ; (B) books: *The Growth and Development of the Negro in Dentistry*, by

Clifton Orrin Dummett (1952); (4) Type of business structure: nonprofit organization; (5) Books published in the following categories: adult nonfiction: histories; (6) Types of editions published other than first editions: none; (7) Publishing objectives related to publishing books to document Afro-American contributions to dentistry.

49. THE NATIONAL PUBLIC WELFARE LEAGUE,
Memphis, Tennessee

(1) Dates of existence: 1914–1930; (2) Major officers: Sutton E. Griggs, founder and President, (1914–1930); (3) Major publications (selected): (A) pamphlets: *The Story of My Struggles*, by Sutton E. Griggs (1914); (B) newspapers: *The Neighbor*, 1919–1930?; (C) books: *Light on Racial Issues*, by Sutton E. Griggs (1921); *Guide to Racial Greatness*, by Sutton E. Griggs (1923); *Stepping Stones to Higher Things*, by Sutton E. Griggs (1925); *The Winning Policy*, by Sutton E. Griggs (1927); *Cooperative Natures and Social Education*, by Sutton E. Griggs (1929); (4) Type of business structure: nonprofit organization; (5) Books published in the following categories: adult nonfiction: social commentaries; textbooks; (6) Types of editions published other than first editions: none; (7) Publishing objectives related to publishing books to: (a) document various aspects of Afro-Americana; (b) assist students and teachers in learning and teaching specific nonreligious academic subjects; (c) change the political, social, and cultural attitudes of Afro-Americans by advancing specific Black ideologies.

50. *THE NATIONAL URBAN LEAGUE, INC.,
New York, N.Y. (Originally known as
THE NATIONAL LEAGUE ON URBAN
CONDITIONS AMONG NEGROES, 1911–1920)

(1) Dates of existence: 1911–   ; (2) Major officers: John E. Jacob, President, 1981; James A. Williams, Director, Publications Department; (3) Major publications (selected): (A) periodicals: *Opportunity: Journal of Negro Life*, 1923–1949; (B) pamphlets: *5,000,000: The Negro at Work in the United States* (Color Line Series) (1933); *Occupational Opportunities for Negroes*, by Lester B. Granger (Color Line Series) (1937); *They Crashed the Color Line* (Color Line Series) (1937); *Guiding Negro Youth Toward Jobs*, by Ann Tanneyhill (Color Line Series) (1938); (C) books (selected): *Ebony and Topaz: A Collectanea*, ed. Charles S. Johnson (1927); *Negro Membership in American Labor Unions* (1930) (this publication was financed and distributed by the National Urban League, although the imprint of Alexander Press appears on the title page); *Unemployment*

among Negroes—Data on 25 Industrial Cities (1930); Unemployment Status of Negroes: a Compilation of Facts and Figures Respecting Unemployment among Negroes in One Hundred and Six Cities (1931); The Forgotten Tenth: An Analysis of the Unemployment among Negroes in the United States and Its Costs: 1932-1933 (Color Line Series) (1933); *Twenty-Fifth Anniversary Souvenir Booklet* (1935); *Racial Conflict: A Homefront Danger* (1943); *Race, Fear, and Housing in a Typical American Community* (1946); *Six Times a Year* (1946); *Spotlight on Gary* (1946); *New Frontiers in the Atomic Age* (1951); *A Study of the Employment of Negroes in the Brewery Industry in the United States* (1951); *A Documentary Report on Housing* (1955); *The National Urban League Re-examined* (1955); *The Urban League Story: 1910-1960, Golden Fiftieth Anniversary Yearbook* (1961); *Where the Lender Looks First: A Case Study of Mortgage in Disinvestment in Bronx County* (1970); *The National Survey of Housing Abandonment* (1973); *The Power of the Ballot: A Handbook for Black Political Participation* (1973); *The Unfinished Second Reconstruction: Proceedings of the 63rd Conference of the National Urban League* (1973); *When the Marching Stopped: An Analysis of Black Issues in the '70s* (1973); (4) Type of business structure: nonprofit organization; (5) Books published in the following categories: adult nonfiction: handbooks; literary anthologies; yearbooks; social, economic, and political commentaries; (6) Types of editions published other than first editions: revised editions; (7) Publishing objectives related to publishing books to: (a) document various aspects of Afro-Americana; (b) portray some aspect of the Afro-American experience; (c) publicize the programs and philosophy of the National Urban League.

51. THE NEGRO PUBLICATION SOCIETY OF AMERICA, New York, N.Y.

(1) Dates of existence: 1941-1943?; (2) Major officers: Angelo Herndon, Executive Secretary and Editor; Directors: Alain Locke, Henrietta Buckmaster, L. D. Reddick, Herbert Aptheker, Arthur Huff Fauset, Dorothy Brewster, Jean Muir, Dashiel Hammett, Bernard J. Stern, Theodore Dreiser, Margaret Keenan, Rockwell Kent, and Ralph Ellison; (3) Major publications: (A) periodicals: *Negro Quarterly*, 1943-1944; (B) books (selected): *The Kidnapped and the Ransomed*, by Kate E. R. Picard (with a foreword by L. D. Reddick) (1941); *Jim Crow's Last Stand*, by Langston Hughes (1943); (4) Type of business structure: nonprofit organization; (5) Books published in the following categories: adult nonfiction: biographies; poetry; (6) Types of editions published other than first editions: reprint editions; (7) Publishing objectives related to publishing

books to: (a) document various aspects of Afro-Americana; (b) portray some aspects of Afro-Americana.

52. THE NEGRO YEARBOOK PUBLISHING COMPANY, Tuskegee, Alabama

(1) Dates of existence: 1910–1928 (Tuskegee Institute took over the publication of *The Negro Yearbook* in 1928, but the Negro Yearbook Publishing Company was used on editions of *The Negro Yearbook* title pages through the 9th edition, which was published in 1938. The 10th edition used "Tuskegee Institute Press" on the title page and the 11th edition bears the imprint of Wm. H. Wise Co., Inc., New York, N.Y.; (2) Major officers: Robert E. Park, President; Emmett J. Scott, Vice-President; Monroe N. Work, Secretary and Editor, 1910–1938; Jessie Parkhurst Guzman, Editor, 1939–1952; (3) Major publications: *The Negro Yearbook* (1st ed., 1914–1915); (4th ed., 1916–1917); (5th ed., 1918–1919); (6th ed., 1921–1922); (7th ed., 1925–1926); (8th ed., 1931–1932); (9th ed., 1937–1938); (10th ed., 1947–1948); (11th ed., 1952); (4) Type of business structure: 1910–1928, a partnership; 1928–1951, nonprofit organization; 1952, a copublishing venture between Tuskegee Institute and the Wm. H. Wise Company, Inc., New York, N.Y.; (5) Books published in the following categories: adult nonfiction: reference books; (6) Types of editions published other than first editions: revised editions; (7) Publishing objectives related to publishing books to document various aspects of Afro-Americana.

53. *NUCLASSICS AND SCIENCE PUBLISHING COMPANY, Washington, D.C.

(1) Dates of existence: 1969?–   ; (2) Major officers: Carl L. Shears, Publisher, (3) Major publications: (A) books: *Among the Living Dead*, by Carl L. Shears (1969); *Niggers and Po' White Trash: A Collection of Stories*, by Carl L. Shears (1971); *Before the Setting Sun; The Age before Hambone*, by Carl L. Shears (1972); *The Black Letters: Love Letters from a Black Soldier in Viet Nam*, by Rita Southall and Carl Shears (1972); *Blackness of My Skin and the Kinkiness of My Hair*, by Carl Shears (1972); (4) Type of business structure: proprietorship?; (5) Books published in the following categories: adult nonfiction: poetry; social commentaries; short-story collections; memoirs; (6) Types of editions published other than first editions: none; (7) Publishing objectives related to publishing books to: (a) document various aspects of Afro-Americana; (b) portray some aspect of the Afro-American experience.

54. THE ORION PUBLISHING COMPANY,
Nashville, Tennessee

(1) Dates of existence: 1901–1913; (2) Major officers: Sutton E. Griggs, founder and Publisher; (3) Major publications: (A) books: *Overshadowed*, by Sutton E. Griggs (1902); *The Hindered Hand; or, the Reign of the Repressionist*, by Sutton E. Griggs (1905) (2d ed., 1905); (3d ed., 1905); *The One Great Question: A Study of Southern Conditions at Close Range*, by Sutton E. Griggs (1907); *Pointing the Way*, by Sutton E. Griggs (1908); *Wisdom's Call*, by Sutton E. Griggs (1911); (4) Type of business structure: proprietorship; (5) Books published in the following categories: (a) adult nonfiction: social commentaries: (b) adult fiction: novels; (6) Types of editions published other than first editions: revised editions; (7) Publishing objectives related to publishing books to: (a) document various aspects of Afro-Americana; (b) portray specific aspects of Afro-Americana; (c) defend the Afro-American against racist-inspired writings.

55. PATH PRESS, INC., Chicago, Illinois

(1) Dates of existence: 1968–1971; (2) Major officers: Bennett J. Johnson, President, 1968–1971; Harmon Cromwell Gilbert, Executive Vice-President, 1968–1971; Milton C. Lamb, Jr., Vice-President, 1968–1971; Wadia Sampson, Vice-President, 1968–1971; Cora Mayo, Vice-President, 1968–1971; Lexia B. Young, Secretary-Treasurer, 1968–1971; Attorney Lemuel C. Bentley, Corporation Counselor, 1968–1971; (3) Major publications: (A) books: *The Myth Maker*, by Frank London Brown (1969); *An Uncertain Sound*, by Herman Cromwell Gilbert (1969); (4) Type of business structure: private corporation; (5) Books published in the following categories: adult fiction: novels; (6) Types of editions published other than first editions: none; (7) Publishing objectives related to publishing books to portray specific aspects of Afro-Americana.

56. THE PICTORIAL HISTORY PUBLISHING
COMPANY, INC., Memphis, Tennessee

(1) Dates of existence: 1933– ?; (2) Major officers: Thomas O. Fuller, owner and Publisher; (3) Major publications: (A) books: *Pictorial History of the Negro*, by Thomas O. Fuller (1933); (4) Type of business structure: private corporation; (5) Books published in the following categories: adult nonfiction: histories; (6) Types of editions published other than first editions: none; (7) Publishing objectives related to publishing books to document various aspects of Afro-Americana.

57. THE PRESS OF R. L. PENDLETON,
Washington, D.C.

(1) Dates of existence: 1886–1930; (2) Major officers: Robert L. Pendleton, founder and owner; (3) Major publications: served as job printer for Afro-American authors who published the following selected books privately: *Samuel Coleridge-Taylor: An Ode of Welcome*, by Maxwell Nicy Hayson (1906); *A Narrative of the Negro*, by Leila Amos Pendleton (1912); *Missing Pages in American History, Revealing the Services of Negroes in the Early Wars in the United States of America*, by Laura Eliza Wilkes (1919); (4) Type of business structure: proprietorship; (5) Job printing done for Afro-American authors who privately published books in the following categories: adult nonfiction: poetry; histories; (6) Types of editions for which the firm served as job printer other than first editions: none; (7) Publishing objectives reflected in the books which the firm served as a job printer were related to publishing books to: (a) document various aspects of Afro-Americana; (b) portray some aspect of the Afro-American experience.

58. J. A. ROGERS PUBLICATIONS,
Chicago, Illinois, (1917–1921?),
New York, N.Y. (1921?–1966)

(1) Dates of existence: 1917–1965; (2) Major officers: Joel Augustus Rogers, founder and owner; (3) Major publications (selected): (A) books: *From "Superman" to Man*, by J. A. Rogers (1st ed., 1917); (2d ed., 1917); (3d ed., 1918); (4th ed., 1919); (5th ed., 1924); *As Nature Leads*, by J. A. Rogers (1919); *The World's Greatest Men of African Descent*, by J. A. Rogers (1st ed., 1931); (2d ed., 1932); *100 Amazing Facts about the Negro*, by J. A. Rogers (1934, 24 editions published from 1934 through 1963); *The Real Facts about Ethiopia*, by J. A. Rogers (1st ed., 1935); (2d ed., 1936); (3d ed., 1936); *Sex and Race*, by J. A. Rogers (1st ed., 1940); (2d ed., 1941); *World's Great Men of Color*, by J. A. Rogers (1940); *Africa's Gift to America*, by J. A. Rogers (1st ed., 1960); (rev. and enl. Civil War Centennial Edition, 1961); *Nature Knows No Color Line*, by J. A. Rogers (1960); (B) pamphlets: *The Five Negro Presidents, U.S.A.*, by J. A. Rogers (1965); (4) Type of business structure: proprietorship; (5) Books published in the following categories: adult nonfiction: historical; social commentaries; collective biographies; (6) Types of editions published other than first editions: revised editions; (7) Publishing objectives related to publishing books to: (a) document various aspects of Afro-Americana and Africana; (b) defend the Afro-American against racist-inspired writings.

59. *ST. LOUIS ARGUS PUBLISHING CO.,
St. Louis, Missouri

(1) Dates of existence: 1912–   ; (2) Major officers: Eugene N. Mitchell, Publisher in 1974; Zelma M. Harris, Editor in 1974; (3) Major publications: (A) newspapers: *St. Louis Argus*, 1912–   ; (B) books: *Immediate Jewel of His Soul*, by Herman Dreer (1919); *The Eagle*, by Thomas Atkins (1936); (4) Type of business structure: proprietorship; (5) Books published in the following categories: (a) adult nonfiction: poetry; (b) adult fiction: novels; (6) Types of editions published other than first editions: none; (7) Publishing objectives related to publishing books to portray some aspect of the Afro-American experience.

60. *SAPPHIRE PUBLISHING CO., INC.,
San Francisco, California

(1) Dates of existence: 1973–   ; (2) Major officers: Board of Directors: Jacqueline Bradford, Patsey G. Fulcher, Aileen C. Hernandez, Jean Kresy, Jessie Minor, Eleanor R. Spikes, Maxine Ussery, E. Anne Warren, Naomi Gray, Anne Chiarenze; (3) Major publications (selected): (A) books: *70 Soul Secrets of Sapphire*, by Carolyn Jetter Greene (1st ed., 1973); (2d ed., 1974); (4) Type of business structure: private corporation; (5) Books published in the following categories: adult nonfiction: social commentaries; (6) Types of editions published other than first editions: revised editions; (7) Publishing objectives related to publishing books to document various aspects of Afro-American womanhood.

61. *THE SUNDAY SCHOOL PUBLISHING BOARD
OF THE NATIONAL BAPTIST CONVENTION,
U.S.A., INC., Nashville, Tennessee

(1) Dates of existence: 1916–   ; (2) Major officers: D. C. Washington, Executive Director, 1959–1974; Cecile Adkins, Executive Director, 1975–   ; (3) Major publications (selected): (A) periodicals: *National Baptist Voice*, 1915–   ; *Adult Bible Quarterly*, 1916–?   ; (B) books (selected): *How to Study and Teach the Bible; Teacher Training Book, National Baptist Convention*, by Samuel N. Vass (1922); *A New Book for All Services*, ed. (Mrs.) A. M. Townsend (1924); *The Colored Baptists' Family Tree*, by William Moses (1925); *The Baptist Standard Church Directory and Busy Pastor's Guide*, by Lewis G. Jordan (1929); *Negro Baptist History, U.S.A., 1750–1930*, by Lewis G. Jordan (1930); *Principles and Methods of Religious*

Education, by Samuel N. Vass (1932); *The Study of the New Testament,* by Samuel Vass (1932); *Commentary on the International Improved Uniform Lessons for 1940,* by J. T. Brown and M. A. Talley (1941); *Unholy Shadows and Freedom's Holy Light,* by Joseph H. Jackson (1967) (Townsend Press imprint);† *Baptist Standard Hymnal* (1974†); *Child's Story Bible* (1974†); *Emergency Addresses and Poems,* by Alice H. Mitchell (1974‡); *Gospel Pearls* (1974†); *Leadership Education Curriculum Handbook* (1974‡); *The National Baptist Pulpit* (1973‡); *Spirituals Triumphant* (1974); *Summary of Christian Doctrine* (1974‡); (4) Type of business structure: nonprofit corporation; (5) Books published in the following categories: (i) religious works: (a) adult nonfiction: denominational histories, songbooks, handbooks, textbooks, teaching guides; (b) juvenile nonfiction: bible stories: textbooks; (ii) secular works: literary anthologies and social commentaries; (6) Types of editions published other than first editions: revised editions; (7) Publishing objectives related to publishing books to: (a) assist clergy and laymen in their understanding and performance of the doctrines, procedures, and history of the Afro-American Baptist denomination; (b) document various aspects of Afro-Americana.

---

† Townsend Press is a division of this publisher.
‡These titles were in print in 1974.

62. *TARHARKA PUBLISHING CO., Annapolis, Maryland

(1) Dates of existence: 1971–   ; (2) Major officers: Phaon Sundiata (Goldman), Editor; (3) Major publications: *Black Manhood: The Building of Civilization by the Black Man on the Nile,* by Phaon Sundiata (1971); (4) Type of business structure: private corporation; (5) Books published in the following categories: adult nonfiction: histories; (6) Types of editions published other than first editions: none; (7) Publishing objectives related to publishing books to document various aspects of Africana.

63. *THE THIRD PRESS, JOSEPH OKPAKU PUBLISHING COMPANY, INC., New York, N.Y.†

(1) Dates of existence: 1970–   ; (2) Major officers: Joseph Okpaku, President; (3) Major publications (selected): (A) periodicals and journals:

---

†Also known as Third Press International.

Journal of the New African Literature and the Arts, 1966–   (Originally published by Joseph Okpaku when he was a graduate student, four years before he founded the publishing firm); (B) books: *Verdict: The Exclusive Picture Story of the Trial of the Chicago 8*, by Joseph Okpaku (1970); *American Negro Slavery and Abolition*, by Wilbert E. Moore (hardcover ed., 1971, paperback ed., 1973); *Drugs: What They Are, How They Look, What They Do*, by Frank Gannon (1971); *How to Get Along with Black People: A Handbook for White Folks and Some Black Folks Too*, by Chris Clark and Sheila Rush (1971); *If They Come in the Morning*, by Angela Davis (1971); *Imperialism in the Seventies*, by Pierre Jalee, trans. Ramond Sokolov and Margaret Sokolov (1971); *Third World Voices for Children*, ed. Robert E. McDowell and Edward Lavitt (1971): *Two Plays*, by Douglas Turner Ward (1971); *Alexander Solzhenitsyn: A Biography*, by Hans Bjorkegren, trans. from the Swedish by Eneberg Kaa (1972); *Gamal Abdel Nasser: Son of the Nile*, by Shirley G. Dubois (1972); *Nigeria Modernization*, by Ukandi G. Damachi (1972); *A Perfect State of Health*, by Peter Way (1972); *Polish Portrait*, by Michael Tarnowski (1972); *Africa in World Affairs: The Next Thirty Years*, by Ali A. Mazuri and Hasu H. Patel (1973); *Cadastre*, by Aime Cesaire, trans. Emile Synder (1973); *Darl*, by Fred Clifton (1973) (An Odarkai Book); *Edward Heath, Prime Minister*, by Margaret Laing (1973); *Fallacy of I.Q.*, ed. Carl Senna (1973); *The Guinea Pigs*, by Kaca Polackova, trans. from the Czechoslovakian by Ludvik (1973); *How the Leopard got His Claws*, by Chinua Achebe and John Iroaganachi (1973) (An Odarkai Book); *Illustrated History of the Jewish People* (1973) (An Odarkai Book); *Illustrated History of the Nigerian People*, by Arthur Pest (1973) (An Odarkai Book); *In the Beginning of Creation: Stories for Children*, by Edward Lavitt and Robert McDowell (1973) (An Odarkai Book); *In the Fog of the Season's End*, by Alex LaGuma (1973); *James Baldwin: A Critical Study*, by Stanley Macebuh (1973); *Justice in the Round: The Trial of Angela Davis*, by Reginald Major (1973); *Klop and the Ustinov Family*, by Nadia Ustinov (1973); *Law Enforcement, Inc.*, by Sidney Becker (new ed., 1973); *Love Poems*, by Sonia Sanchez (1973); *My Talks with Arab Leaders*, by David Ben-Gurion (1973); *Sickle Cell*, by Anthony Cerami and Elsie Washington (1973); *Afo-A-Kom*, by Fred Ferreti (1974); *Dark and Feeling*, by Clarence Major (1974); *Did the Sun Shine Before You Were Born? A Sex Education Primer*, by Sol Cohen and Judith Cohen (1974) (An Odarkai Book); *Drums of War*, ed. George M. Daniels (1974); *Gerald Ford and the Future of the Presidency*, by J. F. Terhorst (1974); *Kasamance; A Fantasy*, by Katherine Dunham (1974) (An Odarkai Book); *Operation Burning Candle*, by Blyden Jackson (1974); *Wood Magic*, by Richard Jefferies (1974); *Annotated Bibliography of Black American Literature*, by Lizabeth Gant (1980); *Indigenous Banking in a Developing Country: The Story of the New*

Nigerian Bank, by Walter Anukpe (1980); *Under the Sroko Tree,* by Joseph Okpaku (1980); (4) Type of business structure: private corporation; (5) Books published in the following categories: (a) adult nonfiction: pictorial commentaries; social, political, and literary commentaries; drama, biographies, histories, (b) adult fiction: novels; (c) juvenile nonfiction: pictorial histories: primers; (d) juvenile fiction: storybooks; (6) Types of editions published other than first editions: revised editions; reprint editions; translations; (7) Publishing objectives related to publishing books to: (a) document various aspects of Afro-Americana and Africana: (b) portray specific aspects of the Afro-American and African experience; (c) assist students and teachers in learning and teaching specific nonreligious academic subjects; (d) enlighten individuals on subjects unrelated to Afro-Americana or Africana.

64. *THE THIRD WORLD PRESS,
Chicago, Illinois

(1) Dates of existence: 1967–   ; Major officers: Haki R. Madhubuti, Editor; Johari Amini, Assistant Editor/Treasurer; Carol Madhubuti, Secretary; (3) Major publications: (selected): (A) books: *Images in Black,* by Johari Amini (1967); *Black Essence,* by Johari Amini (1968); *Paper Souls,* by Carolyn Rogers (1968); *Portable Soul,* by Sterling Plumpp (1968); *Half Black, Half Blacker,* by Sterling Plumpp (1970); *Jacki,* by Luvester Lewis (1970); *Let's Go Somewhere,* by Johari Amini (1970); *The Back Door,* by Phillip Royster (1971); *Blues for an African Princess,* by Sam Greenlee (1971); *Destination Ashes,* by Norman Jordan (1971); *Everywhere Is Yours,* by Charlie Cobb (1971); *Journey to Africa,* by Hoyt W. Fuller (1971); *My Own Hallelujahs,* by Zack Gilbert (1971); *The Redemption of Africa and Black Religion,* by St. Clair Drake (1971); *Black Rituals,* by Sterling Plumpp (1972); *Blackness and the Adventure of Western Culture,* by George E. Kent (1972); *After the Killing,* by Dudley Randall (1973); *Garvey, Lumumba, Malcolm: Black Nationalist-Separatist,* by Shawa Maglanbayan (1973); *Negroes with Guns,* by Robert Williams (1973); *The Destruction of Black Civilization,* by Chancellor Williams (1974); *I Look at Me,* by Mari Evans (1974); *The Tiger Who Wore White Gloves; or, What You Are,* by Gwendolyn Brooks (1974); *Home is a Dirty Street: The Social Oppression of Black Children,* by Eugene Perkins (1976); *Cultural Unity of Black Africa,* by Cheikh Anta Diop (1980); *Enemies—The Clash of Races,* by Haki R. Madhubuti (Don L. Lee) (1980); *To Disembark,* by Gwendolyn Brooks (1980); *How They Made Biriyani,* by Mari Evans (1981); (4) Type of business structure: proprietorship; (5) Books published in the following categories: (a) adult nonfiction: histories;

travel books; social and political commentaries; literary criticism; poetry; (b) juvenile nonfiction: readers; storybooks; (6) Types of editions published other than first editions: revised editions; (7) Publishing objectives related to publishing books to: (a) document various aspects of Afro-Americana and Africana; (b) portray aspects of the Afro-American and African experience; (c) assist students and teachers in learning and teaching specific nonreligious academic subjects; (d) change the political, social, and cultural attitudes of Afro-Americans by advancing specific Black ideologies.

65.   TUSKEGEE INSTITUTE PRESS,
Tuskegee, Alabama

(1) Dates of existence: 1885–1958; (2) Major officers: various managers of the Printing Office; (3) Major Publications (selected): (A) periodicals: *Tuskegee Messenger*, 1906–1936; (B) books: *Industrial Work of Tuskegee Graduate and Former Students during the Year 1910*, by Monroe N. Work (1911); *The Negro in Medicine*, by John Kenny (1912); *The Rural School and Its Relations to the Community*, by Tuskegee Normal and Industrial Institute—Extension Department (1915); *Nebraska and His Granny*, by Rose Leary Love (1936); *The Movable School Goes to the Farmer*, by Thomas Monroe Campbell (1936); *Graphics Arts Survey*, by William E. Boone (1955); *Five County Church Study in East Alabama*, by V. A. Edwards (1955); *The New South: A Symposium and Ceremonies Held in Connection with the Inauguration of Luther Hilton Foster*, ed. Jessie Parkhurst Guzman (1958); *Lynching by States and Race*, by Jessie Parkhurst Guzman (1958); (4) Type of business structure: nonprofit organization; (5) Books published in the following categories: adult nonfiction: histories; educational commentaries; poetry; social commentaries; (6) Types of editions published other than first editions: revised editions; (7) Publishing objectives related to publishing books to: (a) document various aspects of Afro-Americana; (b) portray specific aspects of Afro-Americana; (c) enlighten individuals on subjects unrelated to Afro-Americana or Africana.

66.   THE UNIVERSAL PUBLISHING HOUSE
(also known as THE PRESS OF THE UNIVERSAL NEGRO IMPROVEMENT ASSOCIATION), New York, N.Y.

(1) Dates of existence: 1918–1927; (2) Major officers: Marcus M. Garvey, President, Universal Negro Improvement Association and African Communities League, Inc., 1914–1940; (3) Major publications: (A) newspapers:

212

APPENDIX C

Negro World, 1919–1933 (although there was a demise of all enterprises connected with the Universal Negro Improvement in 1927, the *Negro World* continued publication until 1933); (B) books: *The Philosophy and Opinions of Marcus Garvey*, vol. 1, comp. and ed. Amy Jacques-Garvey (1923); *The Philosophy and Opinions of Marcus Garvey; or, Africa for Africans*, comp. and ed. Amy Jacques-Garvey (1925); (C) pamphlets; *Selections from the Poet Meditations of Marcus Garvey*, comp. and ed. Amy Jacques-Garvey (1927); (4) Type of business structure: public corporation with membership restricted to Blacks; (5) Books published in the following categories: adult nonfiction: social and political commentaries; poetry; (6) Types of editions published other than first editions: revised editions; (7) Publishing objectives related to: (a) documenting various aspects of Afro-Americana and Africana; (b) portraying aspects of the Afro-American experience; (c) changing the political, social, and cultural attitudes of Afro-Americans by advancing specific Black ideologies.

67. *VITA YA WATU (PEOPLE'S WAR) PUBLISHERS (Formerly JIHAD PRODUCTIONS), Newark, New Jersey

(1) Dates of existence: 1967–   ; (2) Major officers: Imamu Amiri Baraka (Leroi Jones), Publisher in 1974; (3) Major publications (selected): (A) Newspapers: *Unity and Struggle*, 1970–   ; (B) books: *Spirit Reach*, by Imamu Amiri Baraka (1972); *Africa and Imperialism*, by Ahmed Sekou Toure (1973); *African Revolution*, by Imamu Amiri Baraka (1973); *African Free School; Education Text* (1974); *Reflections of the Sun* (1974); *Swahili Name Book*, by (1974); (C) pamphlet: *Towards the Creation of Political Institutions for All African Peoples*, by Imamu Amiri Baraka (1972) (reprinted from *Black World*, October, 1972); *Cabral on Nkrumah*, by Amilcar Cabral (1973); *The Political Leader Considered As the Representative of Culture*, Ahmed Sekou Toure (n.d.); (4) Type of business structure: proprietorship; (5) Books published in the following categories: (a) adult nonfiction: handbooks, poetry, textbooks, social and political commentaries; (b) juvenile nonfiction: coloring books; (6) Types of editions published other than first editions: none; (7) Publishing objectives related to publishing books to: (a) document various aspects of Afro-Americana and Africana; (b) portray some aspect of the Afro-American or African experience; (c) assist students and teachers in learning and teaching specific nonreligious academic subjects: (d) change the political, social, and cultural attitudes of Afro-Americans by advancing specific Black ideologies.

68. XAVIER UNIVERSITY PRESS,
New Orleans, Louisiana

(1) Dates of existence: 1937?–1941?; (2) Major officers: various administrative officers within the university; (3) Major publications (selected): (A) books: *The Negro in Louisiana*, by Charles Rousseve (1937); *Arrows of Gold*, by Peter W. Clark (1941); (4) Type of business structure: nonprofit organization; (5) Books published in the following categories: adult nonfiction: poetry; histories; handbooks; (6) Types of editions published other than first editions: none; (7) Publishing objectives related to publishing books to: (a) document various aspects of Afro-Americana; (b) portray specific aspects of the Afro-American experience; (c) assist students and teachers in learning and teaching specific nonreligious academic subjects.

Bibliography

BOOKS

American Book Trade Directory, 1969-1970, The. 19th ed. New York: Bowker, 1969.

American Negro Academy Occasional Papers, The. Nos. 1–22. Washington, D.C.: The Academy, 1897–1924. Reprint New York: Arno Press, 1969.

Bacote, Clarence A. *The Story of Atlanta University: A Century of Service, 1865-1965.* Atlanta: Atlanta University Press, 1969. (This title was published for Atlanta University by the Princeton University Press.)

Bailey, Herbert S. *The Art and Science of Book Publishing.* New York: Harper & Row, 1970.

Bell, Howard Holman. *A Survey of the Negro Convention Movement, 1830-1861.* New York: Arno Press, 1969.

————, ed. *Minutes of the Proceedings of the National Negro Conventions, 1830-1864.* New York: Arno Press and the New York Times, 1969.

Bingley, Clive. *The Business of Book Publishing.* Oxford: Pergamon Press, 1972.

Blase, Melvin G. *Institutional Building: A Source Book.* East Lansing, Mich.: Midwest Universities Consortium for International Activities, 1973.

Bone, Robert. *The Negro Novel in America.* New Haven: Yale University Press, 1958.

Boyd, Richard H. *A Story of the National Baptist Publishing Board: The Why, How, When, and by Whom It was Established.* Rev. ed. Nashville: National Baptist Publishing Board, 1922.

Bradley, David Henry. *A History of the A.M.E. Zion Church.* 2 vols. Nashville: Parthenon Press, 1956–1970.

Campbell, Thomas Monroe. *The Moveable School Goes to the Negro.* Tuskegee, Ala.: Tuskegee Institute Press, 1936.

Carroll, Charles. *The Negro as Beast.* St. Louis: American Book and Bible House, 1900.

Cazden, Robert. *German Exile Literature, 1933-1950.* Chicago: American Library Association, 1970.

Cheney, Orion H. *The Economic Survey of the Book Publishing Industry.* New York: Bowker, 1931.

The Chicago Afro-American Union Analytic Catalog: An Index to Materials on the Afro-American in the Principal Libraries of Chicago. Boston: G. K. Hall, 1972.

Coleman, Robert W., ed. *The First Colored, Professional, Clerical, Skilled and Business Directory of Baltimore City.* Baltimore: Coleman Publishing Co., 1917.

Cronon, Edmond D. *Black Moses: The Story of Marcus Garvey and the Universal Negro Improvement Association.* Madison: University of Wisconsin Press, 1955.

Crummell, Alexander. *Africa and America.* Springfield, Mass.: Wiley & Co., 1891.

Dabney, Wendell P. *Cincinnati's Colored Citizens.* Cincinnati: Dabney Publishing Co., 1926. Reprint New York: Johnson Reprint Co., 1970.

Dessauer, John P. *Book Publishing: What It Is, What It Does.* New York: Bowker, 1974.

Detweiler, Frederick G. *The Negro Press in the United States.* Chicago: University of Chicago Press, 1922.

Dixon, Thomas, Jr. *The Clansman.* New York: Doubleday, 1905.

Dollard, John. *Caste and Class in a Southern Town.* New Haven: Yale University Press, 1937.

Du Bois, W.E.B. *Black Reconstruction: An Essay toward a History of the Part Black Folk Played in the Attempt to Reconstruct Democracy in America, 1860-1880.* New York: Harcourt, Brace & Co., 1935.

———. *Dusk of Dawn.* New York: Harcourt, Brace & Co., 1940.

———. *The Souls of Black Folk.* Chicago: A. C. McClurg, 1903.

Dunning, William Archibald. *Reconstruction: Political and Economic.* New York: Harper & Brothers, 1907.

Dyson, Walter. *Howard University: The Capstone of Negro Education, 1867-1940.* Washington, D.C.: Howard University Press, 1941.

Editors of *Ebony*. *The Ebony Handbook.* Chicago: Johnson Publishing Co., 1974.

Elkins, Stanley M. *Slavery: A Problem in American Institutional and Intellectual Life.* Chicago: University of Chicago Press, 1959.

Feber, Robert, comp. *A Basic Bibliography on Marketing Research.* Rev.
    ed. Chicago: American Marketing Association, 1974.
Franklin, John Hope. *The Free Negro in North Carolina, 1790–1860.*
    Chapel Hill: University of North Carolina Press, 1943.
_____. *From Slavery to Freedom.* 3d ed. New York: Knopf, 1967.
Frazier, E. Franklin, *The Negro Family in the United States.* Chicago:
    University of Chicago Press, 1939.
Frederickson, George M. *The Black Image in the White Mind.* New York:
    Harper & Row, 1971.
Fuller, Thomas O. *Pictorial History of the American Negro.* Memphis:
    Pictorial History, 1933.
Griggs, Sutton E. *The Hindered Hand: or, The Reign of the Repressionist.*
    Nashville: Orion Publishing Co., 1905. Reprint New York: Books
    for Libraries, 1970.
_____. *The Story of My Struggles.* Memphis: National Public Welfare
    League, 1914.
Harris, Abram L. *The Negro as Capitalist: A Study of Banking and
    Business among American Negroes.* Philadelphia: American
    Academy of Political and Social Science, 1936.
Harris, Joel Chandler. *The Uncle Remus Tales.* Rev. ed. New York:
    Appleton, 1908.
Hart, Albert Bushnell. *Slavery and Abolition, 1831–1841.* New York:
    Harper & Brothers, 1906.
Hopkins, Pauline. *Contending Forces.* Boston: Colored Co-operative
    Publishing Co., 1900.
Howard University Library. *The Dictionary Catalog of the Arthur B.
    Spingarn Collection of Negro Authors.* 2 vols. Boston: G. K. Hall,
    1970.
_____. *The Dictionary Catalog of the Jessie E. Moorland Collection of
    Negro Life and History.* Boston: G. K. Hall, 1970.
Hudson, Theodore. *From LeRoi Jones to Amiri Baraka: The Literary
    Works,* Durham, N.C.: Duke University Press, 1973.
James, C.L.R. *A History of the Negro Revolt.* London: Fact, 1938.
Jewish Publication Society of America. *Twenty-fifth Anniversary, April
    Fifth and Sixth, 1913.* Philadelphia: Jewish Publication Society of
    America, 1913.
Johnson, Charles S. *The Collapse of Cotton Tenancy.* Chapel Hill:
    University of North Carolina Press, 1935.
Johnson, John H., and Burns, Ben, eds. *The Best of Negro Humor.* New
    York: Negro Digest Publishing Co., 1945.
Jordan, Lewis G. *Negro Baptist History, U.S.A., 1750–1930.* Nashville:
    Sunday School Publishing Board, 1930.

Kahn, R. L., and Cannell, C. F. *The Dynamics of Interviewing: Techniques and Cases*. New York: Wiley, 1957.

Kelley, Frances Burnett, and Ross, Germain. *Here Am I, Send Me: The Dramatic Story of Presiding Bishop J. O. Patterson, Challenging and Bold Leader of the Church of God in Christ*. Memphis: Church of God in Christ Publishing House, 1970.

Kellog, Charles Flint. *N.A.A.C.P.: A History of the National Association for the Advancement of Colored People*. Baltimore: Johns Hopkins University Press, 1967.

Klineberg, Otto, ed. *Characteristics of the American Negro*. New York: Harper & Row, 1944.

Kolter, Philip. *Marketing Management: Analysis, Planning and Control*. 2d ed. Englewood Cliffs, N.J.: Prentice-Hall, 1972.

Logan, Rayford W. *Howard University: The First Hundred Years, 1867-1967*. New York: New York University Press (under the auspices of Howard University), 1969.

Matthews, Geraldine O.; Phinazee, Annette L.; Hall, Carol J.; and Wynn, Helena M. *Black American Writers, 1773-1949: A Bibliography and Union List*. Boston: G. K. Hall, 1975.

Mays, Benjamin E., and Nicholson, Joseph. *The Negro Church*. New York: Institute of Social and Religious Research, 1933.

Myrdal, Gunnar. *The American Dilemma: The Negro Problem and Modern Democracy*. New York: Harper & Brothers, 1944.

New York Public Library. Schomburg Collection of Negro History and Literature. *The Dictionary Catalog of the Schomburg Collection of Negro History and Literature*. Boston: G. K. Hall, 1962.

Nemeyer, Carol. *Scholarly Reprint Publishing in the United States*. New York: Bowker, 1972.

Nolan, William A. *Communism versus the Negro*. Chicago: Regnery, 1951.

Odum, Howard W. *Social and Mental Traits of the Negro: A Study of Race Traits, Tendencies and Prospects*. New York: Columbia University Press, 1910.

Parris, Guichard, and Brooks, Lester. *Blacks in the City: A History of the National Urban League*. Boston: Little, Brown, 1971.

Patterson, J.O.; Ross, Germain; and Atkins, Julia Mason. *History and Formative Years of the Church of God in Christ with Excerpts from the Life and Works of Its Founder—Bishop C. H. Mason*. Memphis: Church of God in Christ Publishing House, 1969.

Payne, Daniel A. *History of the African Methodist Episcopal Church*. Nashville: A.M.E. Sunday School Union and Publishing House, 1891.

Payne, Stanley. *The Art of Asking Questions*. Princeton, N.J.: Princeton University Press, 1951.

Penn, I. Garland. *The Afro-American Press and Its Editors*. Springfield, Mass.: Wiley & Co., 1891.

Pettigrew, M. C. *From Miles to Johnson*. Memphis: C.M.E. Church Publishing House, 1970.

Phillips, Charles Henry. *The History of the Colored Methodist Episcopal Church of America*. Jackson, Tenn.: Publishing House of the C.M.E. Church, 1898.

Phillips, Ulrich Bonnell. *American Negro Slavery: A Survey of the Supply, Employment and Control of Negro Labor as Determined by the Plantation Regime*. New York: Appleton-Century-Crofts, 1910.

Randall, Dudley. *Broadside Memories: Poets I Have Known*. Detroit: Broadside Press, 1975.

Rogers, J. A. *World's Great Men of Color*. 2 vols. New York: J. A. Rogers, 1946.

Sanders, Charles L., and McLean, Linda, comp. *Directory of National Black Organizations*. New York: Afram Associates, 1972.

Schatz, Walter, ed. *Directory of Afro-American Resources*. New York: Bowker, 1970.

Sinnette, Elinor Desverney. "The Brownies' Book: A Pioneer Publication for Children." In *Black Titan: W.E.B. Du Bois, An Anthology*, pp. 163–173. Edited by the editors of Freedomways. Boston: Beacon Press, 1970.

Smith, Charles S. *A History of the African Methodist Episcopal Church*. Vol. 2. Philadelphia: Book Concern of the A.M.E. Church, 1922.

Spradling, Mary Mace. *In Black and White: Afro-Americans in Print*. Kalamazoo, Mich. Kalamazoo Library System, 1971.

Stuart, M. S. *An Economic Detour: A History of Insurance in the Lives of American Negroes*. New York: A. Wendell Malliet & Co., 1940.

Sumner, William Graham. *Folkways*. Boston: Ginn & Co., 1902.

Tucker, David M. *Black Pastors and Leaders: The Memphis Clergy, 1819–1972*. Memphis: Memphis State University Press, 1975.

Tyms, James D. *The Rise of Religious Education among Negro Baptists: A Historical Case Study*. New York: Exposition Press, 1965.

U.S., Bureau of the Census. *Minority-Owned Business: 1969*. Washington, D.C.: Government printing Office, 1969.

_____. *Negro Population 1790–1915*. Washington, D.C.: Government Printing Office, 1918.

_____. *Statistical Abstract of the United States, 1974*. Washington, D.C.: Government Printing Office, 1975.

_____. *Statistical Abstract of the United States, 1975*. Washington, D.C.: Government Printing Office, 1976.

U.S., Department of Commerce. Bureau of the Census. *Negro Population in the United States, 1790–1915.* Washington, D.C.: Government Printing Office, 1936.

————. Bureau of the Census. *Negroes in the United States, 1920–1932.* Washington, D.C.: Government Printing Office, 1936.

————. Bureau of the Census. *1970 Census of Population: Subjects Reports: Negro Population.* Washington, D.C.: Government Printing Office, 1973.

————. *Historical Statistics of the United States—Colonial Times to 1970.* Part 1. Washington, D.C.: Government Printing Office, 1975.

Vanier, Dinoo. *Market Structure and the Business of Book Publishing.* New York: Pittman Publishing Co., 1973.

Vincent, Theodore G. *Black Power and the Garvey Movement.* Berkeley, Calif.: Ramparts Press, 1971.

Voorhis, Harold Van Buren. *Negro Masonry in the United States.* New York: Henry Emerson, 1940.

Walls, William J. *The African Methodist Episcopal Zion Church: Reality of the Black Church.* Charlotte, N.C.: A.M.E. Zion Publishing House, 1974.

Weiss, Nancy J. *The National Urban League, 1910–1940.* New York: Oxford University Press, 1974.

Wolseley, Roland E. *The Black Press, U.S.A.* Ames, Iowa: Iowa State University Press, 1971.

Woodson, Carter G. *A Century of Negro Migration.* Washington, D.C.: Association for the Study of Negro Life and History, 1918. Reprint New York: Abrahams Magazine Service, 1970.

————. *The Education of the Negro prior to 1861.* Washington D.C.: Association for the Study of Negro Life and History, 1919.

Work, Monroe N., comp. *A Bibliography of the Negro in Africa and America.* New York: H. W. Wilson, 1928.

————. ed. *The Negro Yearbook.* 1st ed. Tuskegee, Ala.: Negro Yearbook Publishing Co., 1912.

Yearbook of American and Canadian Churches, 1975. Nashville: Abingdon Press, 1975.

JOURNALS

Articles

"Aims of the Negro Publication Society." *Negro Quarterly* 1 (Summer 1942): vi.

"Announcement." *Colored American Magazine.* October 1900, p. 1.

"Annual Meeting." *Journal of Negro History* 57 (January 1973): 117–25.

Baker, John F. "PW Interviews Joseph Okpaku." *Publishers Weekly*, October 7, 1974, pp. 6–7.

"Books in Press." *Colored American Magazine*, June 1901, p. 23.

Brown, Sterling, "The Negro Author and His Publisher." *Negro Quarterly* 1 (Spring 1942): 7–20.

Browning, Alice C., and Gayden, Fern, "A Letter to Our Readers," *Negro Story*, May-June, 1944, p. 1.

Chambers, Bradford. "Book Publishing: A Racist Club?" *Publishers Weekly*, February 1, 1971, pp. 40–47.

———. "Why Minority Publishing? New Voices Are Heard." *Publishers Weekly*, March 15, 1971, pp. 35–50.

Christianson, Elin B. "Mergers in the Publishing Industry, 1958–1970." *Journal of Library History* 7 (January 1972): 8–27.

"Copyright Notice." *Negro Digest*, June 1949, p. 1.

"Directory of United States Publishers Issuing New Books." *Publishers Weekly*, Third week in January, 1939–1946.

Du Bois, W.E.B. "Opinion—The True Brownies." *Crisis*, October 6, 1919, p. 286.

Elliot, R. S. "The Story of Our Magazine." *Colored American Magazine*, May 1901, pp. 43–44.

"Finance-Banking," *Survey of Current Business* 57 (August 1977): 5–18; 61 (September 1981): 5–15.

Fields, Howard. "Planned Education Cuts are Devastating to Publishers." *Publishers Weekly* 219 (March 27, 1981): 12–13.

———. "Publishers Back Howard's Book Institute, Now Two," *Publishers Weekly* 220 (July 31, 1981): 14.

Fredrickson, George M. "Two Steps Forward, One Step Back." *New Republic* 492 (December 16, 1981): 33–36.

Gell, Marilyn Killebrew. "Washington Update: The Blue Book." *Library Journal* 106 (May 15, 1981): 1010–11.

Gross, Bella. "Freedom's Journal and the Rights of All." *Journal of Negro History* 17 (July 1932): 241–86.

Hokkanen, Dorothy B. "American Book Title Output—A Ninety Year Overview." *Printing and Publishing*, July 1970, pp. 25–30.

"Introducing." *Negro Digest*, November 1942, p. 2.

Jackson, Luther P. "The First Twenty-Five Volumes of the *Journal Of Negro History* Digested." *Journal of Negro History* 25 (July 1940): 432–50.

Joyce, Donald F. "Arthur Alonzo Schomburg: A Pioneering Black Bibliophile." *Journal of Library History* 10 (April 1975): 169–82.

Kincaid, H. V., and Bright, M. "Interviewing the Business Elite." *American Journal of Sociology* 63 (November 1957): 304–11.

"Library Dollar: Congress Reauthorizes LCSA at Lower Funding Levels." *Library Journal* 106 (October 15, 1981): 1982.

Lofquist, William. "The Printing and Publishing Industry: A Minority Report." *Printing and Publishing*, January 1972, pp. 17–19.

McGirt, James E. "Announcement." *McGirt's Magazine*, September 1903, p. 1.

Mackaye, Milton. "The Birth of a Nation." *Scribner's Magazine*, November 1937, pp. 40–46.

Mason, Marilyn Gell. "Washington Update: Library Priorities and Federal Funding." *Library Journal* 106 (November 15, 1981): 2168–9.

Meier, August. "Booker T. Washington and the Negro Press: With Special Reference to the *Colored American Magazine*." *Journal of Negro History* 38 (January 1953): 67–90.

"The Negro Publication Society." *Publishers Weekly*, April 11, 1942, p. 143.

"Notes," *Journal of Negro History* 6 (July 1921): 380.

Parker, John W. "James Ephraim McGirt: Poet of 'Hope Deferred'." *North Carolina Historical Review*, 16 (July 1954): 330–40.

Parks, Carole A. "An Annotated Directory: The Black Book Publishers." *Black Worls*, March 1975, pp. 72–79.

Porter, Dorothy B. "Activities of Literary Societies, 1828–1846." *Journal of Black World*, March 1975, pp. 72–79.

Randall, Dudley, "Black Publisher, Black Writer: An Answer." *Black World*, March, 1975, pp. 32–37.

———. "Negro Publishers for Black Readers." *Publishers Weekly*, October 22, 1972, pp. 46–52.

"A Series of Articles on Racism in Book Publishing." *Interracial Books for Children*. Winter-Spring, 1971, pp. 6–11.

Shockley, Ann Allen. "Black Book Reviewing: A Case for Library Action." *College and Research Libraries* 35 (January 1974): 19–23.

"S.L.J. News: E.S.E.A. IV-B Trimmed to $161 Million, Block Grant Provision Remains." *School Library Journal* 27 (August 1981): 8.

———. "A Necessary Union: Black Publishers and Librarians." *Black World*, March 1975, pp. 38–44.

Smigel, E. O. "Interviewing a Legal Elite: The Wall Street Lawyer." *American Journal of Sociology* 64 (September 1958): 159–64.

Smith, R. H. "Publishing and Manpower." *Publishers Weekly*, October 6, 1969, p. 37.

Smith, Wendy. "Two H. & R. Symposiums Look at Blacks in Book Publishing." *Publishers Weekly* 219 (March 20, 1981): 13–16.

"Two Lamentable Casualties." *Publishers Weekly*, August 31, 1970, p. 250.

"Unemployed Persons by Marital Status, Race, Age and Sex." *Employment and Earnings* 28 (September 1981): 16.

Waner, Susan. "Howard University Launches Its Own Press." *Publishers Weekly*, March 4, 1974.

Wesley, Charles. "Carter G. Woodson—As A Scholar." *Journal of Negro History* 36 (January 1951): 19-20.
Williams, John A. "Black Publisher, Black Writer: An Impasse." *Black World*, March 1975, pp. 28-31.
Winston, Michael R. "Through the Back Door: Academic Racism and the Negro Scholar in Historical Perspective." *Daedalus* 100 (Summer 1971): 681-90.
Woodson, Carter G. "An Accounting for Twenty-five Years." *Journal of Negro History* 25 (July 1940): 422-31.
_____. "The Report of the Director." *Journal of Negro History* 4 (October 1919): 479-81.
_____. "Thomas Jesse Jones." *Journal of Negro History* 35 (January 1950): 108.
Zummo, Rose Marie. "Outlook Optimistic for Printers and Publishers." *Printing and Publishing*, Janaury 1970, pp. 4-8.

Complete Runs Examined for Book Advertisements
and News of Afro-American Book Publishers

Black Book Bulletin, 1970-1975
Black World (formerly *Negro Digest*), 1942-1951; 1961-1975
The Brown American, 1936-1945
Color Line, 1946-1947
Colored American Magazine, 1900-1909
Crisis, 1910-1975
The Half-Century Magazine, 1916-1925
Journal of Negro History, 1916-1975
The Messenger, 1917-1928
Negro History Bulletin, 1937-1975
Negro Story, 1944-1946
Opportunity, Journal of Negro Life, 1923-1949
The Southern Workman, 1872-1939
Voice of the Negro, 1904-1907

NEWSPAPERS

Cincinnati Enquirer, 10 April 1926, p. 30.
Cincinnati Times-Star, 3 April 1926, p. 18.
Pittsburgh Courier, 9 July 1927, p. 7.
Tennessean, 11 January 1976, p. 9.
Cincinnati Times-Star, 3 April 1926, p. 18.

MISCELLANEOUS ORGANIZATIONAL PUBLICATIONS

Afro-American National League. *The Birth of the Afro-American National League . . . Chicago, Illinois, January 15–17, 1890*. Chicago: Afro-American National League, 1890.

American Negro Academy. *Minutes of the Meetings of the Executive Committee, 1897–1922, Washington, D.C.* Boston: Microfilm by Adelaide Cromwell Gulliver, Director, Afro-American Studies Center, Boston University.

American Society of Free Persons of Colour. *Constitution of the American Society of Free Persons of Colour: Also the Proceedings of the Convention, with Their Address to the Free Persons of Colour of the United States.* Philadelphia: J. W. Allen, 1831.

Black Academy Press. *Supplement, Containing Index to Black Academy Review.* Buffalo, N.Y.: Black Academy Press, 1970.

Cheeks, James E. "Remarks at the Launching of the Howard University Press." Washington, D.C.: Howard University Press, 1974.

"The East: A Model of Nationhood." In *The East*, pp. 3–4. Brooklyn, N.Y.: The East, 1971.

Howard University Press. "Howard U. President Launches First Black University Press in U.S." Washington, D.C.: Howard University Press, 1974.

"A Message from Our Executive Director." In *Winning the World for Christ: Sunday School Publishing Board, National Baptist Convention, U.S.A., Inc., Seventy-Seventh Annual Report, Fiscal Year, July 1, 1973–June 30, 1974.* Nashville: Sunday School Publishing Board, 1974.

National Association for the Advancement of Colored People. *Fourth Annual Report, January 1914.* New York: NAACP, 1914.

Third World Press. *75 Catalog.* Chicago: Third World Press, 1975.

DISSERTATIONS, THESES, OTHER UNPUBLISHED MANUSCRIPTS

Baldwin, Carolyn W. "Denominational Publishing: A Study of Major Protestant Church-Owned Publishing Houses in the United States." Master's thesis, University of Chicago. 1974.

Bullock, Penelope Laconia. "The Negro Periodical Press in the United States, 1838–1909." Ph.D. dissertation, University of Michigan, 1971.

Cook, Raymond Allen. "Thomas Dixon: His Books and His Career." Ph.D. dissertation, Emory University, 1963.

Crenshaw, Esther M. "Negro Publishing Houses." Research project, University of Illinois, 1942.

Hines, Linda Elizabeth. "A Black Sociologist in a Time of Trouble: Monroe Nathan Work, 1866–1945." Master's thesis, Auburn University, 1972.

Lane, Robert Frederick. "The Place of American University Press in Publishing." Ph.D. dissertation, University of Chicago, 1939.

Miller, Mignon. "The American Negro Academy: An Intellectual Movement during the Era of Negro Disenfranchisement, 1897–1924." Master's thesis, Howard University, 1966.

Richmond, Peggy Jo. "Afro-American Printers and Book Publishers, 1650–1865." Master's thesis, University of Chicago, 1970.

Taylor, Alrutheus Ambush. "Fisk University, 1866–1951: A Constructive Influence in American Life." Manuscript, Fisk University Library, n.d.

Tolson, Ruth M., comp. "Hampton Institute Press Publications—A Bibliography." Hampton, Va., 1959. (Mimeographed). Collis P. Huntington Library, Hampton Institute, Hampton, Va.

LETTERS (each addressed to the author and in his personal collection)

Andrews, Naomi, 22 September 1981.
Burroughs, Margaret, 15 September 1981.
Grinstead, S. E., Sr., 1 December 1981.
Jay, James M.,7 February 1976.
Jordan, Casper Le Roy, 7 October 1981.
Jorgensen, Norma M., 27 November 1975.
Madhubuti, Haki R., 22 September 1981.
Martin, Carl, 23 September 1975.
Martin, Robert, 31 May 1976.
Moon, Henry L., 7 February 1977.
Randall, Dudley, 14 September 1981.
Sapphire Publishing Company, 17 November 1976.
Saunders, Doris, 14 September 1981.
Sundiata, Phaon, 23 December 1975.
Tilger, C., 16 January 1976.
Winslow, Eugene, 17 September 1981.

MANUSCRIPT COLLECTIONS

Atlanta, Georgia. Atlanta University. Atlanta University Archives.

Boston, Massachusetts . Boston Public Library. Department of Rare Books and Manuscripts. George Washington Forbes papers.

_____. Boston University. Mugar Library. Special Collections. Trotter-Guardian Collection.

Chicago, Illinois. Chicago Public Library. Vivian G. Harsh Collection of Afro-American History and Literature. "The Negro in Illinois: The Illinois Writers Project." Research studies compiled by the Writers Program of the Work Projects Administration of Illinois.

Cincinnati, Ohio. Cincinnati Historical Society. Wendell P. Dabney papers.

Hampton, Virginia. Hampton Institute. Hampton Institute Archives.

Nashville, Tennessee. Fisk University. Fisk University Archives.

New York, N.Y. New York Public Library. Schomburg Collection of Negro Literature and History. Writers Program. New York (City). Negroes of New York. "Biographical Sketches." Research studies compiled by the Writers Program of the Work Projects Administration in New York City, for "Negroes of New York."

Tuskegee, Alabama. Tuskegee Institute. Tuskegee Institute Historical Collection. Booker T. Washington—Committee of Twelve correspondence.

_____. Tuskegee Institute. Tuskegee Institute Historical Collection. Monroe Nathan Work Papers.

INTERVIEWS

Andrews, Naomi. Lotus Press, Detroit, Mich. 6 November 1975.

Ben-Jochannan, Yosef. Alkebu-lan Foundation, New York, N.Y. (Telephone interview) 9 February 1977.

Browning, Alice C. Vivian G. Harsh Collection of Afro-American History and Literature, Carter G. Woodson Regional Library, Chicago Public Library, Chicago, Ill. 16 November 1976.

Chambers, Bradford. Council on Interracial Books for Children, New York, N.Y. 25 November 1975.

Clarke, John Henrik. Hunter College, New York, N.Y. 24 November 1975.

Diara, Agadem L. Agascha Productions, Detroit, Mich. 7 November 1975.

Feldman, Eugene. DuSable Museum of African American History. Chicago, Ill. 23 September 1975.

Gilbert, Herman Cromwell. 11539 S. Justine St., Chicago, Ill. 24 September 1975.

Grinstead, S. E., Sr. Sunday School Publishing Board of the National Baptist Convention, U.S.A., Inc., Nashville, Tenn. 16 January 1976.

Harris, Charles. Howard University Press, Washington, D.C. 9 December 1975.

Jordan, Casper L. Atlanta University, Atlanta, Ga. 10 January 1976.

Lindsay, Arnett, and Miles, Willie. Associated Publishers, Inc., Washington, D.C. 10 December 1975.

Moyo, Kofi. Third World Press, Chicago, Ill. 13 June 1974.

Nkee, Parama. Vita Ya Watu (People's War) Publishers, Newark, N.J. 18 November 1975.

Okpaku, Joseph. Third Press International, New York, N.Y. 25 November 1975.

Prettyman, Alfred E. Emerson Hall Publishers, New York, N.Y. 26 November 1975.

Pyant, Robert L. A.M.E. Zion Publishing House, Charlotte, N.C. 19 January 1976.

Randall, Dudley. Broadside Press, Detroit, Mich. 7 November 1975.

Ross, David P. Afro-Am Publishing Co., Chicago, Ill. 6 March 1975.

Salaam, Abdoul. Muhammad's Temple No. 2, Publications Department, Chicago, Ill. 17 October 1975.

Saunders, Doris E. The Book Division, Johnson Publishing Company, Chicago, Ill. 4 March 1975.

Toney, Terrance. C.M.E. Publishing House, Memphis, Tenn. 13 February 1976.

Watts, A. Faulkner. Blyden Publishing Company, New York, N.Y. 28 November 1975.

Weusi, Kasisi Jitu. The East, Brooklyn, N.Y. 22 November 1975.

White, Andrew. A.M.E. Sunday School Union and Publishing House, Nashville, Tenn. 13 January 1976.

Williams, James. Publications Department, National Urban League, New York, N.Y. 20 November 1975.

Zu-Bolton, Ahmos. Howard University, Washington, D.C. 2 December 1975.

Author Index

Compiled by Doris Hargrett Clack

The Author Index lists authors mentioned in this work by pages which contain references to their works. References to authors that do not include titles of works may be found in the Name and Subject Index.

Name and Subject Index

Compiled by Doris Hargrett Clack

About the Author

DONALD FRANKLIN JOYCE is Coordinator of the Downtown
Library at Tennessee State University. Joyce is the compiler of *The
Civil War in Books: A Bibliography*, and has been a consultant to
the National Endowment for the Humanities for the past four
years. He was formerly the Curator of, and edited the *Dictionary
Catalog* of The Vivian G. Harsch Collection of Afro-American
History and Literature of the Chicago Public Library, one of the
largest collections of Black literature in the United States.